Astrological Sun Signs of the Cat

by Julie Leiter Member: National Council for Geocosmic Research, Inc., and Astrological Society of Princeton

Aries (March 21–April 20)

A real swashbuckler of a cat with a lot of energy, drive, and daring. Aries cats love being where the action is and will not back away from a fight. With a strong sense of self and a me-first attitude, they hate standing on the sidelines and will try to dominate others around them. Spontaneous and impatient, they are first at the food dish, and the toms are first in line for the queens.

Taurus (April 21–May 21)

A cat who loves the good things in life—a soft cushion, a special place of its own, and gourmet dinners. Laid-back, adagio, and very sensual, Taurus cats choose food, stroking, and massage. So much "good stuff," however, could lead to, well, pudge. Taurus cats are possessive of the things they love, and they can be stubborn. Once habits are acquired, they're hard to break, so train these cats early.

Gemini (May 22–June 21)

A curious and playful cat who doesn't want to miss a trick. Gemini cats are alert, clever, quick-witted, and interested in everything. Variety is the spice of their lives; they choose a little of this and a little of that—but not too much of one thing. They are great communicators and usually enjoy "talking" (or talking back) to whoever is around. Concentration is not their strong point.

Cancer (June 22–July 23)

The homebody of the cat world. Cats born under the sign of Cancer love the security of a warm hearth (or a warm bed). They are sensitive and can be somewhat shy and moody, but they will purr with pleasure at a little TLC. Queens make good mothers, and toms like to be mothered. They love the night hours, and, in their own quiet way, they are very tenacious about getting what they want.

Leo (July 24–August 22)

Truly "the cat who would be king." The Leo cat is proud, regal, and dramatic. Leos like center stage and usually get it. They love flattery and having a fuss made over them. Their vanity, however, will not tolerate belittling, and if you ever make fun of them, they might just go off to seek an appreciative audience elsewhere. But given their royal "due," they will be the happiest and most loving of cats—and lord it over you with the greatest aplomb.

Virgo (August 23–September 23)

A very intelligent and discriminating aristocrat. Virgo cats demand only the best and look down upon anything or anyone who is less than perfect. No dirty litter boxes or day-old food for these connoisseurs—they keep themselves neat and clean and expect their environments to be kept the same way. Virgos have a sense of what seems "right" and can become nervous if things are not "just so." If you win the approval of this cat, you've been bestowed the greatest of compliments.

Libra (September 24–October 23)

Unhappy alone, a good friend to all. Cats born in Libra need interaction with others—felines, humans, or even Fido. Usually very beautiful, they have a refined nature and a love of peace and harmony. Too much discord and loud noise can mean nervousness and misery for them. Libra cats often have trouble making up their minds, like whether or not to go out while you stand there with the door open. But they are so charming and attractive that most humans are happy to be a part of their lives.

Scorpio (October 24–November 22)

The animal of sensuous magnetism. The Scorpio cat is intense, passionate, and mysterious. Scorpios have strong desires and expect to get what they want. They will size up a situation instantly, and they can seduce you into doing whatever they want and have you think it was your idea. In fact, they can push your buttons so expertly that you will enjoy being manipulated. But don't cross swords with them—you are sure to lose!

Sagittarius (November 23–December 21)

A live wire with a yen for adventure. Sagittarius cats are always ready to explore what's just around the corner or go out to conquer a new world. Very athletic, they will delight you with acrobatic feats and yowl loudly if their needs for exercise and activity are not met. Yet as they get older, they will develop a philosophical bent and prefer to sit on the front porch and contemplate where they have been and what they have done.

Capricorn (December 22–January 20)

The status-seeker. The Capricorn cat wants to climb to the top—so watch out for your curtains and look for these cats on the top of furniture or shelving (as close to the ceiling as they can get). Capricorns are serious, cautious, deliberate, and determined, and they work hard at whatever they do. They even work hard at playing! Somewhat insecure, they thrive in a positive environment and appreciate warmth and attention, although they usually won't admit it.

Aquarius (January 21–February 19)

The original "KrazyKat." Aquarius cats are unpredictable, and that's how they like it! Just when you think they're your best friends, they become remote and detached, looking down at you from a distant perspective. Independence and individuality are their watchwords. With a strange quality in their nature, they may appear downright "flaky" because they often can't resist rebelling against what is, upsetting the status quo—just because. Yet they are friendly and generally tolerant of your foibles.

Pisces (February 20–March 20)

A sweet and dreamy cat that finds it easy to "make-believe." The Pisces cat can spend time entertaining both itself and you with imaginary scenarios. Deeply sensitive both physically and emotionally, their hearts yearn for total oneness with you (on their own terms, of course). Their taste usually runs to seafood, and drinking water is less likely to bother them than most members of the feline species. Be aware of what you are feeling when you're with a Pisces cat because they are very impressionable and tend to absorb your moods!

alpha
books

Where to Call When You Don't Know Where to Call

Legal Issues

Animal Defense Legal Fund (707) 769-7771
Information and names of attorneys in your area knowledgeable about the law as it affects your cat.

Grief Support

International Association of Pet Cemeteries (518) 594-3000
Offers referrals to specific cemeteries.

Pet Loss Support Hotlines:
    Michigan State University (517) 432-2696
    Tufts University (508) 839-7966
    University of Florida (352) 392-4700, Ext. 4080
These veterinary schools offer free programs for grieving owners.

Humane Organizations

American Humane Association (303) 792-9900

American Society for the Prevention of Cruelty to Animals (ASPCA) (212) 876-7700

Animal Protection Institute of America (916) 731-5521

Friends of Animals, Inc. (203) 656-1522

The Humane Society of the United States (202) 452-1100

The Pet Savers Foundation/SPAY USA (516) 944-5025

All concerned with humane treatment of animals, each group differs slightly from the others.

Career Guidance

American Grooming Shop Association (719) 570-7788

American Veterinary Medical Association (847) 925-8070

The Humane Society of the United States (202) 452-1100
Offers printed material on various animal-related careers.

National Association of Professional Pet Sitters (202) 393-3317

North American Veterinary Technicians Association (317) 742-2216

Health

American Animal Hospital Association (800) 883-6305
Can provide veterinarian referrals and printed material.

National Animal Poison Control Center (800) 548-2423 or (900) 680-0000
A nonprofit service of the College of Veterinary Medicine at the University of Illinois. Rates vary and will be charged to your credit card. (You might want to inquire about a no-cost poison control hotline in your region.)

San Francisco Behavior Hotline (415) 554-3075
Animal behavior advice from the San Francisco Society for the Prevention of Cruelty to Animals.

For Fun

Cat Collectors (810) 264-0285
For information about kitty collectibles.

America Online (800) 827-6364

CompuServe (800) 848-8199

Microsoft Network (800) 386-5550
To find cat programs and games (and serious information) in cyberspace.

Pet Partners, Delta Society (206) 226-7357
Where and how to train your pet in order to bring it to hospitals and nursing homes for patient enjoyment and relaxation.

The

COMPLETE

IDIOT'S

GUIDE TO

Living with
a Cat

by Carolyn Janik and Ruth Rejnis

alpha
books

A Division of Macmillan General Reference
A Simon & Schuster Macmillan Company
1633 Broadway, New York, NY 10019

For everyone whose life has been touched by a cat and for the cats who have purred their way into our hearts.

©1996 Carolyn Janik and Ruth Rejnis

International Standard Book Number: 0-02-861278-7
Library of Congress Catalog Card Number: 96-084615

98 97   8 7 6 5 4 3 2

Interpretation of the printing code: the rightmost number of the first series of numbers is the year of the book's printing; the rightmost number of the second series of numbers is the number of the book's printing. For example, a printing code of 96-1 shows that the first printing occurred in 1996.

Printed in the United States of America

Publisher
Theresa Murtha

Editors
Dominique DeVito
Nancy Mikhail

Copy/Production Editor
Laura Yockey

Cover Designer
Mike Freeland

Illustrator
Judd Winick

Designer
Kim Scott

Indexer
Jennifer Eberhardt

Production Team
Angela Calvert
Kim Cofer
Tricia Flodder
Laure Robinson
Megan Wade
Christy Wagner

Contents at a Glance

Contents

Introduction

When the folks at Macmillan Publishing asked us to add a book about cats to their *Complete Idiot's Guide* reference series, we were both delighted. What could be more challenging and more fun than writing a cat book! Something unique...something special... something that would collect everything we had learned from the cats in our lives.

The idea grew and grew. Why not a cat book written so that the information is easy to find and easy to read? Why not a cat book that covers everything from the meaning of "ailurophile" to "cats in the zodiac"? Why not a cat book with humor, awe, and that warm, fuzzy feeling, as well as facts and advice? Yes! That would be a book that cat lovers would love. And that's the book we've written for you.

Sometimes *The Complete Idiot's Guide to Living with a Cat* will answer your questions. Sometimes it will help you make decisions, give you advice or suggestions on where to go for more information, or show you both sides of a controversial topic. Sometimes it will catch your attention with bits of information on how cats have influenced our language and participated in our history. Sometimes it will make you smile, sigh, or wonder at the words some of the world's most famous people have written about cats, both their own and others.

This is a book you can curl up with on a rainy day, dip into when you have a few spare minutes, and refer to when you need specific information. Let us introduce you to its six parts.

Part 1: When the Welcome Mat Is Out at Your Place focuses on those first questions everyone has when the idea (or the reality) of a cat in the house takes over. It will help you choose, check out, and welcome this new member of your household.

Part 2: The Masterpiece that Is the Cat takes you right up close to the cat. With a detective's magnifying glass, you'll look at the physical cat from whiskers to tail tip, cat language (audible and otherwise), and the breeds, colors, and body types you've seen or heard about.

Part 3: Home, Sweet Cat-Filled Home gets right into the day-to-day "living with a cat" concerns like food, home furnishings and decorating, cat owner responsibilities and decisions, and having fun. You'll learn about fleas and litter boxes, vitamins and treats, and even cat collectibles.

Part 4: Caring For Your Cat is the grooming and health care section. It also includes some cat psychology, a little sex, kittens, travel, and some insights about the end of a cat's life.

Part 5: Working with Cats explores cats as a career, either part-time or full-time. Here you'll go into the professional show ring, the cattery, the creative and artistic sphere, and the world of the volunteer.

Part 6: Even More than You Wanted to Know! is for the extra-inquisitive mind. You'll go back in history to Cleopatra's relatives and drop in on cats around the world from the nations of Europe to Africa, Japan, China, and South America. You'll also be introduced to the political cats, the writing cats, the musical and artistic cats, and the children's cats of our heritage.

Sugar and Spice

To add fun, extra facts, and new perspectives to the topics you'll be reading about, we've spotlighted items of interest by boxing them. You'll get a clue to the subject matter of each box by the little cartoon at the top. Here's a list of what to expect:

Bet You Didn't Know

Facts and statistics that may surprise you or make you wonder.

Cats in Our Language

Catcalls at the theater, a catty woman, and sitting in the catbird seat—unusual meanings, slang, word histories, and cat phrases that have a special meaning in our language.

Some Helpful Information

Tips on how to do things better, fix things, or get things. These are also warnings about products, practices, and situations that might harm a cat or its caregivers.

It's Been Said

From humor to inspiration, the words of famous people.

Sayings and Superstitions

Proverbs and magical beliefs from around the world.

Tales
Stories about cats from local news items, friends, and distant places and times.

Acknowledgments

Sincere thanks to Illena Armstrong, Michael Brim, Holly and Wayne Carter, Peter Drown, Anne M. and John Johnson, Rachael and Jesse Halpern, Roxanne Hawn, Marcia Morrill, Suzi and Mike Roberti, Dot and Frank Smith, Ronald and Virginia Weimer Vogl, Claire Walter, Joan Witt, and Jane Zeff.

Cat line drawings by Carolyn Janik.

Special Thanks from the Publisher to the Technical Reviewer

The Complete Idiot's Guide to Living with a Cat was reviewed by an expert who not only checked the technical accuracy of what you'll learn in this book, but also provided invaluable insight and suggestions to ensure that you receive everything you need to know about living with a cat. Our special thanks are extended to Karen Commings.

Karen Commings is the author of *The Shorthaired Cat: An Owner's Guide to a Happy, Healthy Pet* and a contributing editor to *Cat Fancy* magazine.

Part 1
When the Welcome Mat Is Out at Your Place

This is an exciting time for you, whether you are adopting your first feline or taking in a companion for a cat already in residence at your place. You have dozens of questions. In the next four chapters you will find dozens of answers, from what you can expect to find at an animal shelter to what to do if it turns out you're allergic to that cute kitty (you can keep him anyway, as you'll learn). Through it all is a dash of humor, of course. After all, this is a time to enjoy yourself and have fun planning for and greeting the new arrival.

Chapter 1

Selecting a Cat

In This Chapter

➤ Points to consider for a first-time owner

➤ Shopping for your second or third or...

➤ Visiting a shelter—or having them come to you

➤ When you are looking for a purebred

You may be about to take the plunge and get your first feline. Or you could already have two or more cats, but you're keeping your eyes open for still another. Those new to this cat business will learn that owners often find it difficult to say "that's enough." The expression "always room for one more" *must* have originated here!

You have many opportunities for finding your cat and plenty of places in your own community that, figuratively speaking (and sometimes literally), hang out the "Cats Here" sign. The experience that awaits you is likely to be curious, touching, funny, or incredible—maybe several of the above. However you hook up with your new pet, you will almost certainly have a story to tell about that match for the rest of your life.

Pop Quiz for Prospective Owners

Are you about to look for your very first cat? Let's go over your thinking about that move.

Why do you want a cat? That seems obvious, of course. You want the companionship of a pet around your place. You look forward to the amusement its antics will provide. There is a vacancy in your life for a pet, and a cat is what will fill the bill. Or maybe you want a pet in order to introduce your children to animals and to the responsibility of caring for them.

On the other hand, perhaps you are Ernie of Ernie's Deli, and you are looking for a cat to keep down the rodent population at the restaurant. That's a valid reason for cat shopping too, as long as you will care for that animal.

Whatever your reason for wanting a cat now, here is an important point to consider: These days a cat's life span can be 15 or 20 years or even longer. Be certain you are ready to make that lengthy commitment.

Cats in Our Language

We are able to trace the word for *cat* back through the mists of recorded history. In the fifth century B.C., the Greeks used the word *ailourus* for felines, meaning "the waving ones." Did that refer to the motion of the cat's tail? Or to how cats themselves moved? Alas, a definition was not handed down with the word. Still, from that word we now have two that are with us today: *ailurophobe*, meaning a person who fears cats, and *ailurophile*, one who fancies them.

Is your life reasonably stable? If you are leaving for college in a few months, moving to England momentarily, or about to divorce, you might want to put taking in a pet on the back burner until things settle down.

Do you have the time to devote to a pet? The cat chosen for work in a store or other setting will find its days full, or its nights if it is working the graveyard shift. But the cat that is brought into a house or apartment as the sole pet has different needs. If you leave for work at 8 A.M., return home at 6:30 P.M., eat dinner, watch some television, and are in bed by 11 to sleep until 6:30 the following morning, puddy is virtually alone more than 20 hours a day, since your sleeping time is not exactly stimulation for him. If you travel frequently in your job, that is worse yet.

It is not kind to take a pet for the enjoyment it can bring you if you cannot offer it some fun in return. In a two-person household where one of you does not work outside the home, the cat may receive plenty of attention. The same for a working household where everyone's hours are staggered.

If your cat is going to be alone a huge chunk of the day, there are ways you can keep it happy (see Chapter 13). You can also try to choose a shy or calm cat who, while certainly friendly, can manage solitude better than the "high maintenance" pet who needs a good deal of its owner's attention.

Another option is to take two cats. They can play with each other, and just knowing another animal is in the home can make a feline more content. Two cats are no more work than one, but are, of course, more expensive.

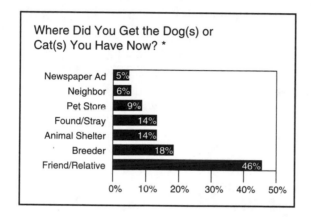

Where Did You Get the Dog(s) or Cat(s) You Have Now? *

* Respondents with more than one pet could indicate more than one source for their animals.

Courtesy of The Humane Society of the United States

Can you afford the cost of cat ownership? Food is a running tab, of course, but there is also cat litter, some toys, regular veterinarian checkups, and perhaps a major vet bill some day for a serious illness or an accident. There might be occasional boarding or pet sitting fees. Will you be able to manage all of that?

Pet ownership is not a formidable expense—except for that major illness tab—but it does call for an ongoing outlay of cash.

It's Been Said
"There are two means of refuge from the miseries of life: music and cats."

—Albert Schweitzer

This brief quiz no doubt set you thinking about the very real changes a pet will bring into your home and how responsible you will be for that little life. You probably passed with flying colors. Here are just a few more points to consider before you go shopping.

Do You Already Have a Cat or Two or...?

Perhaps your dowager 21-year-old cat has recently died. Although you have two younger pets and are naturally missing your companion for his own special personality, you also notice the void his loss brings. Pretty soon, while still mourning Smudge, your thoughts turn to another cat. Not a replacement, of course. There was—and will be—only one Smudge. But the new cat will be a replacement in the sense that he or she will bring your cat complement back up to three. A comfortable number, you feel.

Just be certain that when you go cat shopping you will have the heart to appreciate your new cat for his or her own uniqueness.

Maybe death is not the reason why you are looking for cat #3 (or #4 or...). Perhaps you just plain want another cat. Well, why not? There's no quota system here, but only practical considerations, such as whether your town, landlord, or homeowners association will allow as many cats in your household as you would like, whether you have space for another pet, and whether you can financially care for one more. Oh, and maybe one other thing: Will your current cat(s) accept the newcomer? (There are some suggestions for introducing a new pet to the others in Chapter 4.)

The Choice: A Kitten or an Adult Cat, a Male or a Female

Decisions, decisions. Who can resist the antics of a kitten, a tiny ball of fluff whose face seems to be almost entirely wide, bright eyes? Not many. If you opt for a kitten you are indeed getting moments that will make you laugh out loud as it explores your home and life in general. You can also look forward to what is likely to be a long life for your pet.

But that kitten will grow to be an adult cat. Also, kittens are fragile and subject to illness and injury. Maybe all that kittenish activity will be a little too much for you too. If so, consider the grown-up cat. "Grown-up" can be as youthful as one or two years old, or just plain old (starting at around 10). For adoption purposes, the adult cat can be as young as nine or ten months, just past that cute kitteny stage.

CAT TALES

Tales

Winston Churchill loved cats. He was given one on his 88th birthday, which he named Jock after the friend who gave him the feline. Jock lived at Chartwell, Churchill's famous home, and was a popular attraction there after it was opened to the public. Jock passed away in 1975, well after the prime minister's death in 1964. The curators at Chartwell quickly replaced him with another cat, which they named Jock. Churchill's will stipulated that a marmalade cat should be kept at Chartwell forever, and he left a sum of money to cover room and board for each of the original Jock's successors.

The advantages of an older cat are (1) you can determine its temperament now instead of waiting for it to mature, making your selection a little easier; (2) it has passed through the illnesses of kittenhood; (3) you are spared the sometimes hyperactivity of kittens; and (4) it may have been spayed or neutered. Do not think older cats are not fun, however. They will make you laugh too, with their own special quirks and sometimes outrageous behavior.

The older cat might have some already apparent health problems, and others might crop up sooner than they would with a younger cat. Some mature cats have been neglected or mistreated in the past and may need time to settle into their new homes. However, many more oldsters have been given up because of an owner's allergies, a move, or similar circumstances not related to behavior. And, of course, the older the cat, the fewer the years you will have left with your pet.

Which is better? It's your call. Felines of any age need loving homes.

As to whether your cat should be male or female, that too is up to you. Altered males and females, those that have been spayed or neutered, both make good house pets. Some say you cannot tell the difference in temperament between the two.

One more decision to make here: a long- or shorthair pet. If you opt for the former, remember that the animal will have to be frequently groomed, more so than a short-hair cat.

Of Course Cats and Dogs Can Live Together

Where did the phrase "they fight like dogs and cats" come from? Having your new cat join your Irish setter, or perhaps the setter and your spaniel, can often work out well. See Chapter 4 for introducing everyone to one another and attempting to have harmony reign.

Your Local Animal Shelter

Many towns have an animal shelter, and big cities usually have a few, operated by a variety of sponsoring organizations. Virtually all do a sterling job of trying to find homes for animals that have been lost or discarded. Almost all experience a constant financial crunch too.

You can almost always find a cat you want in a shelter, even a purebred, although they do not find their way into those facilities in the same numbers as the more ordinary "household" cats.

By getting your pet from a shelter you are saving the life of an animal who might have no future at all. Don't worry about the cat you find in this manner. Good shelters screen out animals with serious behavior problems.

Rules and regulations for adoption vary from one place to another, and some screening usually takes place. For example, if you are under 18 years of age, you will probably have to secure the signed consent of a parent or guardian for the adoption. Perhaps the shelter you are visiting does not allow adoptions during the Christmas season, or indeed adoptions of pets as gifts for others at any time of the year. They fear for the well-being of animals adopted for friends or relatives of those visiting the shelter, gift recipients who might not *want* those cats.

Some Helpful Information

If you want to give a cat from a shelter as a holiday, birthday, or other gift, wrap up a cat toy to present to the recipient with a note saying that the kitten or cat is to follow. Or, you might design a clever card on your computer. Some shelters offer gift certificates or cards that you can give along with the toy.

You can usually expect to give a donation of anywhere from $10 to $100 for your pet, which might include spaying or neutering and/or some vaccinations. It's wise to call a shelter first to find out what you need to bring with you.

Look around the shelter you visit. Is it clean? Are the cages clean? Is the staff pleasant and helpful?

Take your time looking at the cats. Perhaps you are sure you want a black kitten, but do allow yourself to become acquainted with some of the others. Maybe some little paw will reach out to you through bars, and the cat you take home will be gray and white, and not at all little. If you see two adult cats in one cage, obviously getting along well, they could be littermates or cats raised in the same household. Give some thought to taking both. It would be a shame to separate good buddies, and, as mentioned earlier in this chapter, having two cats can be a good move for both owner and pet.

Some Helpful Information

Sometimes a presentation of cats will come to you. Many animal shelters bring "petmobiles" to shopping malls, citywide community events, and other places where there are a large number of possibilities for pet adoption. From time to time a shelter will tote a few cages of cats and dogs to the lobby of a major office building for a day or two. Some animal rescue organizations have even set up storefront "branch offices" in busy office areas.

Ask a member of the staff about any cat that interests you. Some details will be on a card attached to that animal's cage, such as the pet's medical history, if it is known, and its present state of health. The staff can usually provide more information based on daily contact. Has that cat been friendly? Shy? Aggressive? What type of temperament do you prefer in your pet? Are there certain personality traits and health problems that go along with that breed? If you can, it is wise to bring every member of the household with you before choosing a specific cat. Some cats could be frightened of children. Some may not like men, others back away from women.

If for some reason the cat does not work out, despite everyone's best intentions, you can return it. Good shelters will take pets back so they will have another chance at a happy home.

Answering Advertisements

"Wanted:" the newspaper or bulletin board advertisement reads, "good homes for five playful, gray, eight-week-old kittens, two males, three females. Call 555-1212."

This is another path to adoption that can work out very well. Cats born in a home, usually of house cats, are already in a good environment and are comfortable around people.

If you have never seen a new litter of kittens before, prepare to spend some time just going "awwww." They will be cute. They will be *adorable*.

When you can finally get down to business, notice the cat mom and her temperament. Ask the homeowners about it too. Is the litter from a house cat, or was it found outdoors? Have they been to a veterinarian? Look closely at the kittens (as if you can take your eyes away from them). Does one seem to be the leader? Is one very shy? Which is the runt, or smallest of the litter? Have they been litter-box trained? See Chapter 3 for an additional checklist of points to note.

It is wise not to take a kitten younger than six or eight weeks from its mother. It is learning much from mom, and that attachment, plus its socialization with littermates, will bode well for its life ahead.

Unless it is a purebred, the cat you find through an ad is usually, but not always, free.

Your new pet could be waiting for you at a local shelter.

Photo by Judith Halden, The Humane Society of the United States

Finding a Cat at the Vet's

Many veterinarians go beyond treating cats and also help to find homes for them. Most allow notices of available cats to be placed on a bulletin board, but some also keep a few strays in the office, just waiting for adoption.

There are advantages to finding your cat through a vet's office. Obviously, it is people who care and are knowledgeable about cats, probably owning one or a few, who place the notices on the bulletin board and bring in pets who need homes. In the latter instance, the vet has probably checked out the animals as well.

You can stop in at a veterinary clinic to look around even if you have never had a pet or have none at the moment. Just one thing: Don't try to adopt office cats, or mascots. The staff will not let anyone have the cuties that perch on their computers, doze on the file cabinets, and officially greet visitors!

It's Been Said
"By associating with a cat, one only risks becoming richer."

—Colette

On the Trail of a Purebred

When you know exactly what you want, and it is not the typical mixed breed that fills the shelters (although a few purebreds do find their way there), then you will want to visit a breeder. You are shopping for a Turkish Angora, for example, or a Scottish Fold.

These animals are bred from a known pedigree lineage to conform to a written standard that describes what, ideally, that breed should look like. These are not common cats in this country, comprising only about 5 percent of the feline population.

It is wise to decide before heading for a breeder if you want a house pet, or a cat to "show." If it's a show cat, try to attend some meetings of a local cat club before definitely electing to enter that arena. It will take work and money.

Breeders know about genetics, temperament, and overall care for the breed, or two or three breeds, that they raise. Some men and women in this field have made remarkable contributions to knowledge about the breed that they specialize in.

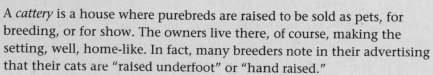

Cats in Our Language

A *cattery* is a house where purebreds are raised to be sold as pets, for breeding, or for show. The owners live there, of course, making the setting, well, home-like. In fact, many breeders note in their advertising that their cats are "raised underfoot" or "hand raised."

You can pay from $100 to several thousand for a pedigreed cat, depending on the breed you want and your geographical location. For the "papers" part of this transaction, you should get a pedigree certificate with the animal's family tree, a transfer certificate that shows you now own the cat, and immunization documents. By all means, shop around from one breeder to another the way you would shop for any purchase. You can find breeders by checking advertisements at the back of cat magazines, by attending a regional cat show, or by contacting cat breeding registries.

Some Helpful Information

Some states have a "pet lemon law" requiring that any dog or cat offered for sale must be accompanied by an official certificate of veterinary inspection. The certificate lists all vaccines and deworming medications administered to the animal and states that the examining vet warrants that, to the best of his or her knowledge, the cat or dog has no sign of contagious or external parasites. Check with your community's Department of Consumer Affairs to see if such a law, or one similar, is in effect where you live.

The Pet Shop Cat

How much is that kitty in the window? Usually quite a bit. This is the expensive way to find a pet because you are paying a middleman—the pet store owner.

Kittens, not full-grown cats, are the specialty in pet shops because they are so irresistible to potential buyers. Many will be purebreds. The problem here, of course, is the background of pet shop kittens. Many are bred indiscriminately (yes, there are kitten mills the way there are puppy mills), where the emphasis is less on care of the animals than future profits. Also, the kittens are subject to disease, certainly stress, and are not used to the love and attention so critical in the early days and weeks of a cat's life.

If you see a kitten you fall in love with at a pet shop and truly want to buy that cat, look around to be sure the store is clean, the animals look healthy (see Chapter 3), and the store owner seems conscientious. Talk to him or her and try to determine as much of the history of that kitten as possible.

Some purebreds wind up in pet stores because they do not conform 100 percent to the standard for that breed. They will not make good show cats, if that is your intention. Ask about "papers" and what the store is ensuring about vaccinations and health-related guarantees. The minimum you should accept is a 14-day guarantee with a full refund. Better yet is one for 30 days against congenital defects, which could be slow to appear.

The Least You Need to Know

➤ Be sure you can afford a cat and will have time for that pet.

➤ Look to your local animal shelter for adoption. Sometimes purebred cats can be found there too, if that is your choice.

➤ Most likely you will find a purebred at a breeder's.

➤ A cat from a pet shop is likely to cost more than you would pay through other sources, and it may come with an unknown genetic and medical history.

Chapter 2

When a Cat Chooses You

In This Chapter

➤ The many ways of coming across a cat

➤ The differences among strays

➤ It takes skill to handle a scared cat

➤ Finding a home for the homeless—your place, maybe?

There is more than one cat owner who came by his or her pet accidentally, almost literally stumbling over that patch of fur. Sometimes the cat or kitten appears around the prospective owner's home, insinuating itself so cleverly into that home life that it finally becomes adopted.

They are everywhere, these lost kittens or adult cats, looking for shelter and a good home. Some day one could bring itself to your attention and make you a rather surprised first-time cat owner. Or, if you have a cat or two at home, you might invite one of these orphans to join your brood.

The Stray, Sort of

One summer, two of four Virginia house cats became parents of a litter of three kittens. Perhaps because there was some renovation work going on in the house at the time and there were three other cats and dogs there, the mother cat seemed to want some peace and quiet for a while. After a few weeks she led her kittens across the street where they took up residence on a neighbor's front porch. The neighbor fed the mother cat and, after they were weaned, the kittens.

But eventually one kitten, all by herself, toddled back to her original house. This cat wanted to be where the action was, and she also wanted to be petted—a lot. The owner welcomed her back and easily found her a wonderful home where, now named Mopsy, she was the center of her people's—and the other house cats'—attention.

Lesson: Some cats, like some people, go after a better life instead of waiting for it to come to them.

The Virginia cat was not a stray, even though she showed up on that owner's doorstep. But some day *you* could hear a plaintive mewing that comes attached to a cat that looks scraggly, or even to a cat that looks fine and fed. The cat can be on your front porch, at your back door, or turn up in your basement. For some folks, a mysterious caller comes into their home through an open window and presents itself on the kitchen counter or the mantel. Voilà! There is a cat from...well, who knows? It seems to want to stay, though.

Look who's come to call...or stay?

Maybe you will meet your stray away from home. You might come upon a litter in a city alley or in woods near your neighborhood. Or you might find a litter of very small kittens in the supermarket parking lot.

It should be said here that there are indoor cats, and there are those who live outdoors but are fed by neighbors. The latter might be tame, but often they are what is known as feral, or wild, cats. It is usually, although not always, too late to bring them into one's home and expect them to settle down and become a serene house pet.

Tales

A couple was walking through downtown in their small community, heading for a furniture store. As they passed a men's clothing shop they noticed the scowling owner in the doorway. Right next to him sat a truly scrawny six- or eight-month-old kitten. "Oh my goodness," said the woman to the owner, "Why is he so thin? Can't he eat?" "He can't eat because he has nothing *to* eat," said the owner shrugging. The couple looked at each other, appalled at the owner's callousness. The man scooped up the kitten with no objection from the store owner. Shopping forgotten, the two headed back home. They named the kitten String Bean, which called for an explanation after a few months because the skinny stray blossomed into a rather sizable cat, always rather shy but very loving around his owners and the other household cats.

Of course, it is not the feral cat that is going to plead to be allowed inside your home, although there are always exceptions. When they become ill or old—or just a little more mellow—a few feral cats allow themselves to be coaxed into the home of the person who has been feeding them. But generally they are not interested in the domestic life, coming within a certain distance of the house only at mealtimes.

However, you might have a chance of finding good homes for the feral cat's *kittens,* if you can get to them early enough (if the cat allows you near them). It would also be good for the always-burgeoning cat population to bring the feral cat to the vet's for spaying or neutering. There is some information on how to catch those elusive felines later in this chapter.

Here is a point to note in the rescuing strays business: More than one kind-hearted soul, new to saving cats, has reasoned, "I'll bring it home, put it in the yard, and give it a good meal. Then it will be able to travel through the neighborhood and someone will adopt it."

Uh-uh. Feed it once, and it will probably consider itself yours, unless you pick it up and deliver it somewhere else. Naming a stray also usually spells doom for your plans to find a home for the fuzzball. In both instances, congratulations are probably in order on the new addition to your household.

Bet You Didn't Know
Spaying is the procedure that removes the reproductive organs of female cats and dogs. Male dogs and cats are *neutered* by removing both testicles. Your vet can explain those procedures to you and advise the best age for sterilization.

HEY!

Handling the Frightened Cat

Who wouldn't be frightened far from what might have once been a warm home, hungry, scared of one's surroundings, and, in some cases, concerned about a litter of even more helpless kittens.

Rescuing an adult cat, or perhaps a mother cat and her litter, will take some careful planning, whether they are found in the bushes behind your home or in that supermarket lot. Normally placid animals can snap and bite under duress or, worse for your purposes, flee and become impossible to catch.

Whether you are catching a cat for your own home, to place for adoption, or to turn over to a shelter, give some thought to this process before setting out.

If you have no cats at home, you will want to be prepared for your stray with cat food and litter, a water bowl, and perhaps bandages if the animal seems wounded.

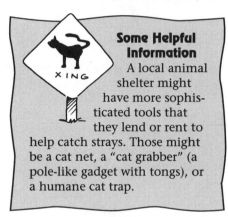

Some Helpful Information
A local animal shelter might have more sophisticated tools that they lend or rent to help catch strays. Those might be a cat net, a "cat grabber" (a pole-like gadget with tongs), or a humane cat trap.

You will need a pet carrier or cage, or at least some large towels in which to wrap the cat. A pair of gardener's gloves or leather gloves will help keep your hands from scratches and bites, but will not offer total protection.

Call quietly to the cat so as not to scare it even more. A sort of "here kitty, kitty, kitty" will do, plus other bits of conversation that, you hope, will put it at ease. When you actually catch it, the cat could be docile, but it is wise to prepare for hisses, scratches, and perhaps bites. Brace yourself for the worst so that you are not surprised and lose the animal.

What we are talking about here is the—at first glance—healthy cat that does not seem feral. The cat that is obviously very sick will call for a different strategy. If it is staggering and perhaps having convulsions, it could have rabies. If there is a discharge from its eyes and nose, it might be suffering from an upper-respiratory infection or even feline distemper.

You will have to choose between trying to rescue this cat yourself or calling for assistance. If the cat goes to a shelter, you must decide whether to pay for its treatment and try to find a home for it, perhaps with you.

A Litter of Very Young Kittens

Step near a litter with the mother cat in attendance and you can expect some fuss from her. If you manage to rescue them all and the mom is still nursing the kittens, you will not have to worry about food for your young strays, at least for the moment. It's when you find a kitten or an entire litter all alone that you will have to see to their meals. Chapter 19 talks about feeding newborn kittens when their mother is not in the picture.

Keep Everyone Separated—For a While

It is wise to keep any homeless cat or kitten separate from your brood until you know the state of its health. You don't want it passing contagious diseases or parasites to your pets.

There is more about having a vet look at a "new" cat in the next chapter, and Chapters 4 and 9 will help you with the settling-in process.

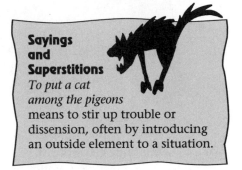

Sayings and Superstitions
To put a cat among the pigeons means to stir up trouble or dissension, often by introducing an outside element to a situation.

You can put your stray in the basement (if it is winter and that space is warm), in a tool shed, or in an extra room or bathroom in the house. It will be quite comfortable with food and water bowls, a litter box (not too close to the food), a bed you have fashioned for it, perhaps a few toys, and, of course, you coming to visit often.

Finding a Home For the Homeless

When the stray(s) you have found, or the one that has found you, has settled down a bit, you will probably have to call a family meeting to decide whether to adopt the cat or kitten, or, if there is a litter, how many, if any, to keep. This will no doubt be a vocal discussion, especially when there are kittens under discussion and you have small children (and sometimes not so small ones) in the house.

Once you have decided who stays and who goes, you have a number of choices for finding homes for your strays. If your find is obviously a house pet, you can put notices on area bulletin boards and run newspaper advertisements under "Pets Found." There is advertising on the Internet. Showing the cats, rather than just talking about them or printing ads, can help enormously in finding them homes. Take the cat (or some littermates) in a carrier or two around to friends and neighbors, folks you know will provide good homes for them. One woman, looking to place a stray she could not keep, took it into her small office for a day, along with all the cat paraphernalia it needed. Sure enough, one of her co-workers adopted it. This works best, of course, in a small, rather informal office where you drive to work. And where you know your co-workers well enough to decide they can be trusted with the adoption.

> ### Tales
>
> A poignant Polish legend suggests the origin of the pussy willow tree. A litter of kittens had been thrown into a river to drown. Nearby willows, seeing the mother cat crying on the bank for her young ones, felt sorry for her and dragged their branches in the water for the kittens to grab on to. Then they stood upright again. Now, every spring the pussy willow tree bursts with little "kittens" of fur.

In "interviewing" applicants from other sources you will have to trust your judgment in deciding who will make a good caregiver for your stray. Other cats in their household could be a sign of commitment to pet care. Ask them where they plan to keep the cat—inside or outside? How many hours a day will the cat be alone? Watch those people too as they become acquainted with the animal. Talk to them about spaying or neutering. They should be for it as soon as a vet says it can be done. It is better to do as the shelters do and not give your stray or kittens from a litter to people looking for Christmas presents, or any kind of gift, for others. Ask that the one whom the present is for come over in person to meet you and the cat.

"She Followed Me Home"

We have all seen television commercials and print ads with a cute child holding a cute dog or cat and saying just that, usually to mom. Oh dear, what's a parent to do?

This can be a good learning experience for a child and might be an excellent opportunity for all of you to gain a new pet.

Some lessons your child can learn from you in this situation are:

1. Just because you found it does not necessarily mean it is yours. The cat very likely has a home, with its owner feeling sad and missing it.

2. It is you and your child's responsibility to try to find that owner.

3. If no one responds, then keeping the cat might be a possibility. But if, say, someone in your household is very allergic to cats or you feel you cannot afford the expense of a pet, you have to help the child understand that adoption is not possible.

If you do keep the cat, the youngster should know about the responsibility of a pet. Talk about how the cat needs to become familiar with your place and might be hiding a lot in the meantime. Cats sleep a good deal and should not be interrupted for play. Ask your child if he or she will be take on the chore of cleaning the litter box (they will, of course, say "yes, yes, absolutely," but sometimes that task eventually ends up with mom).

After talking over the practicalities of cat ownership you can all now settle back for an animated discussion about what to name the newcomer. That can take just seconds for some, but a l-o-n-g period of deliberation for others.

If You Find a Stray Cat

➤ Keep it separate from other pets in your home.

➤ Look for identification so that you can return it to its owner.

➤ If there is no identification, call area shelters and your local pet control office to see if anyone is looking for that animal.

➤ If there is no response from the owner, discuss keeping the pet with other members of the household.

➤ If keeping it is not possible, try to find a home for the cat.

➤ Still no luck? Take it to a shelter, perhaps one that allows cats to live out their lives there.

Don't Feel Guilty

If no one claims your stray, you cannot keep it yourself, and you have been unable to find a home for it, don't feel you have let the poor animal down. You can take it to a shelter, perhaps a facility where animals can stay for the rest of their lives. A veterinarian can give you the addresses of those places in your area.

What would be wrong is to turn the cat loose on the street or in the country, assuming it can fend for itself. It likely cannot, and this time, instead of being rescued by someone like you, it could suffer some misfortune, or even be killed by a car or other animals.

The Least You Need to Know

➤ Sometimes you will almost literally stumble over the cat that becomes your new pet. Strays, unfortunately, are everywhere.

➤ Catching a stray can be quite a job and calls for preparation.

➤ Keep any homeless cat separate from other animals in your home while you are looking for a home for it or until you have it checked out with a veterinarian.

➤ You have a number of avenues available to you when trying to find a home for a cat (or kittens) you cannot keep.

Chapter 3

Say "Ah"

In This Chapter

➤ A close-up look at the cat you are considering adopting

➤ Handicapped animals can thrive in a caring home

➤ That first trip to a veterinarian

➤ Whose cat? Make sure everyone knows it's yours

Whether you get your cat for $45 from a local humane society or pay $1,000 for a fancy one from an area breeder, it is important that you check the animal for obvious health problems before saying, "I'll take this one, please." You are less likely to encounter poor health with a breeder's cat than with one you are considering from a litter of strays, but it *can* happen.

Many problems with a new cat can be fixed, sometimes quickly, at a veterinary clinic. A smaller number are more serious. Some folks want the very ill cat in spite of the bad news they are handed, others return the cat. It is important to know your skills and limitations when considering adopting a pet that is not hale and hearty so that you make the best decision for you and that animal.

What to Look For in a Healthy Cat or Kitten

There are some rudimentary checks you can make to ensure that the animal you want is healthy. Or at least healthy enough to bring you to the next step in this adoption: seeing a veterinarian. Naturally only a vet can tell you what's going on inside that little fuzzball.

Whether the cat is frisky and playing or is sitting off by itself will probably tell you more about the cat's temperament than whether it is sick or well, although naturally a cat that is ailing will not be active.

A healthy cat has clear eyes. If its eyes are runny, it could be suffering from any number of ailments ranging from an upper respiratory problem to feline distemper. Some of those illnesses are easily cleared up with medication, others are more daunting. Watch those eyes as you play with the animal. A cat whose eyes do not follow your moves could be visually impaired or even blind.

Sneezing is also a sign of illness ranging again from a mild infection to a serious condition. Its nose should not be runny either. A cat's nose is normally cold and wet. One that is dry, unless that cat has been snoozing in the sun, could indicate that something is not quite right, perhaps a simple problem easily remedied with medication or proper nutrition.

Sayings and Superstitions

In China it is said that the tip of a cat's nose is always cold, except for one day—June 21, the time of the summer solstice and the longest day of the year. On that day, superstition has it, the cat's nose becomes warm.

Open its mouth to check its teeth and gums. The teeth should be clean and white, the gums not red but a healthy pink. Also look for breathing that is quiet and even, not labored. While you are petting the cat, feel it through its fur. It ought to seem fleshy, not scrawny, but should not have a potbelly, which could be a sign of worms (something else that can be attended to by a vet).

You can clap your hands when the cat is looking away from you to see if it can hear properly but, cats being cats, yours might not turn because it just doesn't feel like it. A vet will have to examine it for possible hearing loss.

Tales

Some cats purr easily, some don't. Some meow constantly, others seem mute. One woman has a cat, now 10 years old, who has never said a word. The woman officially named the cat Tinsel, but nicknamed her Johnny Belinda after the movie in which Jane Wyman played the mute heroine. When the woman moved 1,400 miles away, her two other cats in the car wailed the first 30 miles. Tinsel didn't say boo. Six months later they all moved from an apartment into a house, and again the woman packed the car with the cats. This time it was a two-mile ride. The other two felines were quiet, but Tinsel meowed loudly the entire distance. That was five years ago. She hasn't said a word since.

If you see dabs of black when looking into the cat's ears, the animal probably has ear mites, which are quite common, especially in strays, and can be cleared up easily. A cat constantly scratching its ears or shaking its head is another indication of mites, or perhaps of an ear infection.

Its coat should be shiny and clean. Part its fur to see if there is any sign of sores, hair loss, or other skin problems. If there does seem to be something amiss, you do not need to be leery of taking that animal. Just jot down one more "must-see" for the vet.

While you are looking closely at the fur, check for little black spots the size of a pinhead. (Admittedly, this is a little hard to do with a black cat or one of another dark color!) They might be on its face and around its rear quarters as well. These are flea feces. Yes, yuck. Actually, if the cat has fleas you might see one, or several, jump off its body. Fleas, which can quickly infest an entire house, can be seen to by a vet during your cat's first visit. (See Chapter 15 about your options for getting rid of these super-annoying pests.)

Fleas are only one of several good reasons for keeping your new cat separate from the other animals in your household until it has been carefully examined by a vet. This has been suggested several times so far in this book and relates more to health concerns than possible hissy fits between your current pet and the newcomer.

If the cat you want seems fit and healthy after your inspection, you might want to take it with the proviso that if a serious problem arises from the vet's visit, you have the option of returning that animal.

It's Been Said

"Even the smallest feline is a masterpiece."

—Leonardo da Vinci, whose art includes many studies of the cat in numerous poses

Blind? Deaf? Other Handicap? Still a Good Cat For You—Maybe

You will often see a handicapped cat put up for adoption. It has lost a limb in a traffic accident. Or its hind quarters are partially paralyzed. Or it is now blind. Or it was born deaf, which the new owner did not know. In any event, and for whatever reason, the owner of such a pet cannot keep the animal, and it winds up in a shelter cage.

You should know that a handicapped cat can enjoy life as much as a handicapped human can. We might shoot horses when a leg buckles, but cats and dogs do just fine running about with three legs and can even learn to navigate with partial paralysis. Blind and deaf cats need a bit of extra attention, but their quality of life in a good home is A-1. Pets with these handicaps, or chronic illnesses, can be high-spirited, curious, shy, affectionate, and every other adjective you can attach to a much-loved house pet.

Blindness might be a birth defect, but more often it results from illness or injury. If you decide to keep a cat you know is blind, it will, of course, have to remain indoors (unless perhaps taken outside the house on a leash and watched carefully). Gradually, with your help, it will learn furniture placement and the location of food and water bowls and the litter box. Remember, cats have an acute sense of both hearing and smell. Their whiskers will help guide them too.

Talk often to your blind cat. Your voice will reassure it. Remember, in its dark world it will not know what—or who—is out there. Talk to it before you touch it too, so that you do not startle it. It *will* enjoy its life, thanks to the extra steps taken by you and the others in your household to consider its needs. More than one visitor has said to the owner of a few cats, "Which is the blind one?"

Some Helpful Information

Several cat (and dog) owners around the country have formed support groups for owners of handicapped pets and pets with serious illnesses. They exchange information on medical advances and household tips, and in general they are there for one another in a situation that is not common among pet owners. Ask your vet or local cat club if there is such a group near you. If the answer is no, why not start one? If you want nationwide membership, you can announce your intention in a Letter to the Editor of a cat magazine or on the Internet. For a local group, send a typed notice of your interest to veterinarians in a countywide or regional area for posting on their bulletin boards.

Deafness occurs occasionally in cats, and it is quite common in white cats with blue eyes. Many feel the deaf cat has less of a burden than the blind one, and, in fact, the cat that cannot hear maneuvers equally well in *its* world, which is a silent one. Your vet will help you acclimate your cat, suggesting, for example, that you might walk heavily coming up to it so that it can feel the vibrations of your approach. You can work out a system for letting it know its food is out, although many cats hang around the kitchen at mealtime and do not need you to announce "soup's on."

If you feel, after hearing the veterinarian's diagnosis about defects or other serious incapacitations, that you are unable to look after that cat the way it should be cared for, by all means return it. It could well be adopted by someone who can provide it with a loving home. Then, continue your search for the cat that's right for you.

Photo by Frank Smith

Have your new pet looked at by a veterinarian, whether it was a stray or someone's house cat.

Checking out the Newcomer with a Vet

Most folks who have newly adopted a cat take it to a veterinarian within two or three days. One reason for the hurry is that the cat has been isolated from the rest of the household, or not brought home at all, and the owner is eager to end that separation and get on with a normal life. Also, if there is a serious problem with the cat, the owner wants to know about it before forming too close an attachment to that animal. It might have to be returned to the shelter or other source.

Some shelters have a veterinary clinic on the premises, which makes it especially easy to have a cat examined. No doubt you already have a vet if you have other furry companions at home. If this is your first pet, Chapter 16 talks about how to choose a veterinarian.

What the vet will do that you cannot is, of course, look at that animal with a more practiced eye and check the state of its health beyond what is obvious. The vet can also determine the age of the cat if it is a stray. He or she can tell you if your new pet is male or female, if you do not know, and will also know if it has been spayed or neutered.

Your cat will receive its necessary vaccinations for rabies and distemper, and you will be on record with the vet for annual reminders.

A vet will also check the cat's heart rate, look into its eyes and ears, and take blood samples to check for any number of illnesses. Two of the most serious are feline immunodeficiency virus (FIV), which is a disease in cats that is similar to AIDS in humans, and feline leukemia virus (FeLV). Both are incurable (but keep in mind they are not transferable to humans). There is a more detailed explanation about these illnesses in Chapter 16.

What is important to know here is that many cats can lead a comfortable life for several years with FIV and FeLV, but should be kept indoors and separated from other felines in the house. For some owners that means a one-cat household, but others keep their FeLV or FIV cat on one floor and the others on another level, or they make some other arrangement that allows them to keep the ailing cat.

Sometimes you will be asked to leave your cat with the vet overnight for tests. Sometimes you will take it home, but must return the next day with a stool sample to be checked for worms and other internal parasites. As gross as worms sound—and they certainly *are* gross—that is yet another condition that need not deter you from adopting a particular animal. It can be treated.

How Many Is Too Many Toes?

Do you have cats living with you now? Quick, how many toes do they have? Have you ever checked? Many owners have not and indeed do not know what is the normal number of digits. Is it five? Six? How many?

Five toes is usual, six, seven, and even eight are rare. Sometimes the extra toes are fully formed, while with other cats a bit of a toe might be almost buried behind another one.

Several years ago, the *Boston Globe* reported on a Boston University biologist who had conducted an interesting study. He determined that extra-toed cats could be traced to Boston's early settlement, where they arrived through immigration or on commercial sailing ships. Most ships did have cats aboard, either as pets or to deal with the rat population, and sailors might have deliberately chosen the extra-toed animals for their uniqueness. Docking in Boston and settling there, the cats bred, and eventually their offspring made their way through New England, Canada, and, to a lesser degree, other parts of the country.

HEY!

Bet You Didn't Know A cat with extra toes has a condition known as *polydactylism*. It is the same name as a similar birth defect in humans.

On inspecting a sample of Boston cats, the professor found the multi-toed syndrome in 12 percent of them. But in New York City, which did not see a sizable migration from Boston, the professor found only two-tenths of 1 percent of the felines checked had more than five toes. Philadelphia also had a low number of those animals.

Interesting data, isn't it? One point to consider if you start counting the toes on your new feline and wonder when you will stop is that how many toes a cat sports has no bearing on its health.

Tales

Theodore Roosevelt had a few cats over the years, one of which was "Slippers," a gray cat with six toes. Slippers loved White House diplomatic dinners and always managed to put in an appearance at them. On one occasion an impressive array of ambassadors, ministers, and other beribboned and bedecked guests had to be directed around an object smack in the center of the carpet. It was Slippers, quite happily rolling around and enjoying himself.

That's My Cat: About Identification

Now that you have found and brought home this little treasure, you certainly do not want to lose it. Or if somehow it does wander or become lost, you want to take any measure necessary to ensure its return to you.

It is wise to identify your cat, even though it lives indoors. Actually, many communities mandate some sort of identification in their cat licensing ordinance. You might have discovered that where you live.

The simplest ID is a collar with a metal or heavy plastic tag. These cost around $5 and can be purchased at pet supply stores, veterinary clinics, or through advertisements in cat magazines and cat supply catalogs.

You do not have to be afraid your cat will choke on the collar. Simply purchase one marked "breakaway" or "with an escape feature" that will prevent that from happening.

Bet You Didn't Know

Some estimates say only 2 to 4 percent of cats in a shelter are reunited with their owners. Proper identification could see that percentage significantly increased.

HEY!

If you do not want your name and address on the tag, you might have just your telephone number engraved. Some companies offer a registry service where you put *their* phone number on a tag and the call goes to that office. Their theory is if you lose your cat while traveling with it there will be nobody to answer your home phone if someone calls. But maybe you don't travel much and do not want to spend the money for such a service, which costs about $20 to $30 a year. Then you can use your own phone number on the tag and skip the central service. These companies also advertise in cat magazines and in mail-order catalogs.

*Some cat owners
prefer just their phone
number on an ID tag.*

You might also tattoo your cat. You could use your address or pick an arrangement of numbers—perhaps your phone number. (Some folks use their social security number, but you may not want that in circulation.) A veterinary clinic or animal shelter can tattoo the number onto your cat. You can then register that number at all shelters in your region. If you travel great distances with your cat, you might want to sign up with a national company that offers a national registry, so your pet can be traced if it is lost anywhere in America.

A drawback here is that if your cat is turned in, shelters might not see, or have the time to look for, a tattoo. The marking could be buried under its fur. Also, if a local resident finds your cat, he or she might not know where to call about the tattoo (although if that individual does call a shelter where you are registered, you'll have your pet back).

One growing trend is the microchip. Here a veterinarian "shoots" a pellet the size of a grain of rice under a cat's skin around its shoulder blades, a procedure no more painful than an inoculation. When the lost pet is found and, say, taken to a shelter, the shelter uses a scanner to pick up the chip and identify the animal.

The microchip is a solid means of identification, and surveys are beginning to show successful retrieval rates. But there are a few wrinkles still to be ironed out. What if the cat is picked up by a resident of that community who believes it is a stray and does not know there is a microchip in it? Also, many, if not most, shelters and humane societies cannot afford a scanner for each microchip manufacturer. Companies are trying to cross scan now, which means utilizing scanners that can recognize chips from various manufacturers. That should alleviate incompatibility problems.

Microchipping costs $25 to $40 for a vet to implant, and registration at a manufacturer's computerized database costs another $15 to $35. Your vet can supply you with information about various microchip companies.

Some Helpful Information

Pet ID can be particularly important in times of natural disasters, such as earthquakes, hurricanes, flooding, tornadoes, and hazardous substance leaks that sometimes force residents from their homes. Lost cats with identification are not mistaken for strays and stand a greater chance of being reunited with their owners. If you are leaving your animal with a friend when you evacuate the area, have that person's name and address on a separate ID tag along with your pet's permanent tag.

Imperfect as some means of ID are for a cat, any of them is better than none and raise your chances of your pet's return if you become separated.

The Least You Need to Know

➤ Check the health of a cat as you play with it.

➤ Be sure you can care for a handicapped cat before taking it into your home.

➤ A thorough examination will come from a vet. Make an appointment within a day or so after taking the pet.

➤ You have several options for identifying your pet; identification is an option for some, but mandatory in several communities.

Chapter 4

Welcome Home, Fur Face

In This Chapter

➤ Making room for the newcomer

➤ Choosing just the right name

➤ Helping your cat get along with other household pets

➤ Achoo! Is this wonderful cat making you sneeze?

So there's a new face around your place. What a difference that ball of fur will make in your life! No doubt you are already thinking how dull things must have been around the house before its arrival.

You will be busy for a while as you shop for your new pet, take it to the veterinarian, introduce it to everyone in your household (including your other animals), and generally help it make itself at home. Things will eventually settle down, although with a cat around, every once in a while you can expect the unexpected.

Cat Gear: What You Will Need For the Newcomer

If this is your first cat, you will incur a bit of an expense getting set up. When one woman told a friend that she was planning to get a cat, the friend exclaimed, "Oh, wonderful. I can give you a shower."

Bet You Didn't Know There are more than 57 million cats and more than 52 million dogs living in households in the United States, according to The Humane Society of the United States. A few years ago cats passed dogs as the more common house pet. Not that cats could ever be *common*, of course.

It's Been Said "He loved books, and when he found one open on the table he would lie down on it, turn over the edges of the leaves with his paw, and, after a while, fall asleep, for all the world as if he had been reading a fashionable novel."

—Théophile Gautier, French writer and critic

She was joking, but if this had been her pal's first time out with a pet she could have used the gifts. There is always something, practical or just fun, to give cat owners or the pets themselves.

For your newcomer, you will need water and food bowls, and they should be placed in a spot that is convenient for you and conducive to pleasant and leisurely eating for the cat. That means not in the path of traffic and not near the litter box.

Is there a dog in your household? You might find you have to feed your cat on a countertop or in some other area the dog cannot reach. Otherwise the dog will chomp away at the cat's food. One family put the cat bowls in their attached garage where there is a pet door leading from the kitchen. The door is too small for their Irish setter to wriggle through.

Let's not forget buying the food itself. There is a discussion of what you might choose to feed your pet in Chapter 11.

You will also need some identification for your cat, a point raised in Chapter 3.

What *don't* you need? If money is tight, forget about a cat bed. They are nice if you would like to spring for one, but you can fashion a bed out of blankets or odd pieces of fabric, sheets, or carpeting. Just so it is warm, cozy, and if possible, has some sort of cover or awning (like a cardboard carton resting on its side). Cats love to feel they are hidden even when everyone can see them. Naturally that bed should be in an area where the cat will not be disrupted by family members regularly passing through.

In any event, you are likely to find that where your cat really wants to snooze is on your bed. You will have to decide whether you will permit that. Puddy will also take its 14 or so naps a day on various chairs, sofas, and other comfy spots around your place, so your buying a bed does not necessarily mean your cat will do all its dozing there.

You can also save a few dollars not buying toys. Yes, most cats love to play and need that physical and mental stimulation, but homemade toys, or those that are ready-made, such as paper bags, are easy enough to come by. There is more about playing with your cat in Chapter 13.

The Litter Box

Another purchase will have to be a litter box and some filler for it. Presumably your new cat already knows how to use the box. They learn that easily and quickly as kittens.

The box should be in a space in your home that allows the cat some privacy. Spread some newspapers under the box. If you want to protect the floor underneath, you can purchase a heavy, plastic, see-through floor mat at an office supply store, the kind placed under typists' chairs, and lay that down first with newspapers on top and the litter box on top of that. Those mats cost around $12.

It is important to keep the litter box clean. Cats will often refuse to use a pan that is dirty and opt instead to leave "deposits" around the house. Also, a dirty litter box smells.

A litter box should be cleared of solids daily, and some new litter should be added. Plastic scoopers are sold for that purpose, but they eventually snap in half. Instead, pick up a metal slotted ladle in the housewares section of the supermarket for $2 or $3. It will last forever and just needs washing when you have finished cleaning the litter pan. The pan ought to be washed with soap and water at least once a week, then filled with all-new litter to a depth of two inches.

By the way, unless the litter you buy is specifically marked biodegradable (and flushable), don't pour an entire box of used litter down a toilet or drain. It could cause a blockage.

Some Helpful Information
If you live alone and now have your first cat or two, give some thought to how your pet would fare if something happened to you. For example, you might want to give a neighbor a key to your home so he or she could feed your cat in an emergency. Carry a card with you that states you have a pet at home that needs care.

Those First Few Days

Cats have their own way of coping with the stress of entering a new household. When you put yours down on the floor for the first time, it might scurry under the sofa and stay there for hours, maybe days. Some cats will leap out an open window to get away (of course, you will have your windows closed or screened in anticipation of a fearful flight).

There's always a period of adjustment.

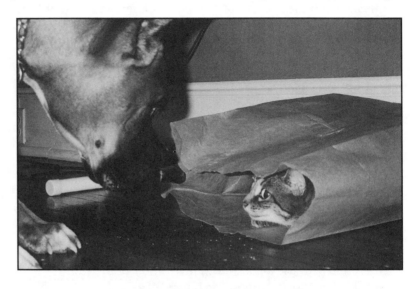

It is hard to tell how your cat will be affected by your surroundings. Maybe this is its first home; perhaps this is its latest after several foster homes or a life on the street. The best way you can help your new pet become acclimated is by giving it plenty of quiet while it gets used to life at your place. That can be difficult, particularly for children, since everyone will want to look at the cat, talk to it, and play with it. Leave it alone, certainly if it is hiding. Even if it is walking around being inquisitive, try to let it wander at its own pace, although you will want to talk to it occasionally in a gentle tone. When it wants some attention, or as one owner put it, "when it needs to be purred," it will come to you. Cats catch a lot of Zzzzzs in a 24-hour day, and a stray, perhaps relaxing for the first time in its life, will spend a good deal of time sleeping now that it feels safe.

Chapter 12 talks about training your cat not to go into certain areas of the house or on some furniture.

MEOW!

It's Been Said

"A house without a cat, and a well-fed, well-petted, and properly revered cat, may be a proper house, perhaps, but how can it prove its title?"

—Mark Twain

Pywacket? mehitabel? Choosing a Name

There are those who look at their new white cat and immediately croon "Come here, Milkshake." The cat has been named, right off the top of the owner's head. No problem.

For others it is a torturous process taking days or weeks. One man, totally stumped at having to name the 11th cat in his life, telephoned friends asking, "What should I call him? Help me out on this." A woman began paging through the dictionary, hoping something would occur to her.

Yes, choosing a name for the new cat is a serious business, but certainly not a scientific one. It's open season here. Some owners select names referring to food (Marmalade, Cookie, Brownie, Peaches, Gumdrop, and, yes, Sara Lee); others select names for where they found that stray (Freeway, Ramp, Chelsea, Treetop).

The mood or personality the pet appears to have can also enter into the naming process. Thus we have Sunny, Tiger, Frisky, Rowdy, and Terminator.

Literary references weigh heavily in the cat-naming arena. The "Pywacket" in this section's title, always popular when writers want to refer to a cat, much like "Rex" or "Rover" are chosen for dogs, comes from the cat in the play, and later the 1950s movie, *Bell, Book & Candle*. The name "mehitabel" came from the feline in "archy and mehitabel," the tale of a cat and a cockroach by Don Marquis. A new collection of their adventures has been discovered and was published in 1996 as *archyology: the long lost tales of archy and mehitabel* (University Press of New England, $14.95).

There certainly is a wide selection of possible cat names with words and names from the worlds of sports, opera, plants and flowers, movies, television, and history. For those who say that is not enough, there are foreign words from which to choose.

If a small child is naming the cat, be prepared for another outlook. If it is all right with you, the cat will be called Peanut Butter or Buster or Hot Dog or Whitey, or after any one of a number of Disney or other fairy-tale characters. One single parent allowed her three-year-old son to name their new stray, and he decided on Cinderella. The cat was later found to be a male, and since the name was certainly also long, it was soon abbreviated to Cinder.

It's Been Said

"I call my cats Shall and Will because no one can tell them apart."

—author Christopher Morley

MEOW!

Pop Quiz: Well-Known Cat Names

1. Who did Audrey Hepburn more or less adopt in the movie *Breakfast at Tiffany's*? _____

2. Who was immortalized by Cleveland Amory in three books, beginning with *The Cat Who Came for Christmas*? _____

3. Who for more than 50 years has been jousting with the cartoon Tweety Bird ("I tawt I taw a puddytat")? _____

4. Who falls into disgrace in the musical *Cats* and sings the haunting "Memory"? _____

5. Who terrorizes the orphaned, but quite determined, pig in the movie *Babe*? _____

6. Who is featured in Edgar Allan Poe's short story, *The Black Cat*? _____

7. Who is Odie's friend in the cartoon strip carrying the cat's name? _____

8. Who became the Clinton White House First Cat? _____

1. No Name   2. Polar Bear   3. Sylvester   4. Grizabella   5. Duchess   6. Pluto   7. Garfield   8. Socks

Whether a name is simple or unusual does not matter as the years go by. That name *is* your cat, and you will always associate it with that pet.

Is there any name *not* to give a cat? Yes, very definitely. Avoid calling it anything demeaning, such as Buttinsky, Uggo, Fatso, or Dummy. Cats are proud, and you are doing them a disservice by attaching a name to them that is not dignified. It doesn't reflect well on you either to come up with something that will cause others to cringe.

Introducing the Pet to Other Animals in Your Home

"The fur will fly" is an expression that could be used right about now when you are bringing home a new cat and you have one, two, or even more cats in your household.

Most of the time these situations work out well after two or three weeks. The cats sort themselves out into a new pecking order, and the newcomer takes its place in the fold. In the meantime, expect hissing, growling, fist fights, and cats chasing one another from room to room.

It is wise to keep the newcomer separate from the others for the first 48 hours or so. You can keep it in a bathroom or bedroom with its food, water, litter, and some toys. Since it will spend much time sleeping, it will not be lonesome. The other cats can smell the newcomer and hear it moving around through the door.

On the second or third day you might position the door so that it is open enough for everyone to meet and sniff, but not enough for a cat to slip in or out of that room. After a day, open the door and allow the newcomer freedom. Don't go out in those early days without putting the new cat back in its own quarters.

Other options include blocking off one floor for the "old" and one floor for the "new" cat, if you can do that where you live. You might also keep the newcomer in an animal cage for a few days with its food, water, and litter box so the other animals can see it and sniff around, but the cat is protected.

Some new cats are accepted easily in a multi-cat household with none of the above dramatics. That is particularly true when the new member is a kitten. Sometimes, one cat tolerates the other but never really grows to like its housemate. Less frequently, an adjustment never comes. If after four weeks or so it looks as if there will never be tolerance in your household, let alone harmony, you have four choices: You can call in an animal behavior therapist to help everyone become adjusted (there is more about them in Chapter 17); you can keep the cats separated forever, perhaps on different floors of your home; you can get used to the idea that one or more of the animals will never be happy about the newcomer (or the newcomer about the others) and learn to live with the occasional hissing or fighting; or you can return the new cat.

There are some felines that prefer to be in a one-cat household and never do adjust or even become at least reasonably accepting of another cat. It is not common, however, for an adoption to fail because of other cats in the house. Hang in there. It does take patience.

Cats in Our Language
A group of cats is called a *clowder*, a group of kittens is called a *kendle*.

Now, about dogs. If you have a dog or two, again, you could have any one of several responses to and by the newcomer, depending on the temperament of each animal. Follow the above suggestions. Dogs and cats *can* get along well, although here too, it is usually a kitten that causes less fuss than an adult cat meeting your dogs.

Bringing Up Baby—and Your Cat

You are certainly a reasonable, rational person. But even sensible types, if they have a baby in the house or if one is on the way, could begin to wonder about old wives' tales about cats and babies. They suck the air from a baby's lungs, you have heard. They lap the milk from its lips.

Some Helpful Information

One very real danger while you are pregnant comes from *toxoplasmosis*, a disease that can be contracted by scooping and changing the litter box of an infected cat and that can affect a fetus's brain and nervous system. Try to have someone else in the household handle that chore. If that is not possible, use disposable gloves while cleaning the pan and disinfect it frequently.

Oh those old wives, how they did babble. The truth is cats don't *do* that. What you might have to be concerned about is the cat that becomes stressed from a lack of attention at this busy time in new parents' lives. That pet could become listless and susceptible to illness. (If the baby is already present in the house when you bring in the cat, that is not likely to be the case, of course.) Pay extra attention to that animal now and after the baby arrives. Try smearing some baby lotion or oil that you will use with the infant on your hands now so the cat can become familiar with the scent. Let it smell the baby's blanket too.

Sayings and Superstitions

A Russian superstition says if you want to be happy in your new home, a cat must move in with you.

A spayed or neutered pet should be more docile than one with raging hormones. Still, it is wise not to leave your cat alone with your infant in the baby's first few weeks, but only because it could scratch the infant trying to get close to it to investigate. Just investigate, not smother.

Could You Be Allergic?

Your eyes are misting as you pet your new cat. But it isn't emotion, it's...could you be allergic to that fur face?

You certainly could. Itchy eyes, a runny nose, and welts similar to mosquito bites on your arm where a cat accidentally scratched or bit you all indicate an allergy.

The problem here is not cat hair, but the cat's saliva, which contains the allergen. When the cat grooms itself, the saliva is transferred to its fur, particles of which float in the air settling on furniture, draperies, and the like, and eventually reaching your lungs.

You do not have to get rid of your pet if you find you have an allergy to it (an exception might be in a household where a child suffers from severe asthma). Many allergists can tell you, rolling their eyes, about even asthmatic cat owners they treat, some in multi-cat households.

What will not work is bathing your cat to keep the loose dander down. Also, too-frequent vacuuming just stirs up the particles of cat allergen, causing you more distress.

You can try over-the-counter antihistamines and decongestants. If that does not help, or if your symptoms become worse, it is best to visit an allergist. There could be other irritants in your life besides your cat, such as greenery or certain foods. The allergist can suggest shots, or if your condition turns out to be asthma, prescribe medications to try to keep it in check. The doctor will also have suggestions for making your home as allergen-free as possible.

The Least You Need to Know

➤ You will have to buy some things for a first cat, but there are other purchases you can do without.

➤ Keeping the litter box clean is important, for the cat's sake and for the sake of visitors to your place.

➤ With a little effort on your part, cats can get along just fine with your other pets and certainly with your baby.

➤ You can still live with a pet if you develop an allergy to that animal.

Part 2
The Masterpiece that Is the Cat

Of course, there's no other cat like your *cat!*

But cats, like humans, share some traits universal to the species. In this section, we'll look at what makes the feline body beautiful (and efficient), how cats communicate with each other and with us, what's passed on from parent to kittens, and, yes, what cats do for us.

You'll surely find your cat in every chapter. But here and there you may also say, "Not my cat!"

Chapter 5

Cats Up Close

In This Chapter

➤ Physical traits that make a difference

➤ The secrets of working feet

➤ How cats groom themselves

➤ The five senses—feline version

➤ Purr facts

You don't have to do a Gallup poll to know that we humans admire cats. Even those people who protest (both loudly and often) that they hate cats often make pro-cat choices. In fact, cat admiration might just be one of the most dependable driving forces in our economy. Will it be a Lynx, a Cougar, or a Jaguar for you?

So what is it that we admire? The graceful body line of the cat sitting proudly on a window sill? The silent stealth and focused control of the hunting

It's Been Said
"Like a graceful vase, a cat, even when motionless, seems to flow."

—George F. Will, American journalist

cat? The almost analytical ability to leap and land exactly on target? The drive that keeps them clean? The love they purr?

Let's take a little time to become familiar with the masterpiece that is the cat.

The Body Beautiful

Grace, flow, and warm soft fur. What else could anybody want?

Spines Alike?

The differences are not in the bones. The number, structure, and location of the vertebrae are almost identical in dogs and cats.

Number of Vertebrae

	Cervical (neck area)	Thoracic (chest area)	Lumbar (middle back area)	Sacral (pelvic area)	Coccygeal (tail)
Dog	7	13	7	3	6 to 23
Cat	7	13	7	3	6 to 24

Well, being human, you might want to know *why* cats are so graceful and agile. If you check out the box above, you'll see that dogs and cats have virtually identical arrangements of their vertebrae (the bones in their spines). So why can a cat leap more than five times its own height? Or jump straight backward when startled? Or twist its body smoothly around seemingly impossible obstacles? Or right itself when falling and land on its feet? A dog can't.

Bet You Didn't Know Cats beat out humans if you're counting bones in the skeleton. The human body contains 206 bones, while the cat body contains 230!

Like some of the more agile breeds of dogs, the bones of the cat are both strong and light, and the body is very well muscled. What makes the cat really different, however, is a flexible skeleton. Feline vertebrae are connected by muscle rather than ligaments. These powerful muscles allow the cat's backbone to flex, extend, and even twist.

Except that pet cats in ancient Egypt may have been somewhat larger, domestic cats haven't really changed much during the 5,000 years that they've lived with humans. Today, most of them weigh about 10 pounds, with a few heavyweights topping 20 pounds. They all have short faces and small broad skulls. Their coats vary from virtually hairless, to short hair (the most common), to long hair. Their coat colors range from white to black with lots of variations of orange and brown in between.

Unlike the scene in the dog kingdom where human control over breeding has produced both the toy poodle and the Great Dane, human attempts to breed for midgets and giants in the cat kingdom have been pretty much unsuccessful. The silhouette of a cat in the window is the same the world over.

On Balance

There she is! Desdemona's walking the top board of the neighbors' fence again. She moves just as though it were a two-foot-wide sidewalk!

She moves just as though it were a two-foot-wide sidewalk.

How does she do it? Some would say the cat's tail acts much like the balancing pole carried by a human tightrope walker. This is true, but that's only a small factor in the ease and careless grace of a cat walking a fine line.

More important is the cat's highly developed sense of balance, which is located in the inner ear. Like most creatures, the cat bases its movements on what it sees, but it also *subconsciously* corrects and augments vision with lightning fast balance messages from the inner ear to the brain. It's this balance mechanism that helps the cat who falls or is dropped to land on its feet, usually unharmed.

Some Helpful Information

The cat's righting procedure seems to work only when a cat falls from a horizontal position. A cat *can* be injured by a fall. Some studies show that cats have somewhat better odds when falling farther (sometimes several stories) because they have more time to right themselves and their spread legs catch more air and act somewhat like a parachute. But there's no accurate way to predict whether or not a cat will be hurt from a fall.

The routine for righting is instinctual and the same for every cat. When dropped upside down, the cat brings its front legs close to its head while spreading its hind legs. Then, using both vision and inner ear balance, the cat bends at the waist and turns the front part of its body a full half circle to bring the head and front feet into a ground-facing position. The spine and hind legs twist to follow and the cat arches its back and extends its legs, ready to meet the ground. All this takes less than half a second!

Cats in Our Language
Catwalk is a word familiar to theater people, boaters, builders, and hikers. It means a narrow walkway connecting two points. A catwalk is often so narrow that you must put one foot directly in front of the other.

But excellent balance and an amazing righting instinct still don't completely explain the careless grace of a cat walking the thin edge of a board. A few humans and some dogs can do it, but we're always holding our breaths as we watch their uneasy steps. They have to *think* about putting one foot directly in front of another. Cats don't.

When walking naturally, the front paw prints of a cat line up right, left, right, left, one *directly behind* the other on an imaginary line that would be under the midline of the cat's body. The hind legs don't come in quite so close, but two inches is enough width for careless comfort.

Paws for Thought

The cat's feet—they are a thing of beauty, power, and awe. And they are precision-designed for a utilitarian function. No cat has ever said, "Oh my aching feet!"

Cats walk on their toes. In fact, the soles of their feet rarely touch the ground. Now this would obviously be uncomfortable for bears and humans, but design is everything and it works just fine for cats. Their feet are shorter and less wide than the feet of other animals their size who walk on the soles of their feet. Their foot bones are also thinner and lighter, and those hard-working toes are very well padded.

The feet of the cat are a dead giveaway to its hunting heritage. Cats can walk silently because their paw pads are soft and pliant. Their retracted claws never click on a hard surface like a dog's nails. And fur between the pads and on the foot muffles sound even further.

All members of the cat family, except the cheetah, have retractable claws. (Which is why the touch of a cat foot can be soft and gentle, or formidable indeed.) The claws are worked by tendons and ligaments in the cat's foot. When the cat is relaxed, the tendons are relaxed and the claws are hidden under the skin and held in place by a ligament. When the cat tightens certain muscles, the tendons and the ligaments in the foot stretch and the claws come forward.

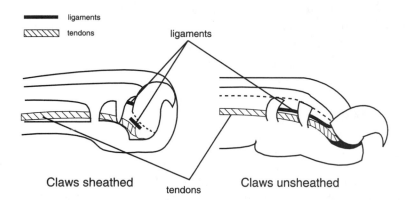

ligaments
tendons
ligaments

Claws sheathed   tendons   Claws unsheathed

Weapons drawn at will: tough tendons and ligaments stretch upon command from the brain to extend the cat's claws. It takes microseconds!

All cats sharpen their claws and scratch. But, honestly, they don't do it to redesign your furniture or to thin the pile on your carpet. It's instinct. In the wild, claws are hunting tools and must remain sharp. Claws are also tools for territorial marking. In Africa, the scratched tree trunk is a *No Trespassing* sign to another lion. So don't be too hard on Mephistopheles when he experiments beyond the scratching post.

Cats also use their front paws for grooming their faces. This is a very important cat activity, and some cats become quite artistic (and compulsive) in its execution.

At the other end of the spectrum, paw pads are another tool (besides scratching and urinating) to mark one's territory. The marking is done through scent glands located on the cat's paw pads. You've probably seen a cat or two standing on its hind legs pressing its front feet against a doorjamb or your leg. The cat is imprinting its scent.

And finally, cat paw pads sometimes serve a purpose similar to that of human sweat glands. The rich capillary blood supply in the pads helps to regulate body temperature. When a cat's body temperature rises, the capillaries dilate and dissipate heat. Sometimes you'll even see moist footprints on a cool surface.

Some Helpful Information

Cats are sensitive to certain chemicals found in fertilizers, insecticides, paints, automotive products, and even the "salts" thrown on sidewalks in winter. In addition to ingesting these poisons when licking themselves for grooming, toxic amounts can be absorbed though their paw pads. If your outdoor cat suddenly becomes ill, check to see what's happening in your neighborhood and tell your vet!

That Sandpaper Tongue

Most cat lovers agree that "sandpaper" is an apt description for the touch of even the most gentle pussycat's tongue. Being licked by a cat is not a pleasant sensation.

But like its feet, the cat's tongue is multi-functional and very efficiently designed for survival of the species. It gets that sandpaper quality from the tiny barbs (almost like hooks) that cover its surface. These *papillae* help predatory cats clean every bit of flesh from the bones of their prey.

But are these tiny barbs useless or a nuisance to our pet cats? Hardly! The backward-pointing hooks are an important asset to the grooming process because they catch and pull dead hair, dirt, and parasites from the coat. They're also a stimulator to new life. The sandpaper quality of the mother cat's tongue probably irritates her newborn kittens. Their protesting cries often clear their lungs and start normal breathing. The licking of kittens' anal areas also helps to start urination and defecation.

The cat's tongue is also its portable goblet. Thin and pliant at the edges, it curls inward to make a very fine drinking vessel. After each four or five laps, the cat will swallow.

As a tasting tool, the cat's tongue seems to be both specialized and idiosyncratic. It can detect even slight changes in the taste of water but has little or no ability to detect sweetness. And, as every cat owner knows, somewhere in the taste buds of the individual tongue are preferences for which there is no accounting. Cat tastes have been known to include cantaloupes and cockroaches, whipped cream and oysters. And, of course, there's always room for a good mouse.

Cleanliness Is Next to Godliness

A child, a dog, and a cat come into the house on a rainy March afternoon. The child stands there dripping. The dog shakes, splattering the rain and mud about. The cat disappears, only to be seen again (after the muddy mess by the door is cleared away) sitting atop the coffee table as pristine as a porcelain statue.

Cats are known for their cleanliness. All members of the cat family (even the big hunting cats) groom themselves every day, and all wash their faces with their paws.

The tongue is the cat's grooming tool. Because of its flexible spine, the cat can reach most body parts with its tongue without undue effort. But not the face and ears. To clean their faces, cats apply saliva to a paw and then use that paw like a wet washcloth, rubbing in ever larger circles until they are satisfied with their cleanliness.

Cats need only be shown the location of the litter box and they'll use it, cleaning themselves afterwards. In fact, cats are so fastidious that they even meticulously clean their genitals after sex. (Perhaps that too should be added to the long list of traits responsible for the survival of the species!)

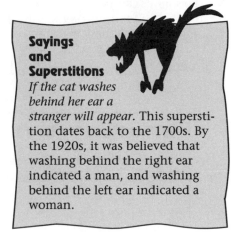

Sayings and Superstitions
If the cat washes behind her ear a stranger will appear. This superstition dates back to the 1700s. By the 1920s, it was believed that washing behind the right ear indicated a man, and washing behind the left ear indicated a woman.

Electronic Ears, Almost

Ear wiggling in humans is usually a comedy routine, for those of us who can, that is. Ear turning in cats is a finely honed survival skill.

Most humans have six muscles associated with the outer ear, and the ears are stationary. Cats have between 20 and 30 muscles, depending on the type of cat, and each ear can rotate independently of the other up to 180 degrees (a half circle). Cats use their outer ears as cone-shaped receptacles to gather sounds to be processed by their brains.

And they gather a lot more sounds than we do. Both humans and cats hear in the lower range down to about 20 cycles per second. In the high range, however, human hearing stops at about 20,000 cycles per second (near the highest notes of a violin). Cat hearing can continue up to 60,000 cycles! That's why *they* hear the squeak of a mouse while *we* sit totally unaware. Mice, by the way, can hear sounds up to 95,000 cycles per second.

Besides having a wider sound range than humans, cats can hear better. The human auditory nerve has about 30,000 fibers, the cat's nerve has about 40,000. So don't be surprised if Felix gets unsettled whenever teenaged Kevin or Debbie play their favorite

Some Helpful Information
No bells, please! A tinkling bell on a cat's neck may warn unwary mice, but it also interferes with the cat's hearing. The sounds can be disorienting, and they are as annoying to the cat as wearing a mask with tiny eye slits might be to a human.

rock music on the boom box. Either separate quarters or a lower volume is probably a good idea.

Catching that Whiff in the Air

Cats in the wild do not track prey by scent. And domestic cats are more responsive to the sound of a can opener than the smell of fish cooking for dinner.

Does that mean that cats do not have a well developed sense of smell? Not at all. They just choose to use what works best for them when hunting: sight and sound. They seem to reserve their sense of smell for recognition and for pure pleasure.

Will a Rose by any Name Smell the Same?

What message the brain registers as a *smell* depends upon olfactory cells. Humans who can't scent-recognize anything much beyond bread baking in the oven have relatively few olfactory cells. Dogs who can track by scent alone have many. Cats fall in between.

Estimated Number of Olfactory Cells

Humans	5 million to 20 million
Cats	60 million to 80 million
Dogs	100 million to 300 million

Besides catnip (which we'll talk about in Chapter 13), many cats have certain smells that they "just love." There's a whole society of patrician cats who have distinct preferences among upscale perfumes. Then there's the blue-collar group who will try to crawl into a shoe just as soon as it's empty of a human foot.

There are people who say that some cats will knock over vases because they love the odor of the stagnant water inside. At the other extreme, you'll see cats hanging around swimming pools, probably enjoying the chlorine odor. Does it make sense? No, but your cat will let you know what it likes.

While the sense of smell seems to serve a hedonistic function in day-to-day cat life, it also serves as a means of recognizing and differentiating what is familiar and what is strange. And it definitely plays an important role in the *ongoing* survival of the species. Yes, sex. A healthy tom can catch the natural perfume of a ladyfriend who might just be receptive to him over a distance that is greater than the length of a football field.

Cats also have an auxiliary scent organ called Jacobson's organ located on the roof of their mouths. When they use it, they make a kind of funny grimace with their mouths, called *flehmen*. Male cats do this more often than females, and the usual stimulant is the urine of another cat.

Ma, He's Making Eyes at Me!

Large for the size of their heads, lustrous, and expressive, cat eyes mesmerize their adoring humans. We see in them a huge range of emotions and motivations including love, anger, joy, curiosity, pain, embarrassment, hunger, and the urge to kill.

Beautiful as they are, cat eyes are designed for the hunt. They can detect minuscule movements in the distance, and they can quickly adjust to changes in the amount of available light. Their vertical pupils can narrow to thin slits in bright light and widen to as much as half an inch in very low light. Their eyelids can move up and down to close either partially or completely over the eye, and they secrete a lubricating fluid to smooth this movement along.

Cats also have a so-called "third eyelid," actually named the *nictitating membrane,* on each eye. It protects the eye and perhaps controls light with thin, pliable tissue that unfolds from the inner corner of the eye. In the healthy cat, this membrane usually cannot be seen.

Besides their extraordinary light sensitivity and movement perception, it was finally proven in the 1960s that cats *can* see color. But they don't seem to care much whether a mouse is gray or brown.

Cats in Our Language

In French, *chatoyer* means "to shine like a cat's eyes." The English borrowed the word and changed it into *chatoyant*. Never heard it? Talk with an upscale jeweler! It means "having a changeable luster or color with an undulating narrow band of white light," and it's used as a compliment in describing many gems.

(Definitions are from *Merriam Webster's Collegiate Dictionary*, 10th edition.)

Contrary to popular belief, however, cats *cannot* see in total darkness. It just seems that way. On a night that we humans would consider total darkness, cat pupils dilate very wide to enable them to use every bit of available light. When sudden light, whether from a fiery torch or car headlights, strikes these wide open pupils, the cat's eyes glow in the dark. This has gotten cats into trouble over the ages because the eerie effect has been associated with evil, magic, and the supernatural. In fact, the glow is the reflection of light on the retina at the back of the cat's eye.

Cats in Our Language

In American English, *cat's eye* has three meanings that have nothing to do with the physical cat:

1. *A gem with a changeable luster:* The precious yellow or pale green cat's eye is a form of chrysoberyl; the semi-precious pale blue-gray cat's eye is a form of quartz.

2. *A marble with eye-like concentric circles:* Flawless ones are considered valuable by many.

3. *A reflector embedded in the road as a guide for motorists in the dark or the fog:* You've probably driven by or over many of them.

What Whiskers Do

So how do cats get around in very dark places? They use their whiskers!

The cat has four rows of whiskers on each side of its face. The upper two rows can move independently of the lower rows, but all whiskers are sensitive to even minute changes in air currents. So you might say that the cat "feels" its way with its whiskers.

Since they usually extend beyond the width of their bodies, cats also quite literally use their whiskers as feelers. With these magic sensing rods, they can test their ability to fit through small places and get around obstacles.

Purr-fect

Well, cats do seem to be quite the perfect hunters. But there's this one extra feature. Why do cats purr?

No one really knows. But we do know *when* cats purr, and we think we know *how*.

Most people believe that purring is a sign of contentment and even affection. Which it probably is. Who hasn't enjoyed the purr of the warm cat curled in your lap? Or looked up from the newspaper because the cat is purring so loudly by the fire?

But cats also purr in situations that are not exactly warm and fuzzy. Newborn kittens purr as they suck for their mother's milk, which may be pleasant for them because they're getting nourishment, but it's also hard work for so young an organism. Grown cats often purr loudly when they are anxious, in distress, or in pain. Sometimes a veterinarian attempting to examine a cat can't hear the heartbeat because the cat is purring so loudly. Some female cats in labor purr. And there are many reports of cats who purred while dying.

For ages many people believed that purring was something like snoring, done while breathing, or something like growling, done with the vocal chords. But it's not. Cats purr with their mouths closed. Most experts believe that the sound is created by two folds of membrane behind the vocal chords, sometimes called the false vocal chords. Like all other cat vocalizing, purring can change in intensity and in pitch. And we still don't completely understand it. Even in this age of technology, there are several theories about how and why cats purr.

Cats are the only animals that purr.

Tales

How the Cat Got Its Purr

In the time before stories were written in books, a princess was given an impossible task. She was ordered to spin 10,000 skeins of linen thread in 30 days, or else the prince she loved would be put to death. The imprisoned princess had only her three cats for company. In desperation, she asked them to help her. The three cats and the princess worked night and day and finished the chore in the allotted time. The cats' reward was the ability to purr, a sound somewhat like the whirring of the spinning wheel.

—from a European folk tale

Now that we've had a closer look at the physical cat, let's go on to unravel some of the many strands of "language" (verbal and otherwise) that our feline friends use to communicate with us.

The Least You Need to Know

➤ The grace and agility of the cat can be attributed to a flexible spine, a well muscled body, and beautifully designed feet.

➤ Cats can hear far better than humans and have an excellent balance mechanism located in the inner ear.

➤ Cat eyes respond quickly to movement and to changes in light, but they *cannot* see in total darkness.

➤ Cats keep themselves clean using their tongues and their paws as washcloths.

➤ Cats purr both when they are content and when they are in pain.

Chapter 6

CatSpeak—It's a Language of Body and Sound

In This Chapter

➤ How cats express affection

➤ What eyes, ears, whiskers, and tails say

➤ The meaning of movements

➤ Cat language and other sounds

Many people go to college to study communication arts, which is really all about how to get messages from one living being to another. Yet without a college diploma (saving loving caregivers many thousands of dollars), cats manage to communicate very well indeed. They even leap effortlessly across language barriers. In fact, a cat can usually teach a human to understand everything that needs to be understood in a matter of days.

Cats also communicate with other cats with tremendous facility. A Maine Coon can tell an Egyptian Mau exactly what she thinks of him, and a Cornish Rex and an Alley can be best friends. Even dogs and other animals quickly pick up enough cat language to get the major messages.

So how do they do it? Let's take a short course in cat communication arts.

Let Me Tell You How I Love You

There are people who say that cats are not affectionate animals. Most of them have never really known a cat. Without ever fawning or begging, without expressing false feelings in expectation of a reward, cats show their thoughts and emotions in genuine, even if usually subtle, behaviors.

It's Been Said

"A cat has absolute emotional honesty; human beings, for one reason or another, may hide their feelings, but a cat does not."

—Ernest Hemingway, American novelist (1899–1961)

The purr is to the cat what the smile is to humans: a characteristic of the species, a sign of contentment, and a means of social communication. The cat purring to your touch is expressing both pleasure and friendliness.

Unlike humans, however, cats also mark what they feel is their own (what they would keep and protect) with their scent. Scent glands are located on the face, behind the ears, in the tail area, and in the feet, and cats use them all. A cat rubbing its body around and against your legs is expressing affection by expressing possession. He or she wants to keep you. The same goes for a cat who stretches its full length to plant two front feet as high on your leg as possible.

Even more a sign of affection is a cat rubbing his or her face against your skin. The cat is marking you lightly with scent, but, more importantly, it is telling you that pleasing you is important. The cat who rubs his face against another cat is expressing both submission and the desire to please.

And then there is gift giving. Just as humans give roses for Valentine's Day and monogrammed golf balls for a birthday, cats give presents to express their affection. Greatly valued in the eyes of the cat are dead frogs on your pillow at dawn or field mice on your doorstep. Don't forget to say "Thank you!"

The Eyes Have It

Some people believe the eyes are a mirror of the mind and read from them both thoughts and feelings. When it comes to cats, there is no way of knowing the accuracy of human readings, except perhaps with your own individual cat. We do have a good deal of information, however, on how a cat's eyes appear in certain situations.

When a cat is interested, attentive, calm, and friendly, its eyes are opened wide but not strained to the maximum width and its pupils are in normal response to the available light. When a cat is frightened, the eyes strain wider and the pupils dilate. When a cat is feeling aggressive or wants to frighten or intimidate, its eyes will narrow into a focused stare. When it is hunting or stalking, its eyes are wide open but very focused and unmoving.

The use of the focused, unblinking stare in both cat hunting and pre-aggression probably accounts for the fact that cats do not like to be stared at by humans. Many cats will respond with quick blinking and turning the head to one side (away from the staring person).

Some Helpful Information

If you are meeting a fearful or timid cat, try catching its gaze, fixing your attention, closing your eyes in a very slow blink, and opening them again also very slowly, all without breaking the visual bond. Some experts believe this action eases tension, intimidation, and anxiety in the cat.

But long, slow, controlled blinking, that's another story in the cat world. In her book, *The New Natural Cat,* Anita Frazier makes a case for the slow blink as a sign of contentment and affection, a kind of "cat kiss." She claims it works as a communication device both between cats and humans and cats and other cats.

The Unspoken Language of Cats

	Affection/ Trust	Need/ Discomfort	Fear/ Defense	Hunting/ Stalking	Aggression
Eyes	eyes wide, pupils normal, slow blinks	varies with situation	eyes very wide, pupils very dilated	eyes wide, focused, unblinking	eyes narrow, pupils focused
Ears	up, forward, and turned slightly to the side	usually up and forward but can vary with situation	horizontal and to the side	up, pointing forward	laid back
Tail	vertical and cocked slightly over the back	usually low	fluffed out, swaying from side to side, or tucked under	low and still except for twitches at the end	wide sweeps from side to side, sometimes fluffed out and still
Whiskers	pointed forward and down	varies by situation, usually forward and up	forward, up, and spread out	forward and tense	forward and up

Ear Signals

Whereas human ears are not much more than turned out flaps, cat ears are almost weather vanes to the prevailing winds of the cat's thoughts. They can move independently of each other, turn a half circle, perk up, hit the horizontal, and go flat. Each position has meaning.

A cat hearing sounds totally inaudible to her human companion might turn one ear toward the source to hear better. Or perhaps hearing a sound in front of her, the cat might turn both her ears slightly forward just as she focuses her eyes.

Cats' amazing hearing and control of their ears, however, may contribute to the bad cat reputation of being inattentive. When you talk to your dog, she'll usually lift her head. Your cat may respond to your voice simply by adjusting the angle of her ears.

A contented, trusting, calm cat will carry his ears up, forward, and slightly to the side. A fearful cat will hold his ears in a horizontal position, out from the sides of his head. An aggressive or defensive cat will pin its ears back against its head. The hunting cat carries his ears up and pointed forward.

Whisker Signs

Cat whiskers are much more than bristle-like face hair. They are guiding tools sensitive to touch, vibrations, and some say even sound waves. And since the top rows are moveable, it follows that they respond to the situations in a cat's life.

A cat walking with her whiskers pointed only slightly forward and down might be attentive, but she is also calm. When the whiskers are pointed forward and up, it is a sign that she is excited or anxious. Even more forward, up, and bristled indicates a defensive or aggressive situation.

About Your Hair, Kitty

Besides humans, no animal is so concerned about the condition and appearance of its hair as the cat. Cats have an excuse, however, since the coat does more than contribute to cat beauty. It also provides warmth in winter and insulation in summer. *And,* it is a defense mechanism.

When a cat is afraid, it makes itself look bigger by puffing out its coat, especially its tail. Each hair stands out as if electrified. Much like the porcupine's hooked quills, this body language is saying, "Don't mess with me!" But the cat's expansion is all just show.

The aggressive or defensive cat who is meeting a challenger may not want to show fear by fluffing himself up. Instead, he will raise the fur over his shoulders, called the hackles, to let the adversary know he should take the challenge seriously.

The welcoming cat.

Tail Talk

The cat's highly developed nervous system extends to the tip of its tail. Sensitive and responsive, that tail is often a signal mechanism for a cat's mood and motivation. Watch it and it will give you messages.

Take "Welcome home!" for example. Your dog will jump up and down, barking gleefully, running in circles around you. Your cat will come out of hiding at a trot, head up, eyes bright, tail erect. In fact, carrying the tail high over the body is always a sign of cat contentment and maybe even a bit of self-satisfaction.

Another common message might be "What's going on here?" or "I'm not sure I like all this." The threatened or nervous cat will hold its tail low and whip it back and forth.

When hunting or stalking, the cat will also hold its tail low, but absolutely motionless except for a possible tiny twitch at the last vertebrae. It's almost as if all the force of control for the tensed muscles must escape somehow through the tip of the tail.

Only when a cat is defeated and fearful will it carry its tail down between its legs. Even the frightened cat who is still ready to fight lifts the tail and puffs it out.

Sayings and Superstitions
Nervous as a long-tailed cat in a room full of rocking chairs!

—American folk saying

Often the cat protects its sensitive tail by wrapping it around its feet when sitting or around its body when lying down. At other times, however, when the cat is sleeping or completely relaxed, it will allow the tail to hang down over the edge of a shelf or a countertop or just extend out from its body on the floor. At these times, there's always the danger of its being stepped on or even having a door shut on it.

Body Language

There have been many pop psychology and self-help books written on human body language. That's because how we do something often means something other than what we're doing. But it's not nearly so complicated with cats. They just do what they do consistently in response to the situation.

Let's take arching the back, for example. This cat act has more than one meaning, but the situation and the manner in which the arching is done will always tell you what the arching means. It's sort of like the words *no* and *know* or *not* and *knot;* they can't be differentiated by their sound, but we don't get them mixed up because of usage.

When a cat arches her back softly and slowly, it is usually to greet you with affection, especially if she is also rubbing against your legs. If she arches her back while you are petting her, she is probably luxuriating in the pleasure of the moment. If she arches her

Sayings and Superstitions
As late as 1910 people still believed that if you should come upon a cat with its tail toward the fire, you could expect bad luck.

back after a nap, she is probably just stretching. But when she arches her back while standing on stiff legs with her hair bristling, she is either frightened or about to fight.

Then there's tapping with a paw. Imagine Griselda sitting on your desk and batting at the pen while you write. She just wants to play. But extend the claws and add a little more power, and the gentle pat becomes a swipe. Swipes give warning or reaffirm the cat social order in the home and in the wild.

Outdoors, the crouch with its tense, motionless muscles is indicative that the cat is about to attack its prey. In the home, that same crouch with all its gathered energy usually means that your cat is about to pounce on a toy.

It's a great life after all!

Photo by Holly Carter

But the best body language, the position that most delights cat owners and observers alike, is the cat's ultimate relaxation pose. There he is, Thunder Toes, on his back, legs outstretched, belly exposed, not a care or concern in the world. This is total trust, total comfort. In the wild, however, a cat's exposing of its soft underside to an enemy is a sign of submission, or an admission of defeat.

Meow Meow

Since cats make sounds that have specific meanings, many experts say that the sounds constitute a kind of language. Studies of cat vocalization show that there are up to 100 different sounds in the cat's vocabulary. In fact, academic studies have been conducted to classify the sounds by vowels and consonants and to record their meanings. But anyone who's lived with a cat has no need of a *study*. You know when your cat is asking for food, wants to go out, is anxious, or is in pain.

Cats in Our Language
"Well, ain't he the cat's meow!" The cat's meow as meaning something exceptionally good or attractive came into both American and British English early in the 20th century. The cat's whiskers and the cat's pajamas were used in exactly the same way.

Sometimes you'll see your cat making mouth motions as if she were meowing, but there is no sound. Well, you've been fooled. There is a sound, it's just out of the range of human hearing. We call it the *silent meow*. Other cats can hear it just fine.

Yes, cats talk. They also understand. Experts estimate that with training and repetition, cats can be taught to respond to 25 to 50 words. They may not always respond exactly as we want them to, but they do respond.

Tales

Many writers have given the cat the ability to speak its feelings. One of the best of these fables is Rudyard Kipling's *The Cat That Walked By Himself*. It is the story of how early wild woman domesticated early wild man by creating a home into which came the dog, the horse, and the cow.

The independent cat, however, hung back and watched until he was sure the cave was a desirable place. Then he said to early wild woman, "I am not a friend and I am not a servant. I am the Cat who walks by himself and I want to come into your cave."

The cat, as in all good fables, encounters some obstacles to his desired entry. But with flattery and a bit of trickery, he proves his worth in the household and wins not only a place by the fire, but also cream three times a day. There are, however, bargains to be made with the man and dog of the house.

The story ends: "But the Cat keeps his side of the bargain too. He will kill Mice and he will be kind to Babies when he is in the house, as long as they do not pull his tail too hard. But when he has done that, and between times, he is the Cat that walks by himself and all places are alike to him, and if you look out at nights you can see him waving his wild tail and walking by his wild lone—just the same as before."

No Words Needed

Humans make sounds that communicate without words: screams, grunts, sighs, moans, and so on. Cats do too, and their variety, range, and volume for so small an animal is truly magnificent. For cats, these communication devices work well from cat to human and even better from cat to cat.

Growls, from low to rumbling, are threats or signs of anger. Hisses and spits communicate displeasure and dislike far beyond a reasonable doubt. On the other hand, sounds called chirping and cooing, for want of better words, indicate pleasure or some specific message. They're often used by mother cats with their kittens.

Sometimes when cats watch prey through a window, you'll hear a kind of chattering of the jaws. This is not considered an aggressive sound, but rather something like anticipation. Toms approaching girlfriends also do it.

Cats under stress, traveling in a cat crate for example, will make a continuous series of long moans quite different from their normal range of communication devices. The sound obviously does not indicate pain, but rather intense displeasure and also frustration at the inability to escape.

Caterwauling

The dictionary definition of *caterwaul*, to make a harsh cry or to quarrel noisily, applies to humans, but who doesn't think of cats calling in the night whenever the word is used!

Cats in Our Language

First found in writing way back in 1749, *catcall* still means a raucous cry, whistle, or other vocal sound made to show disapproval at a theater or sports event. The catcalls at vaudeville performances in the 1920s and at wrestling matches in the 1950s seemed to be part of the show.

The cliché cartoon goes: *Man opens window and throws boot at howling cats.* The common misconception is that the cats are howling in love calls. Nothing could be further from the truth. The raucous noise that is commonly called caterwauling is made by tom cats discussing territorial rights.

When female cats scream it is an entirely different sound and is usually associated with sex. But we'll get to that in Chapter 18.

Talking with Your Cat

Some cats, like the Siamese for example, tell you more than you ever wanted to know. Their conversation seems constant during their waking hours and sometimes during your sleeping hours. Many cats, however, rarely say more than "I'm hungry."

And from the cat's perspective, so it is with humans too. Some talk a lot and some hardly ever.

"But why bother? They can't understand us," say some talk-not-to-the-cat people.

Most experts agree that it is a good idea to talk to your cat. Cats understand more than you might think. They read our body language just as we read theirs. And cats can often sense human emotions. Most important, however, talking with your cat reinforces the bond between you and your feline friend.

The Least You Need to Know

➤ Cats express their affection through their actions, although the signs may be subtle and sometimes missed.

➤ Visual contact is important to cats, and intense staring is considered a form of intimidation.

➤ The position and movement of a cat's tail is an indication of its mood and motivation.

➤ Cats use specific sounds to convey specific meanings. This "language" can be learned by those humans who choose to pay attention.

Chapter 7

It's Hereditary!

In This Chapter

➤ The importance of genes

➤ Coat color and texture

➤ Classifying the body beautiful

➤ Introducing some breeds

It's funny how a lot of things that are said about cats can be said about humans too. And vice versa.

Eric Gurney, an American cartoonist, said, "The really great thing about cats is their endless variety. One can pick a cat to fit almost any kind of decor, color scheme, income, personality, mood. But under the fur, whatever color it may be, there still lies, essentially unchanged, one of the world's free souls."

Hmmm, humans too. So if we're all essentially alike, what makes the Swedes different from the Italians, the Japanese different from the Chinese, and the Nigerians different from the Greeks? And, come to think of it, what makes the Norwegian Forest Cat different from the Egyptian Mau, the British Shorthair different from the Burmese, and the Himalayan different from the Siamese?

The answer is in the genes.

So What's a Gene?

In the 19th century (the 1870s and '80s to be specific), the abbot of an Augustinian cloister in Austria began to study the source of the different shades of green among the edible peas that grew in the monastery garden. He was Gregor Johann Mendel (1822–1884), and his work with hybrid plants formed the basis for the modern science of genetics.

Genetics is the study of heredity—how traits and characteristics (eye color, hair texture, and body type, for example) are passed from parents to offspring. Genes are the substances that determine these traits. Humans, cats, and all other animals get them on the chromosomes, half from the mother and half from the father, that unite in the first cell of conception.

A gene can be dominant or recessive. Let's take length of coat in cats for an example. The gene for long hair is recessive; the gene for short hair is dominant. So a kitten conceived with a longhaired and a shorthaired gene will have short hair. She will be carrying the recessive gene, however, and some of her offspring may be longhaired cats if she mates with a tom who has long hair or who is also carrying the recessive gene. In other words, it takes either one dominant gene or two recessive genes to produce the trait.

Why is all this important in cats? Because genes determine markings, color, coat, body type, breed, and personality. If you are looking for a kitten, you can learn a lot about what the future holds from its parents. If you plan to breed your cat, you can make choices that will affect the litter.

A Tiger Trait

One of the most common coat colorations seen in both pedigreed and non-pedigreed cats is the striped and spotted pattern we call "tabby." These markings have been inherited through thousands of years from the cat's wild ancestors. Only recently, however, has genetic research pinned down the source of the pattern and color changes to a gene commonly called the *agouti* gene.

MEOW!

It's Been Said

"If man could be crossed with the cat, it would improve man but deteriorate the cat."

—Mark Twain

We see cats with the agouti gene as striped or spotted because each of their hairs is banded with alternating light and dark color. The form of the banding and the amount of pigment (somewhere on the sliding scale between black and yellow) determines the pattern we see. In other words, whether your pet looks like a tiger or a leopard.

Shades and Smokes

Many cats look as though they are a solid color until some movement allows our eyes to catch waves of white coat close to the skin. The individual hairs in the coats of such cats are not banded in patterns like the tabby, but change color only once at some point along the shaft.

When only the outer 25 percent or so of each hair is colored (leaving most of the hair shaft close to the skin white), it's called a shade. When 50 to 80 percent of the shaft is colored (leaving from 20 to 50 percent close to the skin white), it's called a smoke.

Shade and smoke coats come in most colors, even black. They do not, however, come in red or cream, which always have an underlying tabby pattern to some degree. And, of course, they can't be all white.

The One-Color Cat

The solid color cat is the result of a mutation (which is a spontaneous change in the genotype) of the agouti (tabby) gene, followed by human control over breeding. Cats of one color do not have the agouti gene of their wild ancestors.

Some solid color cats, the Siamese for example, are pointed. A pointed cat has a light-colored body and darker hair on the points. The word "points" refers to the nose, ears, tail, lower legs, and paws.

Cats that are solid white carry a dominant color blocking gene that keeps pigment out of the skin and hair. This gene also causes blue, green, copper, or sometimes odd-colored eyes (each eye is a different color). It commonly results in deafness in one or both ears in blue-eyed and occasionally copper-eyed cats.

Some Words For the Cat

Although cats from different regions may *look* different, the word for the animal that we call "cat" is similar in many languages over many centuries:

African: *kadis* or *kadiska*

Arabic: *qatt* and *qittah*

Danish: *kat*

Dutch: *kat*

Egyptian: *kut* and *kutta*

French: *chat*

German: *katze*

Greek: Byzantine *katos, katta*; modern word *kata*

Italian: *gatto*

Latin: *cattus* or *catus*

Polish: *kot*

Russian: *koshkas*

Spanish: *gato*

Swedish: *katta*

Syrian: *qati*

Turkish: *kedi* (kittens)

White with Other Colors

Different from the dominant white gene, another gene, commonly called the white spotting gene, is present when cats have colored coats that are also marked with various degrees of white. The colored areas may be tabby patterned, shades, smokes, or solids. The white areas are pigment free.

You've surely known at least one cat named Mittens or Boots. He or she was probably an example of this gene at work with minimal white (less than 25 percent of the body) appearing. Naturally, scientists called this the "mitted" manifestation. A cat somewhere between one-third and two-thirds white is called a "bi-color." A cat more than two-thirds white with some colored patches is called a "harlequin" or a "van."

Tortoiseshell and Calico

Which is which? The two names are commonly mixed-up. The generally accepted differentiation is that the tortoiseshell is a black cat with red and/or orange markings and some white, while the calico is a white cat with patches of red, orange, and black. More important, however, the tortie has a mottled coat coloring, not distinct patches like a calico.

Most tortoiseshell and calico cats are female. When the rare male is found, he is usually sterile.

Sayings and Superstitions

Calico cats are considered lucky in many parts of the world, including the United States and Canada. In Japan, a traditional figurine of a calico cat with one paw raised is often placed near the main doorway in the home with the hope that she will entice financial good fortune inside. In England and Ireland, calicos are called "money cats."

Long Hair or Short, Silken, or Rough

Since the gene for short hair is dominant in cats, it's not at all surprising that there are more shorthaired cats than any other kind. Most mixed-breed cats (cats the British affectionately call "moggies") are shorthaired.

Among pedigreed cats, however, coat is a prime consideration and short hair has a lot of competition. Much careful breeding has gone into creating and maintaining very breed-specific coat qualities. Besides length, texture and thickness are also characteristics that enter into show judging.

Most longhaired cats are descendants or varieties of the Persian, whose thick winter hairs can be as long as five inches. At the opposite end of the spectrum, the Sphynx has a coat so fine and short that he's usually called "hairless." Two British breeds, the Cornish Rex and the Devon Rex, have coats curly enough to have come right out of the beauty parlor. Examples of rougher coats can be seen in the American Wirehair, the Norwegian Forest Cat, the Maine Coon, and the Chartreux.

Bet You Didn't Know
The first breed created in America was the Maine Coon, with a coat as rough and shaggy as its name. Maine Coons appeared in American cat shows as early as the middle of the 19th century. In 1895, a Maine Coon took Best-in-Show at Madison Square Garden.

Body Types

Lots of us still don't want to accept the idea, but it's a fact: not only height but also weight and bone density are pretty much determined by genes in both cats and humans (and other animals too). In other words, you and your cat are probably going to have a body type a lot like your respective parents. Because of recessive genes, however, there's always the outside possibility that either of you might also take after a distant relative.

Predictions regarding probable body weight, size, and shape are usually more accurate for purebred cats than predictions about the human body or the mixed-breed cat body because there are far fewer unknown recessive genes in the pool. Most cat fanciers discuss their cats' body types within the following groups:

➤ *Cobby:* Short, sturdy cats like the Persian. They have a compact body, a deep chest, and a broad head. Humans like them might be called "stocky."

➤ *Semi-cobby:* Somewhat longer but not quite so sturdy as the cobby cat. The American Shorthair is an example. Humans like them might be called "average" or "medium" build.

➤ *Muscular:* Quite long but with good sturdy bones. The Egyptian Mau and the Havana are good examples. In human terms, we'd probably say "athletic."

➤ *Foreign:* Long, elegant cats like the Abyssinian. Their bodies are slender; their tails are long. We might say a woman like them is "lithe" or "svelte"; a man could be called "wiry."

➤ *Oriental:* Very long and elegant like the Siamese. "Intriguing" and "sinuous" might be good descriptive words for humans of this type.

➤ *Substantial:* Large, sturdy cats like the Maine Coon or the Ragdoll. About humans, we'd just say "big and tall."

Personality Counts!

Many people have tried to associate personality traits in cats to their coat colors. You may have heard that black cats are lovers (or roamers) and that white cats are sensitive. Some say that orange cats are comedians and black-and-whites just want to play all the time.

But in fact, no study has proven any of these associations. The personality of the pet cat will probably be somewhat like that of one or both of its parents, but there's no guarantee. The odds are better among the purebreds where there are at least known tendencies within the breed.

Cat Breeds

Some Helpful Information

If you want to know more about recognized cat breeds and their traits, contact several of the national and international cat fanciers' organizations listed in Chapter 22.

Cat registries and cat fanciers' groups are growing throughout the world. Many countries have several different organizations, which in turn recognize and register different breeds. Today there are more than 50 cat breeds in the United States alone. And, believe it or not, that number is still growing, both here and abroad, as knowledge of genetics allows breeders to emphasize selected traits.

To introduce you to every breed would take a book by itself. Instead, let's take a brief look at some of the best known and some of the most unusual. For your convenience, we've grouped them as: Longhairs, Shorthairs, and Orientals.

Longhairs

Sometimes looked upon as the pampered aristocrats of the feline world, longhaired cats require careful grooming by their owners. Most owners, however, will tell you that their cats are worth every single extra minute.

The Persian

The Persian is probably the ancestor of all longhaired cats.

Some say it is the earliest of the longhaired cats and ancestor to them all. The Persian today can be found in more than 60 varieties and color variations. The Himalayan variety looks like a longhaired Siamese. The red Peke-Face variety is bred to look very much like a Pekinese dog. And the delicate Chinchilla has a sparkling white coat that is lightly tipped at the edges with black in the face, ears, and along the back.

Persians are a small, cobby breed with large round eyes and a large head. Their placid nature and even disposition make them a popular candidate for apartment living. Busy, career-oriented owners, however, must remember that each Persian in the house will need about 15 minutes of grooming time each day!

The Maine Coon

One of the largest cat breeds, the Maine Coon was developed by crossings between Angora cats brought into the United States by British sailors and the semi-wild cats of the Maine forests and coastline. Although this cat does look like a raccoon, crossings with the raccoon are biologically impossible.

An excellent hunter, the Maine Coon is equipped for survival. It has long legs and large paws that can be used almost like hands. But it is a gentle giant and a good family cat.

The Norwegian Forest Cat is similar to the Maine Coon in appearance and temperament, but it is a separate and very ancient breed.

The Maine Coon was the first breed originated in the United States.

The Turkish Van

The Turkish Van is a cat who loves to swim!

White with spots of auburn color on the head and tail, the Turkish Van was discovered around the shores of Lake Van in Turkey. And guess what: they love to swim!

This is a sociable cat with a soft voice. The coat is semi-long (not nearly so long as the Persian), and the eyes are amber or blue. They'll do laps in the pool with you if you let them.

The Ragdoll

The Ragdoll is among the most easygoing of all cats.

This is an all-American breed from the 1960s in California that is rarely seen outside North America. Probably the most laid-back of all cat breeds, Ragdolls will relax completely (they will actually go limp!) when picked up (hence their name) and will rarely fight for any cause. They are both non-aggressive and non-complaining, and they are said to have so extraordinary a tolerance for pain that injuries can go unnoticed. Being so mild-mannered, they do better living indoors where they will have some protection.

Ragdolls are large cats, as large as the Maine Coon, with semi-long fur and blue eyes that give more than a hint at their white Persian ancestry. Most experts believe there is also some Siamese in their background.

Shorthairs

Shorthaired cats far outnumber their longhaired cousins. Virtually all cats born in the wild are shorthaired since that gene is dominant. There is, however, great variety among cats with this coat characteristic.

The American Shorthair

The American Shorthair is the cat people think of when they hear the word "cat."

The American Shorthair is the cat you are most likely to find on your doorstep. It's what most people visualize when they think of a cat. And, of course, it is very similar to the breed from which it probably descended, the British Shorthair.

The oldest recorded coloring on the Shorthair was the tabby, which is still both common and popular. Shorthairs also come in the solid colors: white, black, blue, cream, chocolate, and lilac. Or, if you prefer, you can choose tortoiseshell, calico, pointed, shaded, smoked, tipped, bi-colors, and vans. In other words, this is the most variety you're ever going to get in the cat world.

The American Wirehair is exactly like its cousin except for a coat that got, perhaps, a little too much perm. It first appeared in Vernon, New York in 1966.

The Scottish Fold

The Scottish Fold is a cat with a teddy-bear face.

This breed is an example of a spontaneous mutation. In 1961 on a farm in Perthshire, Scotland, a farm cat gave birth to a white kitten with folded ears. She was named Susie, and two years later she bore a kitten who looked very much like her.

Further breeding showed that when Folds are bred to cats with normal ears, half the litter will be Folds. When Folds are bred to Folds, however, kittens may be born with a skeletal disorder where the vertebrae of the tail become fused and cartilage grows around the toes. It's important to remember, therefore, that this breed should always be mated with American, British, or Exotic Shorthairs, not with other Scottish Folds.

Folds are easygoing, loving, and intelligent cats with soft voices and tolerant dispositions. They do well in families.

The Chartreux

The Chartreux is a breed naturally occurring in France, where its dense, water-repellent, blue fur is much admired. With a large sturdy body and slender legs, it is both strong and agile and is an excellent hunter.

This breed is sometimes confused with the blue-coated British Shorthair, but most American and French breeders keep the two breeds separate. The Chartreux is particularly loyal to its owner and its home. Many people believe the breed originated with the Carthusian monks in the 16th century.

The Chartreux is called the blue cat of France.

Orientals

Many new breeds have been derived by mating the ancient Siamese type cat with other purebreds. All have the lithe and graceful body type of their forebears.

The Siamese

The Siamese is intelligent, affectionate, and a great talker.

The Siamese is the extrovert of the cat world. It greets everyone, demands its due attention, and expresses its opinion on everything. Some people are bothered by its rather loud voice, which it uses more or less constantly, others love the ongoing conversation.

Despite being a small, graceful, slender cat, the Siamese will usually dominate other cats in the household. Most Siamese love children and do well in family situations, even though they may consider one particular adult as their own. They are very intelligent and, like other aristocrats, can sometimes be moody.

The Abyssinian

The Abyssinian is an agile athlete.

Many people believe that the Abyssinian breed is the ancestor of all others, being the cat of ancient Egypt. It has a medium-sized body and long legs that combine with excellent musculature to produce the look of a fine athlete. The breed also has the energy of an athlete and needs space to exercise. Oh, and it loves to play in the water.

Abyssinians are intelligent, affectionate, and interact well with their owners. They will learn tricks and usually enjoy showing off and being praised. They do not like to be left alone for long periods of time, and they do not like to be crowded.

The Oriental Longhair

The Oriental Longhair has a Siamese body with a semi-long coat.

Called the Oriental Longhair even though its coat is only semi-long, this breed combines many of the qualities of the Siamese and the Persian. It is thin and graceful but also strong and well muscled. The texture of its coat is fine and silky. The tail plume is especially long and feathery.

The Oriental Longhair usually gets along well with other pets in the family and with the family members too. It's an especially curious and inquisitive cat and expresses its affections openly.

Your Moggie

The vast majority of cats in homes around the world have no pedigrees. You may be able to recognize traits in your cat's physical makeup or personality that align him or her with one of the established breeds, but you can't really prove anything. And it doesn't matter. Your cat is an individual and precious as such—just like his or her human!

The Least You Need to Know

➤ The physical features and personality traits of your cat are determined primarily by its genes.

➤ Coat color and texture is an identifying characteristic in the cat world.

➤ Cats are sometimes classified by body type.

➤ The number of cat breeds is growing as genetic knowledge is used to bring out desired traits.

What Cats Do

What *do* cats do?

"Not much," say the ailurophobes.

"More than you can imagine," say the ailurophiles.

Who's right? Both. And an infinite number of answers in between.

Your perception of what cats do and how valuable their contribution to life on this planet is all depends on your standards of measurement. Is function and achievement most important to you? Are relationships and quality of life most important to you?

Or, perhaps bettering the quality of individual lives is an immense achievement. In the opinion of many, that's what cats do.

They Catch Mice, Don't They?

In the 19th century, the French artist Theophile-Alexandre Steinlen did many drawings of cats catching mice.

Yes, and their amazing ability as mousers drew them from the wild into domestic life in ancient Egypt. There, cats kept civilization's earliest silos free of pests. Cats shared mousing honors with ferrets in ancient Greece. By the middle ages in Europe, cats had a mixed reputation, often feared as the embodiment of the devil, but respected as the foe of rodents. They were still secretly welcome in barns and grain storage buildings.

Cats in Our Language

Although the Latin word for cat is *cattus,* medieval documents almost always refer to the cat by the function it performed: *musio, muriceps,* or *murilegus,* which mean *mouse catcher.* It's probably not coincidence that occupation-derived surnames were just coming into being at that point in history. The person who ran the mill might be called *John the miller* and later *John Miller.* The blacksmith might be called *John the smith* and later *John Smith.* Good thing *the mouse catcher* didn't catch on.

Barn cats are still found around the world today. Studies show that with a daily ration of milk to keep them thinking of the place as "home," barn cats are effective at virtually eliminating mice in a barn. They have more trouble with rats; they are often able to keep the rat population from expanding and thereby potentially ruining a stored crop but are rarely able to eliminate the rodent completely.

It's usually not far from the barn to the house and many an ancient farm wife must have brought a favorite cat or two into her home. "After all, mice can get into the kitchen too!" was certainly the thought. So it happened that the protective house cat became a cross-cultural tradition that has traveled down the centuries. And it's still going!

In 1979 Sissy Wieczorek hadn't been in her newly built house three months when she brought home a six-toed yellow tabby. "We want to make sure no mouse chooses this place for a home," she said. "You know the mice can tell when there's a cat in the house." Her family hasn't seen a mouse in 17 years, and Claudius, the cat, is still doing just fine.

Bet You Didn't Know Among today's preserved papers from Ireland in the 5th century, there's a list that names items considered especially helpful to women in the home. The cat appears on that list!

In 1995 Claire and Tom Harris moved into a renovated barn as their first home. They brought with them their three cats, Rosencrantz, Guildenstern, and George Eliot. "Well, we'd rather live with cat hair than mouse droppings," said Tom. "And besides, we like the cats."

The Cat Police

Aptly named after the Les Miserables *character, Javert Cat brings in another one.*

83

Wherever there is food, either stored or discarded, there is an attractive area for mice, yet mice are definitely unwanted in public places. So what's the solution? Owners and caretakers of these areas have used cats to do battle almost since people have gathered for work, meetings, travel, and entertainment.

There are cat police at work in stadiums, bus and train stations, warehouses, post offices, churches, stores, and even manufacturing plants. In fact, cats are often used to control mice wherever humans leave their apple cores and sandwich crusts or store the ingredients that will make their apple pies and hoagies. The cat/human partnership goes back a long way!

Through most of our agricultural history, grains have been ground into flour at mills. Here was a gathering place for foodstuffs that was always being resupplied. What mouse could resist the sacks sitting about the floor? And what miller didn't have at least one cat! Today there are few waterside mills in the United States, but the work of the cat continues elsewhere.

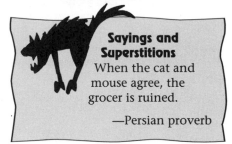

Sayings and Superstitions

When the cat and mouse agree, the grocer is ruined.

—Persian proverb

Prior to the middle of the 20th century, encounters with mice and their droppings were a major problem for people who went out of their homes to purchase food. Supermarkets did not yet exist and most people shopped at the corner grocer. Many of the commodities sold there were delivered and distributed in burlap sacks that could easily be chewed through by mice. Virtually every grocer had a cat.

Even today, if you look closely in the pet food aisle, you may see some 25-pound dog or cat food bags that are chewed through near the corners—a dead giveaway for mouse infestation. And, yes, there are still some supermarket cats employed in the biggest and best stores.

HEY!

Bet You Didn't Know

A mouser that worked for Shepherd & Son Ltd. in Lancashire, England has been noted in several record books. He was a tabby named Mickie who was on mouse patrol in this wholesale/retail business from 1945 until his death in 1968. During that time he accrued over 22,000 dead mice to his credit.

Tales

How valuable is a mouse catcher? The British still tell a story that came down from an epitaph long since destroyed by the Great Fire of London (1666). The headstone that stood above the body of Dick Whittington, the man who was mayor in 1398, 1406, and 1419, read:

> Beneath this stone lies Whittington,
> Sir Richard rightly named,
> Who three times Lord Mayor served in London,
> In which he ne'er was blamed.
> He rose from indigence to wealth
> By industry and that,
> For lo! he scorned to gain by stealth
> *What he got by cat.*

So what did Dick Whittington get by cat?

Popular legend has it that Dick Whittington was a poor orphan lad who went to London to make his fortune. A kind merchant found him starving in the streets and assigned him to work helping the cook. But the cook was cruel and Dick ran away.

Resting by the side of the road, he heard the bells of the church of St. Mary-le-Bow in London. They seemed to say: *"Turn again, Whittington, thrice Lord Mayor of London."* So he went back to the merchant master who, somewhat later, allowed all his servants to partake in sending a cargo of merchandise to Barbary. Dick sent his cat.

As fortune would have it, the King of Barbary was much troubled by mice, which Dick Whittington's cat promptly and efficiently destroyed. So the king paid a great sum for the cat.

Dick Whittington used the money to start up a successful business. He married his merchant master's daughter, was knighted, and became not only thrice Lord Mayor of London, but also the city's richest merchant. He died in 1423 leaving his vast fortune to charity and the public good.

The epitaph on the headstone was real. The man was also real. Is the story real? Who knows. But every young British entrepreneur would like to have Dick Whittington's cat!

In Business

Why would a business that does not deal in food keep a cat? Cats are living in more and more small offices, accounting firms, advertising firms, lawyers' offices, and just about everywhere else in American enterprise. Why?

Because cats do more than catch mice. They have a calming effect on people. Watching and interacting with a cat can put the battles and frustrations of the business day into perspective. What is the value of stroking a soft, warm, purring animal when you want to kick the trash can? A lot.

It's Been Said

"You can't look at a sleeping cat and be tense."

—Jane Pauley, American journalist

Bookstores seem especially attractive to working cats. Somehow feline forms just "look right" draped over the assortment of bestsellers or curled up in an empty spot on a shelf. Christopher Cronin, a theater sound designer, commented: "Every bookstore should have a cat. A cat comes up and checks you out as you browse, communicates a bit, and then lets you know he'll be around should you need help."

In many pet supply stores, the role of the working cat goes beyond greeting and companionship. Cats actually model the latest in pet wear as well as attract repeat customers who come to "visit" their favorite cats.

Sayings and Superstitions

When the cat's away the mice will play.
This saying occurs in many languages around the world. In the scheme of things, the cat symbolizes the authority figure who keeps underlings in line.

While the spotted Dalmatian is still considered the traditional fire company mascot, there are many, many more firehouse cats than firehouse dogs. In Great Britain, theater cats are considered instruments of good luck and much in demand. And throughout the western world, there's many a place of worship that has its resident cat to greet the people before every service.

Messages Beyond Understanding

Cats very often seem to know something we don't know, something that's coming or about to happen. Do they have ESP—extrasensory perception? Where do they get these messages? No one seems to know. But the cat has been associated with the supernatural from the time it became the cat-as-we-know-it in ancient Egypt.

In addition to their primary job (rodent control), cats have been weather predictors at sea almost as long as there have been ships. An excited cat rushing about and pursuing her tail was said to predict a coming storm. The saying was: *The cat has a gale of wind in her tail.*

A cat seen washing behind its ears still predicts imminent rain on land or sea to many people in many countries.

In ancient China, cats were honored as protectors of the hearth and used to predict earthquakes. "That was then," you say. Well, not much has changed in a few thousand years. Many people in earthquake prone areas around the world still swear by their cats.

Cats in Our Language
Since 1665, the name for the nine corded whip used for flogging unruly sailors was *cat-o'-nine-tails*. It was not formally abolished as a form of civil punishment for crimes of violence until 1948!

One couple who had moved to Kentucky after experiencing several California quakes said Shirley, their cat, knew every time a quake was coming. "She would get agitated," they said. "She'd go in and out, in and out, every 2 or 3 minutes. It was like she wanted to escape, but she kept coming back in to get us. She wasn't usually more than 15 minutes off, even when the rumblings were minor. After her second or third prediction, we always believed her."

Some cats work at detecting smaller "rumblings" and more subtle signs. There are innumerable cats who wake their owners every morning just before the alarm clock rings. Newspapers have reported cats who woke their owners when a fire started or a gas line was leaking. *Cat Fancy* magazine reported a Siamese cat in a group home in Dickinson, North Dakota who could predict imminent seizures in the residents.

How do they know? Is it some kind of magical witchcraft after all? Probably not. Cats are extremely sensitive animals. They can hear and smell better than we can, and their whiskers are sensitive to minute movements in the air. It's great to know that they are willing to use these extraordinary senses to help their humans.

Tales

Many stories and myths of cats helping humans have come down to us over the centuries, but the most famous of all is still *Puss in Boots*. This tale first appeared in Italy in 1530, then in France in 1585. By 1697 it had reached England. The newest and most beautifully illustrated of many American editions appeared in 1995.

In the story, a marvelously accomplished cat befriends a penniless young miller. The cat uses his quick wit and several ingenious tricks to pass off the miller as the *Marquis of Carabas* and secures for him not only great wealth, but also a princess bride.

Therapists and Visitors

Science is just beginning to understand the important role emotions play in illness and health. As we become more aware of this mind and body connection, we are also learning how the relationships between humans and their pets can affect the physical and emotional well-being of both. Cats have been known to lower blood pressure, alleviate stress, and help dispel depression. Slowly we are beginning to make them a part of therapy teams for both children and adults.

Dr. Philip Pizzo, chief of Pediatrics and head of the Infectious Disease section of the National Cancer Institute, believes that hospitalized children benefit tremendously from contact with animals. The contact seems to serve as a kind of bridge to their home environment. Speaking of a pet therapy program, he said, "It's a way to comfort children. It simply provides a spiritual fortitude that helps them deal with the difficulties they face. My assessment is that it enhances dignity."

Pet visitation programs in nursing homes and mental hospitals also provide pleasure with dignity for adults. Many of these patients were forced to give up their pets when they entered these long-term care facilities. When a pet visitor program is implemented, the often tedious and sometimes lonely days are broken up by the recurring opportunity to hold a soft and affectionate animal. Both men and women are grateful.

In a journal she kept during the two years in a nursing home before her death, Joyce Horner, a poet, novelist, and teacher, wrote about her wish to have a cat to pet despite her extremely crippled and deformed arthritic fingers. In a magazine, she had read about a hermit in the 6th century who had given up all his possessions for God's sake, except his cat "with which he played oft and held it in his lap deliciously." The story, she says, "made me wish for a cat then and there."

Fortunately, pet therapy and pet activity programs are growing across the nation. Dogs have led the way in this new venture, but cats are coming into their own. In fact, according to one Texas program director, there are more special requests for cats than for dogs.

Some Helpful Information

If you are interested in animal assisted activities or animal assisted therapy, you can contact the *Pet Partners* program of the Delta Society at 289 Perimeter Rd. East, Renton, WA 98055-1329. Their phone number is (206) 226-7357, and their fax number is (206) 235-1076. This organization offers a national registration system for pets and volunteers. It also does training for volunteers and sets up health, skills, and aptitude screening for pets. They offer a newsletter, handbooks, and other printed materials.

Home Bodies

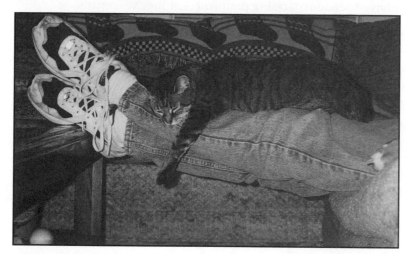

But what do most cats do?

Photo by Holly Carter

But what do *most* of the cats we know do? They live with us. They sleep, they eat, they play, they purr, and they welcome us when we return home. They are our friends and companions. We keep them because they are interesting and because they are interested in the things we do and, in fact, in our just being alive.

In some ways, cats seem almost human. In some ways, they seem better. Aldous Huxley said, "If you want to be a psychological novelist and write about human beings, the best thing you can do is to keep a pair of cats." Ernest Hemingway took his advice and kept many cats.

And finally, they are beautiful. There is an art gallery in Clinton, Connecticut that leaves several sculpture pedestals vacant whenever an exhibit is mounted. These are for the cats who live in the gallery and invariably compete favorably with the art.

MEOW!

It's Been Said

"Sometimes he sits at your feet looking into your face with an expression so gentle and caressing that the depth of his gaze startles you. Who can believe that there is no soul behind those luminous eyes!"

—Théophile Gautier, French writer (1811–1872)

The Least You Need to Know

➤ Cats are, and always have been, outstanding performers at mouse control.

➤ Cats are entering the American workplace as stress relievers, companions, models, and receptionists.

➤ Some cats seem to catch messages before they can be perceived by humans.

➤ The company of cats can improve the health and happiness of humans.

Part 3
Home, Sweet Cat-Filled Home

Your new companion is beginning to settle in now as he explores his home and certainly keeps you on your toes.

In the next several chapters, you'll read about all the decisions you'll have to make, from selecting pet food to checking for household hazards to whether your pet should be kept indoors or allowed out. Heavy stuff. But there's fun here too, like playing with your cat and relaxing with some cat-themed books, movies, and magazines.

Chapter 9

Settling In, For Both of You

In This Chapter

➤ Cats are intelligent, although teaching them tricks can sometimes be...tricky

➤ Declawing: is it necessary or just cruel?

➤ The many poisonous substances around your home

➤ Other household threats

Once your cat is more or less assimilated into your household—there might still be some hissing between the newcomer and your other pets—there are household decisions to make and actions to take.

If this is your first cat, you will have to look at your home as one big potential source of danger for your pet. That fluffball, whether she is a kitten or an eight-year-old, will no doubt be into *everything* as she explores her new turf.

Cats Can Be Taught a Thing or Two

Are cats intelligent? Well, *yours* is, of course, but what about all the others? Actually, it has been difficult to judge cats' smarts because it is hard to test them. They do not react well to the action/reward system of grading that scientists use with lab rats and mice. And while a dog will beg and perform tricks for praise or affection, few cats will so demean themselves or stand still long enough to be trained.

However, it is generally believed that cats are neither more nor less intelligent than other domesticated animals. Scientists working with cats note that they certainly can learn to respond to selected stimuli, and they show quite a bit of ingenuity. Of course, even without scientific tests, those of us who are owned by cats know they can indeed be very smart, clever, and even sly. And communicate? A cat expresses herself in many different ways—using her voice, her tail, her ears, the position of her body, and purring and licking her owner. All of that is "talking."

Those who have had their cat tear from an upstairs bedroom down to the kitchen in 10 seconds when he hears the can opener hit the tin of Tuna Treat will know that cats are quick-minded (they also have great hearing). There are cats that can open the refrigerator door as well as doors to outside the home (usually the latch kind that can be lifted).

A cat is apt to know his own name. Will he come when called? He might if he is so inclined. He can also learn perhaps 25 to 50 other words (dogs can learn a few more), most of them dear to his heart, such as "eat" and "treat." He will probably also respond to your own special terms of endearment, and his little ears pick up to "no," "stop," "stay," "down," and other reprimands, although it could be the stern tone of your voice that makes him obey.

What about tricks? Can you teach your cat to dance with a lampshade on her head? You can *try*. You might be able to train her to do simple tricks, such as sitting up and reaching for a treat or toy, with *much* repetition and with no session lasting more than 10 minutes, which is about the length of a cat's attention span. Your success will depend on the cat's intelligence and mood of the moment, along with the difficulty of the trick.

You are likely to have more luck teaching your pet no-nos, and scoring a few points in that area will make most owners happy enough. There is more about this in Chapter 12.

Also in the brainy cat department is the question of how cats find their way home when lost, or how they travel thousands of miles to rejoin an owner. Chapter 10 talks about that phenomenon.

MEOW! **It's Been Said**

"Some Cats is blind, and stone-deaf some, But ain't no Cat wuz ever dumb."

—Anthony Henderson Euwer, American poet and writer

MEOW! **It's Been Said**

"By and large, people who enjoy teaching animals to roll over will find themselves happier with a dog."

—Barbara Holland, writer

MEOW! **It's Been Said**

"I love cats because I love my home; and little by little, they become its visible soul."

—Jean Cocteau, filmmaker and poet

Big Decision: To Declaw or Not to Declaw

Here are the two schools of thought on this major issue: "He's going to be an indoor cat, but I don't want my furniture ruined, so I'm having him declawed." And "Declaw? Never. How would *you* like to have your nails pulled out one by one and be forced to walk around on stumps for the rest of your life?"

Which is the right way to go here? It is don't declaw. In fact, these days many veterinarians will not perform that operation.

But what about your home, you say? What about scratches to *you*?

Chapter 12 goes into ways of repelling your pet when it tries to sit on or scratch furniture, and Chapter 17 talks about the cat's reasons for doing this and other types of destructive behavior.

All of those suggestions mean a little more work for you. But they will bring the results you want without having to subject your pet to that loathsome operation.

Bet You Didn't Know Sometimes the entire nail bed in a declawed cat is not removed and one or more claws will begin to grow again. These are usually quite different from the original claws, however, and are misshapen and of no use to the animal.

Common Household Poisons

There are some products around your home that might as well carry a skull and crossbones on them as far as your pet is concerned. These include most cleaning agents, which should be kept out of reach. You might even want to invest in interior latches, sold at hardware stores, that keep kitchen, bathroom, and other cabinet doors from being opened by toddlers and curious cats.

Even drinking water from the toilet could cause your cat harm if you have cleaned the bowl with chemicals and their toxic residues remain in the water. It's best to keep the toilet lid down.

Keep the inquisitive one in another room when carpets are being cleaned and when fumigation is going on. Also be careful of products used on furniture to waterproof it or make it stain resistant. Using aerosol sprays near a cat's food or water bowl can also cause it harm.

The problem isn't just their eating cleaning supplies and similar products, it is also their walking through those substances and then washing and licking it off themselves.

If your cat does somehow ingest a toxic substance, you will notice any one, or a few, of these symptoms: drooling, respiratory difficulties, vomiting, fits, a staggering gait, and even unconsciousness. Get the animal to a veterinarian without delay. Do not try home-made formulas, which could be toxic to pets or at the least waste valuable time. If a vet is some distance away, call and follow his or her directions for emergency treatment. You might also ask around at veterinary clinics and animal shelters for the number of a local poison control center, which might offer free advice.

Some Helpful Information

If your pet seems to be in trouble from a toxic substance, you can also call the 24-hour National Animal Poison Control Center, a nonprofit service of the College of Veterinary Medicine at the University of Illinois. A veterinarian will answer the phone, or you will be handed over to one. You can call (800) 548-2423 for a charge of $30 per case, or (900) 680-0000 for $20 for the first five minutes and $2.95 for each additional minute (the typical call lasts 10 minutes). Your fee covers any follow-up calls. Payment is by credit card only.

The Greenery Around Your Place

Cats love to nibble on grass, which can be a good digestive aid. Their chewing on it can help them cough up a furball. But an indoor cat, not likely to find a lawn in your living room, could start chomping on any green leaves it finds, such as plants on a tabletop or small trees on the floor.

Cats love to nibble grass, a good digestive aid. You can grow a small pot for your indoor cat, if you like.

Photo by Frank Smith

The list of harmful house plants is a lengthy one. For example, avocado, dieffenbachia (also known as the mother-in-law plant, or mother-in-law's tongue), English ivy, philodendron, the sturdy pothos, and the spider plant are bad for cats. So are the asparagus fern, Boston ivy, ficus (weeping fig), and shefflera.

If your cat goes outside, it might find other kinds of landscaping that could be bad for it.

Cats should avoid azaleas, boxwood, buttercup, chrysanthemum, iris, laurel, lily of the valley, morning glory, oleander, poison ivy, and yew. Ask your veterinarian if he or she has a complete list of plants and flowers harmful to pets. You might inquire at a poison control center near you too.

"Good grief," you say, "outdoors is one thing, but it sounds like I can't have *any* houseplants." But you can. For one thing, some cats never bother a plant. Yours could be one of them. Also, you can hang the toxic greenery up high, or keep it out of a paw's reach. Try sprinkling cayenne pepper on the soil of your plants, the smell of which will repel your pet (you'll have to keep sprinkling though—the odor will fade and need to be refreshed). You can also grow catnip indoors for your pet to nibble on and to divert it from the bad stuff. There's more about catnip in Chapter 13.

Safe plants for a cat to be around include begonias, coleus, dracaena, ferns, grape ivy, and several varieties of peperomia. Most cacti are safe, except for the pencil, peyote, and the candelabra cactus, which are poisonous.

Bet You Didn't Know
Marijuana as a pot plant in some ways acts on your cat the way catnip does. If she eats it, she will experience both the stimulating and relaxing properties of catnip, plus, perhaps, hallucinations. But the similarity ends there. Your cat might have a seizure from marijuana and could easily die from it.

Some Helpful Information

Besides chewing on plant leaves, cats will sometimes take up the unlovely habit of urinating in the pots. This is more likely with large-sized floor tubs, where they jump in, begin scratching the dirt, and water your plant for you. To discourage this habit, you might cover the dirt with cypress mulch or similar chips, loosely arranged playing marbles, or small pebbles, all of which disguise the smell of and access to the earth, while still allowing water and air through to the plant.

Jingle, Belle

As much as cats love Christmas—and some of them become adorably freaky when holiday decorations are brought out of storage—this holiday brings a new set of perils to the merry-making pet. Greenery that is either poisonous or otherwise dangerous to cats includes such favorites as holly, mistletoe, and even pine needles. In recent years, the poinsettia has been absolved of causing illness to cats, although you might still want to keep yours away from it as you would other plants.

Tinsel, angel hair (a synthetic substance that looks like a mop of golden hair and can be separated and placed in tree branches), glass ornaments, the hooks that hold ornaments to the tree, real berries, the water at the base of the tree (especially if you have added a chemical to it to prolong its life), and much of your Christmas tree are harmful to a pet. Try to place safe ornaments, such as small stuffed or wooden toys, on the lower part of the tree where the cat might be able to swat at them from the floor and get them into its mouth, and place the other decorations on higher branches. Either on the bottom or on the entire tree, substitute narrow ribbon for those hooks.

Then there are the lights. Cover cords to outlets with wire camouflage so your cat cannot bite through them or stab them with its claws.

Let's see, should I climb those draperies or…I know! I'll run up the Christmas tree!

For the gymnastic feline, be sure the tree is anchored by wire, string, or a hook to some part of a wall or the ceiling in case he attempts to scale it and it topples. Actually, an artificial tree might not interest your cat at all and spare you some of the worry.

Keep an eye on your pet when exchanging gifts—this goes for all gift-giving occasions—so that he does not swallow the ribbon used for wrapping presents.

Whew, that's certainly a lot more work for you during an already busy time of year, isn't it? Still, all you would need during those hectic days is an unexpected, frantic dash to the 24-hour veterinary clinic with a *very* sick cat. So it does pay to cat-proof your holiday decor along with your other furnishings.

Other Puddy Perils

How much mischief can a two-year-old toddler get into? Multiply that a few times and you will have some idea of where the curiosity of a cat, especially a kitten, can lead that pet. Using just the kitchen as an example, you will have to make sure there is no room for the cat to squeeze behind the refrigerator. Also watch that it does not get on top of the stove while it is lit. Cats love warmth and hidden places, so you will *always* have to check the clothes dryer before turning it on. Check the washing machine and even the dishwasher. When you have the refrigerator door open, glance inside before you shut it. It is amazing how quickly a kitten can leap into that appliance while your back is turned. When you think, "Where *is* that cat?" you will often be astonished at where the little whiskers turns up.

If you see your pet gnawing at electrical wires, you can buy wire camouflage strips at a hardware store. Naturally, you will want to keep her away from open windows and balconies.

Some Helpful Information
Your cat could find itself in trouble through no fault of its own. Consider buying a pet decal to stick on a window of your home to alert the fire department or anyone else in an emergency situation that you have animals inside. You will find these at pet supply stores and in mail-order catalogs. The ones with a blank for you to write in the number of pets in your household are best, so all can be accounted for in a crisis.

Bet You Didn't Know
A study on "high-rise syndrome" in cats, conducted a few years ago by the Animal Medical Center in New York City, found that of the 132 cases they considered of cats that fell, 10 percent of the animals were euthanized (sometimes because the owner could not afford treatment). Of the survivors, although many were seriously injured, the most serious were those that fell five to nine stories. There is a complicated explanation for that, having to do with the rate of speed at which objects drop, depending on the height from which they fall.

Are you now feeling a little overwhelmed at all the threats to your cat from your home itself, plus its various plants, bottles, and powders? Are you wondering how you are going to keep one step ahead of your pet?

We have a suggestion that can help, especially if you are a first-time pet owner. Take a pad of Post-it notes, mark a number of sheets "cat," and stick them to the washing machine, clothes dryer, window ledges, cabinets under the kitchen and bathroom sinks, and all other sources of danger to your pet. Eventually you will automatically think about the cat when you are near those appliances or parts of the house, and then you can remove the strips. After a while, being careful really does become second nature.

The Least You Need to Know

➤ Of course cats are smart, but their capabilities, instincts, and reactions differ from other domestic animals.

➤ Training is certainly possible, although for most owners, training them to stay off counters and certain pieces of furniture, plus other good behavior you want around the house, is more likely to be successful than teaching a cat "tricks."

➤ Skip declawing and try other ways to keep your home furnishings from being attacked.

➤ You will need to cat-proof your home against poisons and potential trouble spots.

Chapter 10

Citizen Cat

In This Chapter

➤ Indoor versus outdoor cats

➤ Many communities have leash laws even for cats

➤ When your pet is lost

➤ Who has custody of the cat in a divorce?

Just as you have obligations beyond your front door as a citizen of your community, so too does your cat. Or let's say you do *representing* your cat. Although you may let your furball do almost anything he likes, your neighbors and the folks down at city hall are not likely to be so indulgent. You can read about minding your civic p's and q's in the next several pages.

There are other legal matters that affect your cat, such as divorce and your will. For a little bit of a thing, your pet crops up more often than you would think in many areas of your life that touch on the law.

Should Yours Be an Indoor or Outdoor Cat?

About half of all companion cats live exclusively inside. The remainder either go in and out or live outdoors 100 percent of the time. Check your community laws. Some prohibit "owned" cats from roaming freely.

What is the current buzz on the indoor/outdoor issue for pet owners who have a choice?

A cat *can* live a happy life indoors, and that is what professionals interested in cats' welfare are suggesting more and more these days. Sure, there are country cats, farm cats, and barn cats that can lead long lives outside, but there are many perils to life outdoors for other companion pets in built-up locales: traffic, other cats and animals, dangerous terrain, poisonous plants and food, and *people* who poison, torture, or kill cats.

Dr. Franklin Loew, dean of Tufts University School of Veterinary Medicine has said, "There are four keys to longevity in cats. One is luck; two is proper nutrition; three is health care, including appropriate vaccinations; and four is keeping out of harm's way." For most owners, harm's way is the great outdoors.

Bet You Didn't Know The typical cat living exclusively or mostly outdoors has an average life span of about 3 years. That's compared to 12 to 16 years or so for an indoor pet.

There is a compromise here: a controlled outdoors experience, where cats can feel the breeze on their fur, watch leaves fall at their feet, and even come precariously close to a bird or two. Some owners—with the space to do this, of course—rig up a shelter or a run made up of wood or wire fencing for their cat in the yard. Others keep their pet on a leash tied up out front or back so that they can experience the outdoors. Some take their cats for a stroll around the neighborhood. Really. There is more about the correct way to do this coming up.

There are also fencing systems that keep your cat confined to its own property when outdoors. Check cat magazines for advertisements for these products.

Finally, your community might just make the indoor/outdoor decision for you, as you will see in the next few pages.

Courtesy of The Humane Society of the United States

The Pet Door

You have probably seen these advertised as a major convenience allowing your cat to go in and out of your home at will. The door comes in a variety of sizes and can be easily installed by a novice (making sure it is the right height for the cat to step through). A common style is a rubber flap that allows ease of movement by the cat going in and out and a slide that moves vertically up and down if you want to close the door at times. Some feature an indicator that tells you whether your cat is in or out, while others open only after matching a magnet that is on your pet's collar, which registers when that animal approaches, letting it in. Cats without that magnetized collar cannot enter.

Bet You Didn't Know Sir Isaac Newton is said to have invented the cat door for the use of his own pets.

Pet door kits can be found at hardware stores and home centers for around $30 to $70 or so, depending on the size you choose and the number of special features you elect. If the door you want will be between two inside rooms, you might want to skip the kit and create a less expensive entry of your own design with no need for a flap.

If you have a toddler around, you will want to make certain the opening isn't large enough for the child to squeeze through. Depending on your cat's smarts, it might take a while to train it to use the exit. One family, who installed a pet door leading from the kitchen to the attached garage where they kept the cat litter, was never able to train the cat to nose its way through. So they cut off the rubber entry flap, figuring the waste of heated/cooled air from the now-open pet door was minimal. The cat quickly went through the unblocked opening.

Tales
You might enjoy the visitors that enter through your pet door. One man occasionally sees a strange blond cat who follows his calico, Maggie, inside his house. He calls the cat Kato, after America's most famous house guest of the O. J. Simpson murder trial. When Kato shows up, the man just picks him up and puts him outside again.

You will also want to make sure your pet door is far enough away from bolts and locks to deter burglars from inserting gadgets that can open your house door from the inside. Finally, you know that if your cat comes in after touring the neighborhood, so can other felines. Hmmm. Some manufacturers offer products that are difficult to swing open, such as the door the cat pulls out when he is ready to come back in, making it impossible for a friend to follow him through without learning just how to do that. There is also the previously mentioned magnet that serves as a code to the door.

Local Laws that Can Affect Your Pet

In many communities, a cat, even one kept indoors, must be registered and licensed with the appropriate local government agency. There is, of course, an annual fee for that tag. Rabies inoculations are often required each year too. Rabies, you say, for an *indoor* cat? Well, if your cat should accidentally slip out of the house, he will need that protection in the outdoors. Also, if a rabid bat ever got into your place—not totally outside the realm of possibility—you would be glad your pet had that preventive shot.

Some towns do not allow "owned" cats to roam the streets unleashed any more than they do dogs that have a home.

Your local government can fill you in on leash and other pet laws in your area. If you violate a cat-at-large law, you might be charged a fine of anywhere from $15 to $1,000.

Sometimes you must answer to both your town and your residential community for a roaming cat. Many single-family home, condominium, and cooperative developments and mobile-home communities have bylaws that state, among other dos and don'ts, that there can be no more than a specific number of pets per household and that they are allowed out only on a leash. If you are considering moving, be certain to ask your real estate agent or the seller of the home you are considering buying to show you the bylaws *before* you make a deposit on any property. While the laws can be changed during your residency in those communities, you will have input about changes then.

Restrictions can also apply to those in rental apartments. Some buildings or complexes allow pets; others do not or limit their number per household.

An exception to the no pets rule is federally funded developments designated exclusively for renters who are disabled or elderly.

This can be a complicated area. Usually, if you sign a lease with a no pets clause, you must not have, or subsequently acquire, companion animals. However, at least one exception is New York City, where there is an ordinance prohibiting landlords from enforcing the no pets rule if a tenant has lived openly with his or her animal for three months or more.

> **Cats in Our Language**
> *Cat on a hot tin roof* does not, of course, refer to a cat roaming from one rooftop to another. It means being nervous or edgy.

If you have a problem or questions in this area, you can call the Animal Legal Defense Fund at (415) 459-0885 for information or the name of an attorney in your community knowledgeable about this legal specialty.

The Cat in Winter: A Checklist

Keep these points in mind when the north wind doth blow where you are:

✓ It is best to keep cats indoors when the temperature plummets. Their fur coats are not that protective; they can suffer from hypothermia just like people.

✓ If your cat does go out, check its paw pads and between its nails regularly for salt and deicers. These products can irritate paws, and when they are ingested after the cat licks its feet clean, they can cause more trouble.

✓ Antifreeze has a sweet taste cats like, but even a few drops can be lethal. Make certain there are no puddles in your garage. You might want to switch to a *propylene* glycol instead of the highly toxic *ethylene* glycol-based product. One brand is Sierra; call (800) 289-7234 for local retailers. Another brand is Sta-Clean; call (800) 825-3464. The safer products will cost a little more than the other brands.

✓ When your car is parked outdoors, knock soundly on the hood before getting in and turning on the ignition. The knock should scare away any feline under the hood or the vehicle itself, two spots cats often head to for shelter from the cold.

Walking Matilda

Of course you can walk your cat. It isn't just dogs that are permitted to enjoy a stroll around the neighborhood. In fact, as mentioned earlier, you might live in a community where your cat is allowed out only on a leash, so you will dutifully *have* to walk it if it likes to get beyond your property line.

When starting this adventure, you might want a harness and lead for the animal so that it will not escape at the first sight of an alluring bird. This is better for a cat than a leash attached to its collar. Let the cat wear the harness a bit around the house so that it becomes used to it before going out.

Your cat is...well, a cat, and not Fido. When it is outside, it will not walk in a straight line, but will wander this way and that, sniffing and investigating sights and sounds. But that's okay. Being a good citizen, you will not, of course, allow your pet to chew the geranium beds of the folks down the street. You might want to keep her off lawns in the summertime too. Some may have been treated with dangerous chemicals.

The ambling cat could well pick up fleas, although you don't have to have an outside cat for an infestation in your home. Still, it's wise to keep a close eye on your pet for any manifestation of that serious cat—and household—problem.

Some cats are eager to go for a stroll, others quite definitely are not. If yours seems to fight the harness, or going outside at all for that matter, drop the whole business. She can, as mentioned elsewhere in these pages, live quite happily indoors.

If Your Cat Is Lost

You might want to reread the section of Chapter 3 that discusses placing identification on your pet in the event it becomes lost, which can happen even if yours is an indoor cat. For example, if you hold your front door open a second too long, the cat may dash out before anyone can catch him.

If you lose your pet and you live in a community with leash laws even for cats, your pet could have been picked up and transported to the local animal shelter. You might have to pay a fine to retrieve it. As Chapter 3 brings up, you have several identification choices for your cat. It's wise to choose one as soon as you bring the animal home. While none of them guarantees its return, identification certainly helps.

Less than 5 percent of lost cats brought to animal shelters ever find their way back home to their owners, so you will have to work to see the return of your pet.

First, of course, search your home. Surprised at that rather obvious suggestion? Those of you who have searched for your cat for 10 hours, frantic and teary-eyed, convinced he was gone forever, only to have him turn up sleeping in the back of a bureau drawer you had opened that morning, will know the wisdom of that suggestion. Searching means everywhere, not just the cat's hangouts. Obviously he is somewhere else, so look where you would never expect to find him.

Then search your neighborhood, even ringing neighbors' doorbells and asking about your AWOL pet.

If you still have no luck, drive slowly around your community getting out of the car at times to hunt on foot. You might bring a box of cat food with you to rattle and lure your cat out if it is hiding.

If the cat is identified by a microchip or a tag listed with a central directory, you will want to follow the directions for a lost pet issued with those items.

Some Helpful Information

Help! Your cat is up a tree. What can you do? You are supposed to let it make its way back down, the theory being if it could climb up, it can reverse the process. A cat's claws curve downward, though, making the ascent easy. Returning, it has to back down out of the tree. Waiting for a cat to figure this out is when most folks panic and call the local fire department. Try setting an open can of cat tuna (strong smelling to attract your pet) on the highest branch you can reach and then wait for the explorer to descend.

It's 10 P.M. Do you know where your people are?

Photo by Frank Smith

You can phone area animal shelters to see if they have your cat. Call them frequently because if the animal eventually shows up there, you will have to rescue it pretty quickly before it is offered for adoption or is euthanized.

Draw up a flyer with a picture if possible, a description of the animal, and the location where it was last seen. You might also note if you are offering a reward for its return. Close with your name and/or phone number. Put the flyers on bulletin boards at nearby stores, places of worship, schools, and anywhere else where a person who might find your pet will look.

You could have some success with an advertisement in your local newspaper's classified columns under "Pets Lost" too. If you have a daily paper and a weekly neighborhood publication, try both.

The Radar that (Sometimes) Gets Them Home

What about those television news features and newspaper accounts about cats that followed their owners 2,000 miles from their old home to their new home crossing unfamiliar, rugged terrain, but arriving in one piece at the astonished owner's door weeks, even months, after their parting? Could your lost cat find its way back from that distance? How do they *do* that, anyhow?

No one is exactly sure how pets perform this feat. The reasons remain the cats' own, but the subject does tantalize those conducting studies. Some say the cats use the sun as a guide, others point to the animals' excellent sensory perception.

Tales

There is a true story told of a cat that was left behind at a family's vacation home at the end of summer. It turned up a month later at their permanent residence a few hundred miles away—a home it had never seen—carrying a kitten in its mouth. But this tale gets better: The cat went back to the vacation locale, brought back another kitten, and then made three more trips, eventually transporting five kittens!

Two German scientists performed an interesting experiment. They took some cats on a drive around their city, weaving in and out of streets to throw off the cats' sense of direction. Then they returned to their lab where the cats were put in a large maze with several exits, all of them facing different directions. The overwhelming majority of cats chose the exit that lay closest to their home.

How *did* they do that?

108

Puddy and Your Personal Life

Legalities can crop up here too. Some divorce settlements involve pet custody issues and haggling over pet visitation rights. Pet custody is even written into some prenuptial agreements. These days in the who-gets-what of negotiating, the pet often comes in just below the children in importance, but certainly well above any other family possessions.

Another issue that comes under the heading of paperwork is your will. Have you made a provision for your cat? You say you haven't thought about it? Unless your next of kin already knows your wishes, it is smart to have a clause in that document providing for your pet(s). Perhaps there is someone you can name who will care for her, someone whose consent you have already secured, of course. You might elect to give that individual a sum of money for at least a bit of the pet's care. If there is no one who can look after the animal, investigate facilities that keep cats alive and healthy for the remainder of their lives. Your vet can apprise you of where those homes are in your area.

It's Been Said
"But thousands die, without this or that, Die, and endow a college, or a cat."

—Alexander Pope

It is also possible to leave money to an animal welfare organization or foundation, either one near you or a national group. An attorney can guide you in the wording of any of the above-mentioned clauses or bequests.

The Least You Need to Know

➤ Keeping your cat indoors is the best guarantee of a safe life.

➤ Your community and residential development could determine whether you may have a pet and other aspects of its life.

➤ Identification on the animal can make the search for a lost cat easier.

➤ Don't forget naming someone to care for your pet in your will.

Chapter 11

Mealtime—High Point of a Cat's Day

In This Chapter

➤ A regular feeding schedule and a regular dining spot

➤ Nutritionally balanced commercial food

➤ Do cats need vitamins?

➤ About special treats

Soup's on! Come and get it! Chow time! Those are usually welcome words to a human's ear. The sound of a can opener grinding through the lid of a tin can or the rattle of a box or bag of cat food at certain times of the day are equally sweet music to a feline.

Food is of major interest to all cats, but especially to those that live indoors and focus their days around dining. That's fine. We have much to choose from in pet food these days that's delicious (we're assuming) and nutritious (we know), so there's no reason for your furry friend to become bored with the menu. And there's certainly no reason for him to be malnourished.

Well Now Isn't that Special

Just as we have *our* eating hangouts at home, most cats like to know they can find their meals in their own spot, in the same place, when the dinner bell sounds.

The spot should be out of the path of household traffic and near no offensive odors. Certainly it ought to be a good distance from the litter box.

The "table setting" will include a food dish and a water bowl with fresh water poured daily. The latter is a nutritional necessity. A cat might lose up to 50 percent of its overall weight and survive. But if it loses just 15 percent of its water weight, it will die.

Most folks feed their cat twice a day, a morning meal and another meal in the late afternoon or early evening. Some spread that food across three meals. Try to stick to a schedule. No doubt your cat will give you a hand by wailing when meal time is near.

Some Helpful Information

In some households with a dog and a cat, the dog eats the cat's food as well as its own. You can move the cat's food up to the kitchen counter where the cat can jump to eat it but the dog can't. Or, if you are in a house of a certain style, you can keep the door to a garage, cellar, or pantry closed, put in a pet door big enough for the cat but not the dog, and put the cat's food in that area. In a multi-cat household with cats on different diets, it's possible to buy a pet dish rigged for just one cat (the bowl has a matching collar for the cats you want to keep out of that bowl, which emits a tone to the cats to discourage them from eating from that dish). See ads in cat magazines and catalogs.

The Pet Food Selection These Days

Cats are carnivores. They must eat meat. Most of the popular commercially prepared cat food available contains all the nutrients your pet needs—protein, fat, vitamins, and minerals. In fact, our furry friends are eating more balanced meals than many of their owners!

The reputable pet food companies are constantly experimenting with the content and taste of their foods. This is a huge business, as you might have noted from the length of the pet food aisle at the supermarket. In the United States, cat food sales *doubled* during the 1980s to reach *$2 billion a year*—more than the amount spent for baby food.

If you are new to cat ownership, the can, envelope, box, or bag of cat food will tell you how much to feed your pet. You might want to experiment with different brands, with moist versus semi-moist versus dried, and with various flavors until you find a few your pet prefers. Some folks feed one type in the morning and another for the second meal.

"I Have a Question..."

Many pet food companies answer consumer questions about their products and may offer free pamphlets on a variety of subjects relating to pet care.

Here are some telephone numbers. Check the label of the product you are inquiring about for the company manufacturing that meal. For example, 9-Lives is a product of Heinz Pet Products. Offices listed are open during regular business hours in their parts of the country:

➤ Friskies Petcare Company   (800) 258-6719 (PST)

➤ Heinz Pet Products   (800) 252-7022 (EST)

➤ Kal Kan Foods, Inc.   (800) 525-5273 (PST)

➤ The Quaker Oats Company   (800) 4MY-PETS (CST)

➤ Ralston Purina Company   (800) CAT-CARE (CST)

Producers of special dietary meals for cats usually have trained nutritionists and other specialists that can answer an owner's more involved questions. There is no charge for talking with these staff people:

➤ Hill's Pet Nutrition Line   (800) 445-5777 (CST)

➤ The IAMS Company   (800) 525-4267 (EST)

➤ Pet-AG   (800) 323-0877 (EST)

Incidentally, the most costly products are not necessarily the best nutrition-wise, or the ones your pet will prefer. Whatever its cost, just be sure the item you choose is labeled "complete" or "nutritionally complete."

Cats prefer their food at room temperature. Moist food can stand out 45 minutes or so, but then it should be taken away and the uneaten portion should be scraped into the garbage. Cats like to nibble, go away, come back for more nibbles, and so on. But canned food can become quite unappetizing if left uneaten all day, not to mention potentially dangerous in warm weather. Some owners have a small bowl of dried food always available to their pet so it can munch round-the-clock.

113

Some Helpful Information

In 1978 scientists discovered that taurine, a colorless amino acid, was essential in a feline's diet to prevent eye problems leading to blindness. Pet food companies responded to this news by adding that ingredient to their cat foods. In 1986 a link was found between a lack of taurine and heart disease in cats. The amount of taurine that was currently in cat food was not enough, so manufacturers raised the level. Taurine is not included in dog food ingredients because dogs have no need for it.

In recent years many pet food companies have focused on specialized markets, coming out with meals for kittens, for seniors, and for the pudgy cat. Some manufacturers have also developed products to help prevent LUTD (lower urinary tract disease). Besides LUTD, there are other health problems where symptoms can be alleviated to some extent with specialized diets. Talk with your vet about any special foods, some of which can be found easily at the supermarket. Others are manufactured by newer companies and can be purchased at the veterinarian's clinic, a pet supply store, or from a mail-order catalog.

Some Helpful Information

Some owners prefer homemade food for their cats. Be sure to check with your veterinarian before introducing such a diet, however, since you will have to be careful that your pet is receiving all of the protein, vitamins, and minerals it needs. You also might want to read *The New Natural Cat* by Anitra Frazier with Norma Eckroate (Plume, $12.95) or *Dr. Pitcairn's Complete Guide to Natural Health for Dogs and Cats* by Richard H. Pitcairn and Susan H. Pitcairn (Rodale Press, $15.95).

Never switch to a new diet for health reasons without first checking with your vet. If you do get the green light, introduce the new food in what your cat is now eating a little at a time, gradually easing out of the old diet. Starting out overnight with totally different meals can cause gastrointestinal upsets to your pet.

While your cat is likely to show some preferences for certain flavors of cat food, don't let it narrow its meals to one choice. Eating just liver, for example, is not good. Feeding it only fish could cause a vitamin B deficiency.

Giving your cat prepared *dog* food, which might be tempting if you have a dog in the house, is a definite no. Their meals are not interchangeable. The meat content in prepared dog foods is not high enough for cats, and certain amino acids and important vitamins are missing.

About Vitamins

Thanks to complete prepared commercial foods, cats do not need special vitamin supplements.

Veterinarians say they see more health problems with pets suffering from vitamin excesses, or toxicities, than those related to vitamin deficiency. Keep in mind that if your cat food contains at least the required amount of some vitamins—and some foods contain several times that dose—giving your cat still more vitamins could harm it.

Table Scraps and Other Treats

The tendency to feed one's pet some food from the table starts early in many households. After all, if we find that roast turkey absolutely delicious, why not pass that enjoyment on to the cat?

Thus is born a habit that becomes difficult to break as your cat rushes to the kitchen each time you do, hoping for any snack from leftover meat loaf to cantaloupe. Occasional bits from the table are not likely to harm most cats. But those snacks shouldn't be a regular occurrence. If it is eating commercial cat food, your pet does not need the food *you* eat. You may discover that: (1) she finds some of it indigestible; (2) too many nibbles combined with the regular pet food meals she is scarfing down have piled on the pounds; and (3) she is becoming a fussy eater, preferring the table scraps to cat food. It should be pointed out here, however, that some cats have no interest at all in human food.

Messalina waiting for the pizza delivery.

Photo by Frank Smith

It can be dangerous for your cat's health, and it is certainly nutritionally inadequate, to feed her raw meat. Never put your cat on a vegetarian diet either. Cooked chicken or turkey is a feline favorite, but be certain that what you set out has no bones. Besides being boned, fish must be carefully cut up and should never be served raw. Avoid giving tuna fish for humans to your cat; stick to cat tuna. Break the food you serve into small pieces. Some cats have a hard time digesting milk or cream, but surprise, they don't need either.

Finally, if you give your pet people meals *instead* of cat food, it may eventually suffer from malnutrition! Your food will not constitute the balanced chow a cat needs.

Nibbles sold commercially as cat treats should also be handled as just that—a treat and not a dessert after every meal. They are not formulated to be complete meals—just tasty extras from time to time. And don't make the mistake one owner did, until she was filled in by a friend, and shake out a whole package of treats into the cat's food bowl as dinner!

Tales
Dr. Samuel Johnson, a giant among 18th century English writers and one of the great gourmands of history, often went to the market to buy oysters for his cat, Hodge. It is said he did not want to ask the servants to undertake the errand lest they take a dislike to the cat for that reason.

Pudgy Petunia: Feeding the Overweight Cat

Your cat *looks* like a couch potato, but she isn't sprawled on the sofa watching television and downing chips and brewskies (well, maybe she *does* spend a good deal of time on the sofa). How did she pile on those extra pounds? The same way we do—eating more than we can work off with exercise. (By the way, there is no reason to expect a spayed or neutered cat will automatically gain weight.) You might want to have your pet checked by the veterinarian to be certain her thyroid gland is functioning properly, which could be a medical reason for weight gain. If everything is fine there, you can talk with your vet about knocking off some of those pounds. Obesity in cats can lead to arthritis and diabetes.

Some pet food companies have brought out "lite" lines for the chubby kitty. You might ask your vet about them. Although it is difficult to tell just how lite the manufacturer means since calorie counts are not required on labels, you can call the pet food company for more information (see "I Have a Question..." earlier in this chapter).

You might also try engaging your cat in more activity. Some suggestions for fun and games can be found in Chapter 13.

The Finicky Cat

"He's a very finicky eater. But then aren't all cats a little fussy?"

Nooooo, they're not. Most owners who say this have a spoiled cat rather than a delicate eater. Yes, spoiled.

There are all sorts of reasons cats start to turn up their noses at certain foods, but most date to our seemingly harmless efforts to offer our pets ever more delicious meals. The animal then becomes so selective it has us jumping through hoops trying to please it.

What can you do with a fussy eater? Steel yourself to ignore its meowing when you put down food you know it has eaten before and apparently enjoyed. Don't reach for something new to appease it. Leave that dish out for 15 minutes. If the fluffball hasn't eaten it, pick it up and take it away. Put down the same kind of food for the next meal. If he still won't bite, feed him a small amount of his favorite meal, but not enough to satisfy him. Keep up that feeding program until Mr. Particular learns that refusing one dish is not going to lead to something better.

Bet You Didn't Know

If the pictures of your cat you carry around in your wallet are not enough, you can now have a credit card featuring puddy's puss. Ralston Purina Pet Products has introduced a MasterCard with a picture of your pet. MBNA American Bank, N.A. issues the card with no annual fee. It helps support the Purina Pets for People Program, which helps senior citizens adopt household pets from animal shelters. Call MBNA at (800) 386-2722.

A few cats are truly finicky, but their number is small. Some purebreds fall into this category. If a cat has had poor eating habits since kittenhood and must be coaxed to eat—even if its heart desire is not the best, most nutritious food—then that is what you will have to do to keep it from starving. In most cases, however, the cat has just been cleverly manipulating its owner.

Cats on the Table

Cat salt—Finely grained salt formed from bittern, which is the bitter water solution of salts that is left after ordinary table salt has been crystallized out of a brine.

Cat thyme—A European germander, or plant of the mint family, with aromatic foliage.

Catfish—A name generally given to a large class of fish characterized by having no scales. The fish also has long barbels, or feelers, around the mouth. That, along with its habit of lashing its long tail as it swims, is probably why its name carries the prefix "cat." Most are freshwater fish found in this country and in Europe under a variety of local names.

Catlap—A weak drink usually served to the ill or infirm; sometimes a derogatory term for a weak drink.

Catmint—An herbaceous plant with aromatic leaves. Its young shoots can be used, although sparingly, in green salads.

Cattail millet; Italian millet—Species of grain-bearing grass grown in prehistoric times and still used, especially in parts of Asia and Europe. The best variety to eat is golden millet, which is yellow in color and makes a coarse bread and a porridge; also used in the preparation of the North African dish *cous-cous*.

Pussy's paws or pussy's-toes—A hoary herb with small, usually white, flowers.

The Aging Cat's Nutritional Needs

Sayings and Superstitions
A 16th century British superstition suggests that when you first get a cat you should butter its paws. When it licks off the butter, it will like the taste so much it will never want to leave home.

Like older people, older cats sometimes eat less and seem to want familiar, favorite dishes. Tuna is one preference, perhaps because of its strong smell, which manages to reach a cat's fading senses.

Your veterinarian can help you decide what's best for your old cat, taking into account health problems it may have developed in its later years and the fact that its protein requirement is likely to be different from what it was during its growth and reproductive years. Perhaps a special diet from one of the commercial food companies making special products for "seniors" will fill the bill perfectly at this time in your cat's life.

What the Outdoor Cat Might Eat

The outdoor cat and the outdoor/indoor cat can easily find a dinner or snack outside.

Not all cats are hunters—they must have been taught how by a mother who hunted and not all eat what they catch. In fact, the cat well fed by its owner might play with and kill its prey, but not bother dining on it at all. It will abandon it or bring it to the owner in one of those gift presentations that cat people shudder at receiving.

Cats hunt mice, rats, young rabbits, squirrels, and, although not to the extent you would think, birds. If they do eat their catch, each part of that prey supplies the nutrients and minerals a feline needs. From the muscle of those animals it obtains protein. From the bones, intestines, and other organs it gets vitamins, minerals, and other necessary nutrients. The prey supplies the cat's fluid requirements too.

> **Cats in Our Language**
> When talking about an object, "something the cat dragged in" means messy almost beyond recognition. When referring to an individual, as in "Boy, I look like something the cat dragged in," it means slovenly.

In the wild, a cat might eat about a dozen small meals a day, a habit you'll also notice with many house pets as they return to the food bowl several times in a 24-hour period.

The Least You Need to Know

➤ Try to maintain a regular feeding schedule for your pet.

➤ Most commercially sold cat food contains nutritionally balanced meals.

➤ Don't overfeed your cat or give it too many table scraps.

➤ Finicky eaters are usually spoiled and can be cured with an attitude adjustment from both of you.

Chapter 12

Good Housekeeping

In This Chapter

➤ The fur flies—everywhere

➤ The benefits of a scratching post

➤ Pet stains

➤ Training your cat

He's here, he's there, he's everywhere, that cat. Can you have a relatively tidy, attractive home in spite of him?

Of course you can, with some thought and preparation. You might want to read Chapter 17 about now. It talks about why your cat might be engaging in behavior destructive to your home and actions that could be symptoms of illness. What we talk about here, however, are practical tips for maintenance, repair, and decorating, keeping in mind that in homes with pets there *will* be traces of the little dears here and there. After all, it's their home too. Cat owners understand that. Most will be happy just keeping it all under control.

Will the Cat's Bed Be the Same as Yours?

Many owners do not want their pets to sleep on the bed with them at night or indeed to jump on the bed at any time. Cats can be trained, through repetition and other suggestions in this chapter, to stay off the bed. They usually have the whole house or apartment to search for a place—or two or three—to snooze during the three quarters or so of the day that they sleep, so don't feel you are being too severe shooing them off the bed.

Cats in Our Language

We all know how cats doze off for brief periods of time throughout the day. A short, light nap for a person is called, of course, a catnap.

The word *catnap* has been around since the 1820s. Maybe that's when we humans first acknowledged that many of us have been imitating cats all along by catching brief sleeps whenever opportunity presents itself.

Then there are those who delight in having their pet beside them, head on the pillow or snuggled under the covers, at bedtime. The music these owners fall asleep to is the soft purr of a contented pet. Unfortunately, what they often wake up to—and too early at that—is that pet sitting on the owner's head, licking her face, or reaching out with its paws, and claws, to wake up the sleepyhead. There's some accommodating to do by both parties if you let your cat on the bed. Many a cat's slumber has been disturbed by an owner's restless tossing.

Some cat beds are large enough for a sleepover.

Photo by Rachael Halpern

Official Cat Beds

As we noted in Chapter 4, you might want to buy a cat bed to keep your pet's snoozing quarters separate from your own. Prices range from about $15 on up to over $100.

Whatever style you choose, a cat bed should be washable, or at least have a washable mat or cushion. It ought to be made of fire retardant materials too. Plastic is best for not harboring the dreaded fleas.

Giving cats their own place to sleep should keep them from the digging they do with their claws when they are about to settle down, kneading that could harm bed linens or living room upholstery if a pet chose those spots for a nap.

It's Been Said
"What fun to be a cat!"

MEOW!

—Christopher Morley, American writer

About that Litter Box

Cats are the perfect pets because you don't have to walk them. They just use the litter box.

Oh yes, that litter box—filling it, cleaning it, and first of all, of course, deciding where it should go around your place. There's more about this subject in Chapter 4. Here we'll concentrate on where the box fits in your home.

Most folks opt for an out-of-the-way spot, naturally, both for their sake and the cat's. Cats do like their privacy when heading for the litter pan. The chosen area is usually an extra bathroom, the garage, the basement, or the porch. In some homes, alas, there are few choices. A small apartment, for example, may have just one bath. The owner can keep the box under the sink if there is no cabinet, sewing two pieces of fabric around a strip of elastic and making a "skirt" to put around the sink. The cat can go through the curtain-like opening where the material meets. If there is no space under the sink, owners are often forced to keep the litter box elsewhere in the bath, and never mind that it won't be out of sight.

Here's another idea: If you have no space ideally suited to a litter pan, put it in the corner of a living room or a spare room with an inexpensive decorative screen around it, hiding it from view. These are available commercially.

You can try a covered litter box, which certainly keeps the filler from spilling, but your success will depend on whether your cat is receptive to that concept. And whether he'll *fit* into that closed space. Some bruisers don't.

> **Some Helpful Information**
>
> If you hate the litter box enough and have nearly the patience of Job, you might want to toilet train your cat. This is a system involving placing the litter pan next to the toilet, gradually raising it until it is level with the toilet, and then, with a few extra steps, moving the cat over to the toilet. Simple, huh? Paul Kunkel explains it all in *How to Toilet Train Your Cat: 21 Days to a Litter-Free Home* (Workman Publishing, $5.95). It's illustrated, of course.

Hair! It's Everywhere

Little balls of fur move, like tumbleweed, across your bare wood floors at the slightest puff of air. Cat hair clings to your carpets. And look at the sofa and club chair (assuming your cat is allowed on them). You can almost see puddy's outline in left-behind fur on the spot he favors for his naps.

Cat hair can be both sticky—adhering to some surfaces—and elusive, as it flies away from others while you are trying to clean it up. You can keep it to a minimum by regularly brushing your pet, but you'll still have to clean.

An upright vacuum cleaner is likely to do a better job on your rugs than the canister type. It goes deeper into the pile. It's better for flea control too.

Frequently sweeping bare wood floors might be followed by a quick once-over with a wet mop if the surface has a sturdy coat or two of polyurethane so that you aren't washing untreated wood. Some folks vacuum wood floors, which is fine if you can do it without scratching the wood.

Tales
A New Zealand woman identified only as Fiona has a cat who has dragged 60 items of women's underwear filched from neighbors into the house. "Obviously, my stuff wasn't good enough," Fiona remarked.

—An item in *Newsweek*, May 20, 1996

It is possible to vacuum upholstery too, of course, but for quick fixes for hair on sofas, chairs, and beds, run a damp cloth over those spots.

You can also buy products that will pick up fur. One company, 3M, puts out something called Pat-it, a sticky sheet of pet hair remover that can also be used for lint. Just dab it on the furniture's furry spots.

The cleaning product that won the 1995 best of year in *Cat Fancy* magazine is called "FURniture Magnet," from the company of the same name. It wipes hair off furniture and can be washed and re-used. Call (800) 738-4247 or (800) PET-HAIR for more information.

Maybe you don't have to buy anything at all. Check your kitchen drawers for a rubber jar opener. Rub that on the hairy surface, in one direction, and it'll pick up enough fur to make another cat. It's cheap too, around $1 or so if you have to spring for one. You can often find these household aids in the supermarket around shelves of food in jars.

Scratching Posts, Wanted and Unwanted

R-i-i-i-p. Is there a sound more bloodcurdling to a cat owner than hearing her cat tear upholstery? Scratching bare wood, especially if it is Granny's heirloom rocker or something equally valuable, is probably almost as dismaying. Scratching at—even climbing—draperies also makes the blood run cold (an alternate window covering might be blinds, shades, or valences).

Cats have a very real need to scratch. They have scent glands in their feet, and when they scratch, they not only sharpen their claws and shed old, loose nails, but also mark their scent. Scolding them for doing what comes naturally will only confuse them.

You need a scratching post so that your cat can be happy clawing and you can be happy at what he's *not* tearing. (You need to have your pet's nails clipped regularly too.)

Some Helpful Information

There is a relatively new product in the war against scratching: soft vinyl claw caps that are glued onto your cat's nails and replaced every month or two as the nail is shed. The cat doesn't mind the caps and can still scratch, only now his nails are blunt with a plastic coating and not liable to do harm. The nails are advertised in cat magazines, available at veterinary clinics, pet supply stores, and through mail-order catalogs. Your vet can put them on your pet, although as you watch you might learn and do it yourself next time. Or maybe not.

A scratching post is just that—a chunk of wood or other sturdy material covered by a rug (use the underside, since its good side will send your cat the message it's all right to claw at carpets), sisal rope, burlap, corrugated cardboard, or some equally sturdy fabric appealing to a cat. Its only purpose is to provide the animal with an outlet for scratching (and, incidentally, stretching). It ought to be at least three feet long, as long as the length of your pet, and anchored so that he can't tip it over. What you are simulating here is a cat scratching at tree bark.

You can buy a scratching post or you can make one. Set it down near your cat's bed so it can exercise its need to stretch out and claw at something when it wakes from sleep.

You need to make the objects your cat likes to scratch—and which you don't want him to—unappealing to him.

Tales
A woman was visiting a friend's home and noticed her friend's cat standing tall and scratching along the length of a wood-sided chair. The cat seemed to have already left long claw marks on both sides of the chair. "What're you going to do," said the cat owner, shrugging, when her friend called it to her attention. "Lida Rose is distressing it for me," she said, referring to a method of marring furniture to make it appear aged.

Some Helpful Information
The last few years have seen the appearance of slipcovers that can be easily fitted to sofas and chairs without sewing or having to be custom fitted. They come in a variety of good-looking patterns, costing as little as $100 for a sofa. They replace those huge, dowdy "throws" of old, and are relatively inexpensive cover-ups for damaged upholstered furniture. Look in stores or home furnishing catalogs.

Take a sheet of contact paper, sticky side up, or two-sided tape, and run it along where you *don't* want your cat, tacking the ends to keep it firm. When he jumps up, he won't stay *there* long. Or you can use aluminum foil, which makes a crinkly, tinny sound your cat also won't like.

Or take a can filled with coins or pebbles and a piece of string tied to the can. Tack or tape the string across the scratching area. When the cat scratches, the can will fall near him and the noise will startle him. He's not likely to go back there.

Keep your traps in effect a week or two after your cat stops attacking those items, just to be sure your plan is working.

Spraying the animal with a water spritzer can also be effective. However, it must be done as you catch him in the act, and you won't always be there then. It can be a good back-up when you *are* around, though.

There are citrus and menthol-based sprays sold for this purpose too, odors your cat will find offensive but which won't harm your furniture. Check cat magazines and your vet's office for items advertised or sold there. Eucalyptus oil is also a turn off to cats. You can try sprinkling a little on threatened upholstery.

While you are saying "hands off" to some things, you should at the same time be guiding your cat to the scratching post (you might need two if your home is large), where you are offering him an okay alternative to his first choices.

You might smear the surface of the post with catnip to make it even more alluring. Guide his paws over the post in a scratching motion. You can put some of his toys near there and play there with him. Regularly place a treat at the top of the post, and praise your pet lavishly each time you see him clawing away. Of course, all of this will take some time and patience.

What Cats Don't Like to Scratch

If it's your style, you can decorate with leather or Naugahyde, neither of which seem to interest most cats. They prefer nubby to smooth surfaces. They might want to nap on such a sofa, but not scratch it. Other smooth surfaces that don't hold much interest for them are marble and lacquer-finished pieces.

Cats might scratch wicker furniture, but it takes a long time for those claw marks to become visible, and they can often be easily covered by light sanding and repainting those spots.

When it comes to fabric, felines prefer (meaning like to scratch) material with some substance for them to dig into with their nails. For example, they don't care much for chintz (polished cotton) because it's too smooth. However, tweeds and other rough textures are perfect.

Bet You Didn't Know
There are paper dessert napkins out these days printed with cat-themed messages, such as "If you want the best seat in the house you'll have to move the cat."

Rugs—Out Damned Spot

Even a house or apartment with hardwood floors will have an occasional area rug. Have you noticed how cats love to play with an area rug? Oh, you have.

Maybe your cat moves it around until it's clear across the room and rolled up a bit too. You might want to buy undercarpeting or tape that are sold with the purpose of keeping an area rug in the area you've chosen for it.

In a home with a cat or two, area rugs and wood floors are much easier to keep clean than wall-to-wall carpeting. Flea control is easier too (they love to burrow into wall-to-wall carpets), although fleas can also head for cracks and crevices in wood floors.

Now, about "accidents" on rugs. They will happen, and you are likely to find yourself eventually with several products from the supermarket or veterinary clinic that can be used for cleaning. Which is best? Each owner has a favorite. You will probably have to conduct some home tests to see what works on your particular carpet. Some liquids or sprays might leave more problems than they take away—widening a stain, for example, or discoloring that patch of rug.

To clean urine from a floor can be especially important because you don't want your cat returning to

Some Helpful Information
Heloise, the newspaper columnist, offers "Heloise's Cat-Care Hints" for $2. Send a self-addressed stamped (55 cents) envelope to Heloise/Cat, P.O. Box 795001, San Antonio, TX 78279.

that area and making it a secondary litter box. You also don't want your home to smell. Use paper towels to get up as much liquid as possible. Then rinse with water. Blot the area with paper towels, then rinse with distilled white vinegar (this can also be used on upholstered furniture). Let it air dry.

If there is still an odor when the spot is dry, cover it generously with baking soda and leave it for several days, covered with a sheet of plastic if your cat has used the area often. Clean up the baking soda with a dust pan and brush, not a vacuum cleaner, which can be harmed by the powder.

Cats in Our Language

A room being too small *to swing a cat* is a terrible expression when you think about it. Some say it is a sailor's term, referring to the space needed to swing the whip known as the cat-o'-nine-tails. Others argue that can't be right because the cat-o'-nine-tails was not used until about a century after the phrase was first recorded. The correct origin seems to be lost in the mists of history.

"Tired nature's sweet restorer, balmy sleep!"
—Edward Young (1683–1765) in "Night Thoughts"

The Least You Need to Know

➤ Decide where you will and won't allow your cat and be consistent in following through on those dos and don'ts.

➤ You can still hide a litter box in a small house or apartment.

➤ A scratching post will offer your pet an acceptable place to claw away, a very real need of cats.

➤ There are ways of training your cat to keep away from certain places and furnishings around your home.

Chapter 13

Fun and Games For You and Your Pet

In This Chapter

➤ Cats—exercise and playtime

➤ Inexpensive toys found around your home

➤ The delights of catnip

➤ Taking pictures of your pet

All cats are different in breed and in temperament. But they do have a few important things in common: they need exercise, they like to play, and they like—*love*—their owners.

Put all of that together, add some inspiration on your part when it comes to fun and games, and you wind up with many enjoyable moments spent with your pet. Call it quality time. Call it bonding. The result is a closer, happier relationship on both sides and as much understanding as possible between the two of you.

Cats and Exercise

Cats need regular exercise or movement, from kittenhood to old age, just the way humans do to stay in fit condition. If you can spend 15 minutes a day with your pet, getting it to move around or playing with it, you'll have a healthier, happier feline on your hands.

First, a point that applies to all of the suggestions in this chapter. As you know, there are shy cats and outgoing ones, cats that play well with other cats, and those that seem to prefer human companionship. Of course you'll want to gear your play activities toward your own pet's temperament and preferences.

MEOW!

It's Been Said

Cats certainly know how to disappear at play or any other time. Dr. Louis J. Camuti, the American veterinarian and cat specialist, has said, "A cat determined not to be found can fold itself up like a pocket handkerchief if it wants to."

A game many cats love that is excellent exercise is tossing a ball, or even paper scrunched up to form a ball, and letting your pet run to it. Expecting it to bring the object back to you might be asking a bit too much. Unlike dogs, cats do not seem to know almost instinctively to bring the ball back to you so you can throw it again. You might be able to train your pet to bring it back by using patience and rewards it considers pleasurable—attention and praise from you or a kitty treat.

A growing number of owners are taking their indoor cats out for walks, using a harness. The cat gets outside in a controlled environment and gets to move those furry little legs. The owner gets some exercise too.

All cats need regular exercise.

Photo by Illena Armstrong

132

Inexpensive or Free Toys, Games, and Enjoyable Pastimes

Cats love to hide. Paper bags provide a fascinating diversion, as do cartons. Some cats love it if, when they've hopped inside a box, you fold over the flaps so they are completely hidden for a while.

Tales

A retired teacher decided to turn an empty carton into a plaything for his cat, Bonkers. He turned the box upside down and cut out a front "door" for the cat. He sliced another square from the top so the cat could stick his head up out of the box. Bonkers watched all of this intently. When the man was finished, he stepped aside and waved the cat over. But the animal headed instead for a sliver of cardboard a couple of feet away that had been discarded as the man carved the box. He tossed that bit of paper around for days, having a wonderful time. He never went near the carton. Go figure.

Tie almost anything—bird feathers, a cork, an empty spool of thread, a pine cone—to a piece of string, elastic, or wire and swirl it around for your cat to catch. Or you can fasten the contraption to a door handle so it swings free for the cat to swat.

Many cats love playing under the bed covers. You can box with your pet when it's beneath the comforter and you're not without having to worry about scratches. When you change linens, you are likely to find your cat smack in the middle of the bed waiting for you to make the new sheets billow, which seems to delight many adult cats, not to mention kittens, as they run around the top of the bed.

Some cats are fascinated by wind-up toys like a toddler's very small car or truck. Others are wide-eyed at bubbles you blow in the air in their direction, which you can buy for about $2 in a store's toy department.

Some Helpful Information

51 Ways To Entertain Your House Cat While You're Out by Stephanie Laland (Avon Books, $7.50) offers tips with illustrations for low- or no-cost playthings to keep kitty amused. Here's one: Put a few walnuts (in their shells, of course) in an empty tissue box and tape over the opening. Cut a paw-sized hole in the side of the box and rattle the box in front of your cat. He may spend hours scratching at the box and moving it around trying to get all the walnuts out.

There are a few cautions here. Be sure your toy, homemade or store bought, does not have detachable parts your cat can chew off and ingest or is not so small that the animal can swallow the whole thing in one gulp.

Be very careful about offering your pet any length of string, yarn, or ribbon. Many an owner has made a fast trip to the veterinary clinic after the cat has swallowed a mouthful of one of those substances. They can cause serious intestinal damage.

One of the simplest, and probably most popular, diversions for your pet is the windowsill. Cats can sit for hours watching what's passing and dozing off. They will make those strange cackling sounds at birds they see, track falling leaves, and, most important for an indoor pet, feel the warmth of the sun. Many cat people make sure any home they move into has windowsills wide enough to accommodate their cat!

If your home does not, you can purchase what is advertised in cat magazines as cat perches or shelves, which can be hooked onto a windowsill and give a cat a comfortably covered spot from which to look outside. They cost around $35.

If You Have Money to Spend

If you have a front and/or backyard, you might want to put in a birdhouse or bird bath to keep your indoor cat entertained. A bird feeder will hold its interest too, and it can be affixed to an exterior wall of a house or apartment, or on a fire escape.

Consult gardening books to see what you can plant that will attract butterflies to your garden, which will entrance your cat when she's sitting on the windowsill.

You can get pretty fancy for your pet. Kitty condos, or gyms, costing anywhere from $50 to $200 or so, usually consist of a several-foot-high building with entrances and ledges where your cat can climb and perch. They are available at pet supply stores and through mail-order catalogs.

It's Been Said

"When I play with my cat, who knows whether I do not make her more sport than she makes me?"

—Michel de Montaigne (1533–1592)

If there's a handy person in the family, he or she might construct some stairs just wide enough for the cat against the side of a wall leading straight up and ending near the ceiling. Cats love height. Yours can spend hours on the top stair surveying his realm below. Some do-it-yourselfers erect a catwalk across a kitchen or living room ceiling that can fit in nicely with the decor as a sort of decorative beam. Add a spot in the room for the cat to get up to that plywood plank, and perhaps down again on the other side.

The Pleasures of Massage

One of the most relaxing things you can do with your cat, while still accomplishing something, is the massage. You can almost feel your blood pressure drop as you rub your little friend, and you can see and feel him relax. Ahhhh—for both of you.

You can conduct a cat massage standing up, sitting, kneeling (perhaps on a rug or your bed), lying down with the cat alongside you, or even standing with the cat on a high table like a human massage.

You most likely know how and where your cat likes to be petted and scratched. Now focus that attention on all of him, from gently rubbing your thumb on his forehead to an equally gentle running of your hand along his tail.

Your cat will most likely roll over and stretch during all of this, or perhaps fall quietly asleep. Some, post-massage, will jump up raring to go.

The cat massage serves a few purposes. Besides being relaxing for both of you, moving your hands along your cat's body will allow you to check for irregularities, such as lumps, so that you can have the animal checked by your vet as soon as you notice any changes. If the animal cries when you touch a certain spot, that's another signal to call the vet. Finally, you can also look for fleas and other pests while you are kneading away.

Some points to watch out for: Your cat could easily become overstimulated at some point during a massage and begin scratching or biting, or just scurry off. It's time to stop then. Also, don't massage your cat when it is ill, although it is tempting to think that a nice rub will help it feel better.

Bet You Didn't Know
Here are two French terms to help with your massage: *Cat effleurage* is a series of gentle strokes, moving downward with both your hands, one on each side of the spine. *Cat petrissage* is gently kneading your pet, exerting slight pressure from your thumbs.

Some Helpful Information
How to Massage Your Cat (Howell Book House, $9.95) will take you step-by-step through this art and offers tips for special cats and situations, like massaging the long-whiskered pet.

Whee, Catnip!

Massage, and now catnip. Oh to be reincarnated as one of our own cats, right?

Just one whiff of this unique herb sends most cats into a reaction that humans might call ecstasy. The cat rolls over, purrs, growls, and sometimes leaps into the air. Some become aggressive and bop a fellow house cat on the noggin. Interestingly, catnip has both a stimulating and a relaxing effect on them, although cat reactions vary. There is a small minority of cats who get no bang at all from catnip, although they might eagerly munch on its leaves.

What *is* that stuff anyway?

Catnip is a member of the mint family, related to more familiar kitchen herbs like sage and thyme. It used to be a common plant in herb gardens and was once the base for a quite popular beverage in England—dried catnip leaves in boiling water. The tea was said to have a calming effect. It's a rare person today who brews a cup of catnip tea for himself after putting some of the herb out for his cat, but if you like, you certainly *can.*

The chemical that gives your cat a buzz is called nepetalactone, which is set into action by smell and then works on the cat's nervous system. It is safe and non-addictive.

Tales

Some 20-plus years ago, a graduate student, Leon Seidman, searching for some *great* catnip for his cat, W.B., was steered by friends away from commercial products and toward the pharmaceutical department of drugstores where it is sometimes sold in jars along with other herbs. His cat rated the stuff he brought home four-star. That summer Seidman visited a back-to-nature farmer friend in West Virginia and found catnip galore, some of it growing wild. He filled his car with it, headed back home to Maryland, and began a small business selling what he called Cosmic Catnip. Today, Cosmic Pet Products, Inc., of which Seidman is president and his wife, Pamela, vice president, packages 130,000 to 140,000 pounds of catnip annually for sale in the United States, Canada, and Europe. The catnip is grown in western Maryland, the finest spot in the world for that product, Seidman contends. No other company claims to produce more, according to the Pet Industry Joint Advisory Council, a Washington-based trade group. Seidman says his largest competitor is Hartz Mountain Corporation.

Because it distracts a cat and does have that soothing effect, you might want to give your cat a little before it must travel, when you are busy moving, or at any other time of stress (perhaps those are times for a nice cup of catnip tea for *you*!).

However, like anything special, it should not be available 24 hours a day. Put it out for a while, then take it away for a few days. You don't want your cat always hyped, or in a perpetually lethargic state. Catnip should not be given to a cat going outdoors either, since the animal might be unable to care for itself while under its influence.

Since the scent eventually fades, every once in a while you might want to freshen a catnip toy by rubbing the herb all over it.

You can grow your own catnip too. Depending on where you live you might keep a pot outside on a window ledge, have an outdoor herb garden, or, if conditions are right, set a plant inside your house or apartment. Pet supply stores and mail-order catalogs offer starter kits. If you have quite a little outdoor patch going, give some thought to harnessing that power into catnip gifts for friends and their pets.

Bet You Didn't Know Some 79 percent of surveyed pet owners give their pets holiday or birthday presents, according to a national survey conducted by the American Animal Hospital Association (AAHA).

How Cats Play Together at Home

You can enjoy many games with him, but your cat is still playing with a human. Romping with another feline, however, he plays different games with rules we'll never comprehend. That is one of several good reasons for having two cats. Only with another cat can a cat be, well, a cat.

The two will wrestle, chase each other from room to room, or sit together on a windowsill, facing each other or back to back. If Sidney jumps onto the counter to lick the butter dish, Samantha will watch. Next thing you know, *she's* on the counter licking the butter dish. Cats set both good and bad examples for each other.

CAT TALES

Tales

In a note to a Mrs. Patterson in 1908, Mark Twain said the following of his cat Tammany's kittens: "One of them," he wrote, "likes to be crammed into a corner-pocket of the billiard table—which he fits as snugly as does a finger in a glove and then he watches the game (and obstructs it) by the hour, and spoils many a shot by putting out his paw and changing the direction of a passing ball. Whenever a ball is in his arms, or so close to him that it cannot be played upon without risk of hurting him, the player is privileged to remove it to anyone of the three spots that chances to be vacant..."

Cats being together can be especially important during long days when their owner is at work or away on business or vacation. Even when they're not playing together, the cats will be reassured and comforted by each other's presence.

There is the occasional cat who does not *like* his feline housemates, which means none of the above good will reigns in *that* household.

Cat Pet Peeves

➤ Water, unless it's for drinking

➤ Being talked down to

➤ Owners vacationing without them or, worse, taking them along

➤ Loud, sudden noises

➤ Being decorated with ribbons, funny hats, and so on.

➤ Owners turning over in bed just when the cat is comfortably snuggled there and dozing off

➤ Trips to the vet

➤ Car rides, since they're almost always trips to the vet

➤ Being told they're the biggest, fattest cat that person has ever seen

➤ Being tripped over or stepped on

➤ Not getting a table scrap they've sat patiently waiting for for 15 minutes

➤ Dogs, sometimes

Photographing Your Cat

This can be fun for you, although the cat might wonder what on earth you're trying to get her to *do.*

It is not so much a trick to taking photos of pets as it is a mind-set you will need that is different from shooting humans. For one thing, you will have to wait until your cat is in the mood for pictures, unlike an adult or child who will, presumably, pose for you when *you* like.

Good times to keep a camera handy are just after a cat eats, when it's licking itself and presumably relaxed, and just as it is awakening from a nap and stretching, looking adorable and also at ease.

Since a cat sleeps so often, does that mean you have to have a camera around your neck all the time at home? Pretty much, or at least always handy if you want to snap the type of charming pictures that makes everyone who sees them say "Awww."

Get down to the cat's level too. Many amateur pet photographers shoot the pet as they are standing and looking down, which misses details that can make a photo, like the cat's face or expression. Most times, it's best to get within three feet if you can, depending on the limitations of the camera you are using and the shot you are trying to capture.

If your pictures turn out well, consider sending them to one of the cat magazines as a way of sort of immortalizing your pet in print. Those publications regularly feature photos of readers' pets.

The Least You Need to Know

➤ All cats, from kittens to seniors, need exercise and play.

➤ Look around your home for low- or no-cost toys for your pet.

➤ By all means, introduce your cat to the wonders of catnip.

➤ Take pictures of your cat for a photo album or perhaps for publication in a cat magazine.

Chapter 14

Vicarious Cat Pleasures

In This Chapter

➤ Cat books in several genres

➤ Cats in cyberspace

➤ Audiocassettes for you

➤ Videos for you and your pet

For most of us, our delight in the cat in our home leads us to seek more information about cats and more of them to look at and admire. Cats, we want more cats!

They certainly are out there. Since cats surpassed dogs a few years ago as the primo pet in American households, they have become especially prominent on the national landscape, showing up in books, movies, on television, and, increasingly, on the Internet. You can hardly turn around these days without seeing cats in some form or another, which is, of course, as it should be.

Cats in Today's Mystery Novels

Mystery stories and the mysterious cat seem to go together, a match not unnoticed by writers. If you are a mystery fan, you're in luck. You can combine two of your favorite interests.

Have you discovered Lilian Jackson Braun's *The Cat Who…* series? If not, you will not only enjoy the books, but also the knowledge that there are nearly 20 in the series, promising you many happy hours of reading. These stories, combining mystery and humor, feature the eccentric billionaire (there's a story there) Jim Qwilleran and his detective Siamese cats, Koko and Yum Yum. The two most recent adventures of the three characters are *The Cat Who Said Cheese* and *The Cat Who Blew the Whistle*.

Cat Crimes is another excellent series. Each book of the four or five published so far comprises 15 or so short stories by some of America's top mystery writers and features cats, naturally, in one role or another.

Computer Cats

Are you online? If you're a cybersmartie you can skip this section. But if computer talk is moving too fast for you, as it is for many of us, that first question asks whether you have subscribed to a particular service that broadens the use of your computer to allow you access to all sorts of additional information.

You subscribe to a service with a modem, which you purchase for about $100 and which is attached to your computer. The service you subscribe to then offers you all its material transferred through that modem. The company bills your credit card. Rates are all over the place, but they are dropping rather quickly these days. Generally, you can expect to pay around $20 a month for 20 hours of use and perhaps $3 for each hour beyond that.

What can you learn about cats from this addition to your computer? A *lot*, as those who are already on-line know. It can be fun too. The two major services—America Online and CompuServe—have pet forums that offer you information on many aspects of living with a cat—health, behavior, showing cats, pictures of cats, and more—written by authorities in the field. There's also usually a "chat room" where you can exchange questions and stories with other cat owners who use that service.

Some Helpful Information

Here's some fun in mixing cats and computers. *Catz* is, well, a cat living in your computer. It periodically scampers unbidden across your screen. It eats, it plays, it purrs, and, of course, it takes a few catnaps. You can play with it too (and hear it purr). In fact you can spend a *lot* of time with your computer kitty when you could—should—be working, but ah well…. *Catz* is available on CD-ROM (PF.Magic) and on the Web (http://www.pfmagic.com).

You can reach America Online at (800) 827-6364 and CompuServe at (800) 848-8199. Microsoft Network at (800) 386-5550 is a relatively new online service and is moving up fast in popularity. All three can eventually introduce you to the World Wide Web, which offers even more exploration opportunities.

Cat Publications

There are two major cat magazines, *Cat Fancy* and *Cats Magazine.* Take a look at both. They feature stories about cat care and behavior, lots of photographs, special columns, advertising, a breeder's guide, contests for readers, and more. It's easy to pick up each and quickly find yourself immersed in a particular article that's a must-read for you.

A one-year subscription to *Cat Fancy* is $25.97 for 12 issues. Write to *Cat Fancy,* P.O. Box 52864, Boulder, CO 80322, or call (303) 666-8504.

Cats Magazine costs $21.97 for one year or 12 issues. Contact *Cats Magazine*, One Purr Place, P.O. Box 420236, Palm Coast, FL 32142, or call (904) 445-2818.

The cover price of each is $2.95.

If you think only dogs matter in the United Kingdom, you're mistaken. *Your Cat,* which advertises itself as "The U.K.'s best-selling cat magazine," addresses cat owners there in a full-color monthly publication filled with short articles and consumer tips that, while geared to its U.K. readership, can be useful to cat owners everywhere. There's lots of advice and input from readers too.

Some Helpful Information
A subscription to a cat magazine makes a welcome and unique gift for a child of 10 or older who loves cats. Besides being quite readable for 10- or 11-year-olds, the publications often have special features for kids and publish their poetry and letters to the editor.

One feature that might interest cat lovers in the United States is a pen-pals column where U.K. readers, starting at around nine years old and going up to beyond retirement age, list their names and addresses looking for a match. Would *you* like to write to a fellow cat lover overseas?

The magazine is rather pricey in the United States—about $5.50 a copy—and is sold only in certain bookstores, one of which is Barnes & Noble. For subscription rates, write to *Your Cat* at EMAP Pursuit Publishing Ltd., Bretton Court, Bretton, Peterborough, Cambs, PE3 8DZ, England.

Natural Pet: Holistic Care for Your Best Friends is a glossy magazine with articles on natural foods, herbs, cures, flower essences, and rolfing (massage) for cats, dogs, turtles, birds, and horses.

The magazine is published bi-monthly. A one-year subscription (six issues) is $17.95. Contact the subscription department at P.O. Box 420543, Palm Coast, FL 32142, or call (904) 445-4608. The cover price is $3.95.

Bet You Didn't Know

HEY!

You can, of course, buy greeting cards with pictures of cats on them. Now you can buy cards to send *from* your cats. The cover of one, a seemingly old magazine illustration of four cats, each on a piano stool, carries the line: "You're the best cat sitter around!" Inside reads, "Thanks for taking care of us!" Cards include invitations to pet parties, apologies from pets, and some cards from owners and others looking for something a little different, such as the card sent to a cat on "Gotchaday" (a cat's actual birthday is sometimes not known) and the announcement of a new cat addition to the family or a new litter. There are also cards for dogs and for vets to send their furry patients. For a free catalog, call "Litterature" at (800) 639-1099.

Finally, there is the excellent *Catnip* newsletter, published by Tufts University School of Medicine in North Grafton, MA. The eight-page (or so) monthly covers a variety of topics, specializing, as you might expect, in the health and behavior of cats. There are some letters from readers and brief items about how owners came by their cats, solved a particular problem, and so on. This is a nicely, although not lightly, written magazine, and what little artwork there is breaks up the text and is composed of sketches, not pictures of cute cats. Still, the newsletter can be an invaluable resource for the pet owner.

Catnip costs $30 per year (U.S.) and $42 per year (Canada). For subscription information, write to *Catnip*, P.O. Box 420014, Palm Coast, FL 32142, or call (800) 829-0926.

Read a Good Cat Story Lately?

Cats do turn up in books other than mysteries, of course.

If you are new to being owned by a cat, you'll find that your bookstore or library offers much to delight and inform you, both in novels and non-fiction.

Cleveland Amory's tale about his very special pet, Polar Bear, *The Cat Who Came for Christmas*, first appeared in 1987. It's hard to see how any cat lover would not be moved by the book. The story is about how Amory, who acknowledged himself to be primarily a "dog person," came by a distinctive cat that changed his life; the story continues in *The Cat and the Curmudgeon*. In 1994 *The Best Cat in the World* was published, completing the

144

trilogy. Yes, this last book includes more adventures of the feline and the writer/animal rights activist Amory, but it also brings down the curtain on Amory's days with Polar Bear and introduces readers to his new cat companion, Tiger Bear, Amory's first kitten. Indeed, when he initially met the stray Tiger Bear, the little guy was less than a month old.

Desmond Morris and Roger Caras have written many books on various aspects of cat life and health. If you enjoy cat tales, look for *The Cats of Thistle Hill: A Mostly Peaceable Kingdom*, by Roger Caras, who relates many stories about the more than 10 cats who live with him and his family on their Maryland farm, along with 20 or so other animals and the workers who care for them.

Thistle Hill is in the warm, fuzzy vein, and so are the books of the late James Herriot, the British veterinarian-turned-writer. *James Herriot's Cat Stories* is perfect for the cat lover, although you might be just as interested in his writings about other animals.

Here is a relatively new cat book: *The Dog Who Rescues Cats: The True Story of Ginny* by Philip Gonzalez and Leonore Fleischer, with an introduction by Cleveland Amory. The slim book was published in 1995 following an article about Ginny and her owner that appeared in *Good Housekeeping* magazine.

Philip Gonzalez is a young New York steamfitter who became disabled after an industrial accident. Friends urged him to adopt a pet, and so he adopted a dog named Ginny, a gray, badly abused one-year-old mixed breed from a shelter.

What a dog Ginny turned out to be! She literally rescues cats—abandoned, starving strays, many of whom are handicapped as well—and steers them toward Gonzalez, who at first reluctantly, and then almost with a mission, saves the cats. While it's a canine who's obviously the star of this ongoing tale, cats of every description figure prominently. You'll find yourself rooting for each bedraggled little creature man and dog find, first to get well, then to live happily ever after.

> **It's Been Said**
> "What I like about a good author is not what he says, but what he whispers."
>
> —in "Afterthoughts" by Logan Pearsall Smith (1865–1946)
>
> MEOW!

> **Some Helpful Information**
> You probably have friends who are cat lovers. Why not share the cost of a book, magazine subscription, or audio- or videocassette with them, forming your own lending library. You'll keep up on what's new with cats at a fraction of the cost all those purchases would cost one person.

A Half Dozen Cat Tales Worth the Search

While some of these books and short stories can be found in libraries and bookstores, others may be out of print. However, you might be able to find a copy at a used or rare bookstore.

1. *The Silent Miaow* by Paul Gallico. Describes how a stray wins over her new people and is written by a masterful writer who has penned books in such diverse subject areas as *The Poseidon Adventure* and the *Mrs 'Arris* series.

2. *The Black Cat* by Edgar Allan Poe. A truly ghastly short story about a man and his cat where the feline is the moral arbiter. The fainthearted should skip this one—you won't get past the first few pages.

3. *The Cat* by Colette. Set in 1920s Paris, this is the tale of a husband and his childhood pet who is one of the causes of trouble in his marriage.

4. *Cat in the Rain* by Ernest Hemingway. An early Hemingway very short story of a going-through-the-motions marriage. The wife wants more—a particular cat, for one thing.

5. *The Cyprian Cat* by Dorothy L. Sayers. A mystery, minus her titled sleuth, Lord Peter Wimsey, that takes place during a summer holiday. The mystery is not who dunnit, but rather...well, why spoil your fun?

6. *Particularly Cats...and Rufus* by Doris Lessing. This prolific author looks back on a life with cats in Africa, where she spent some years of her childhood, and in England.

Finally, the artwork of Britain's Lesley Anne Ivory in books, calendars, and notepaper is finding wide appeal in this country. Her charming stories are on small themes (*Cats in the Sun* and *Cats and Carols* are two), and her drawings are suitable for framing.

Tales

A true story that almost seemed to be fiction appeared in newspapers in several parts of the world early in 1996. Fire broke out in a Brooklyn, NY garage, trapping a cat and her five kittens. The cat brought one kitten out of the building in her mouth, left her in a safe spot, and then went back for the next. She continued until she had taken out the last one. The firefighters named her Scarlet because of the patches of red that could be seen on her skin through the fur. Four of the kittens were not seriously injured, but one died.

Scarlet was taken to the famed North Shore Animal League on New York's Long Island, where she recovered nicely. She was not blinded as people first feared after her eyes were blistered shut in the blaze. By early summer, the shelter had received more than 1,000 phone calls from around the world offering to adopt Scarlet or one of her kittens. Scarlet and her family are now all in loving homes.

Look and Listen: Audio- and Videocassettes For You

The most recent cat star in films has been Sassy, who appears in the movies *Homeward Bound* and *Homeward Bound II: Lost in San Francisco*. In both films, Sassy, voiced by Sally Field, and two dogs, Chance and Shadow, are lost and trying to find their way back to their human family, experiencing numerous adventures along the way.

Going back a decade or so, *Harry and Tonto* starred Art Carney and told the warm tale of a man traveling across America with Tonto, his remarkable cat companion.

Small but meaty roles have been played by felines in *Babe*, the movie about a pig who wants to be a sheepherder, and *Breakfast at Tiffany's*, the 1960s film based on the novel by Truman Capote and starring Audrey Hepburn and George Peppard.

That Darn Cat, starring Hayley Mills, is a Disney film of the '60s. In 1996 Disney released in video the cartoon, *The Aristocats*.

Thanks to today's technology, if you missed a decades-old movie in the theater, you can usually rent the video. Most rental stores also have enormous catalogs of movies in print, so you can order from them if you want to purchase a particular film.

> **Some Helpful Information**
> Another way to enjoy cats vicariously is stamping, which can become quite an addictive pastime. You'll want cat rubber stamps, which you can use to create decorative packages and notepaper and, taking the hobby a step further, to design and make jewelry. *Rubberstampmadness* is the publication in the field. Write to Dept. CF, 408 SW Monroe, No. 210, Corvallis, OR 97333, or call (541) 752-0075. A one-year subscription (six issues) is $24, a sample issue is $7.

Besides movies starring or featuring cats, there are now a few dozen special videos out about cats. They offer information about cat care, cat stories, cute cats, and careers with cats. You might want to rent first before plunking down money to buy one.

A point to keep in mind for both video- and audiocassettes: A growing number of public libraries carry shelf after shelf of movies and books on tape that can be borrowed with just a library card, costing you nothing at all. Unless, of course, you incur a fine for their late return.

"Happy is the house that shelters a friend."

—Ralph Waldo Emerson

Audiocassettes can also be rented at shops specializing in books on tape. You're not likely to find older books to listen to, except perhaps for some classics, but certainly the current, popular ones stand a good chance of showing up in cassette form.

The beauty of audiocassettes is that, unlike reading, you can listen to tapes while driving, walking, washing the car, and so on.

Sayings and Superstitions
In Great Britain, cats in the theater are considered good luck. Most theaters over the ages have had a resident feline.

Here are two you might like to track down:

Garrison Keillor and mezzo soprano Frederica von Stade make music in *Songs of the Cats*, featuring 20 tunes written by Keillor. Or sort of—all are given the Keillor homespun touch we have come to expect, but the music is generally familiar, sometimes several tunes in one song. (One sample lyric is "Don't take your cats to town, son, leave your cats at home, Jim.") Songs include "Dance to My Cats," "Guilt and Shame," "Beethoven Chased by Rossini," "Eine Kleine Kat," and "Out in the Catskill Mountains," certainly a broad subject selection. Keillor entertains listeners with some of his well-known chats and poems too.

Accompanied by a very occasional, appropriately placed "meow," *Classical Cats: Music for Your Cat* is strictly music, and quite soothing too, for both a person and the feline on his or her lap. Selections start with "Stretch and Yawn: Welcome to the Day!" which is actually "Peer Gynt Suite No. 1" (Grieg), played here by the London Festival Orchestra, and end with "Time for a Cat Nap, Prelude to The Afternoon of a Faun by Debussy," also performed by the London Festival Orchestra. Bravo!

...and For Your Furball Too

It had to happen. If *we* stretch out on the sofa watching a video, why can't our cat?

That's what a number of entrepreneurial types asked themselves, and in the last few years, they have delivered a spate of videos especially for cats to watch. No longer will puddy have to sit through your shows, although it should be said here that many cats become fixated on certain moments in particular television programs. Some like to watch animals (specifically birds and other cats) or cartoons. Others are into sports. Many react to the theme music from certain programs. Of course, cats can still watch people television, but how nice that they now have programs just for them.

What exactly *do* they have here? As you might expect, what fascinates cats in real life is what's on celluloid for them—movies about birds, mice, fish, cats, and various other animals.

Bet You Didn't Know Before Garfield and Odie, there was the team of Tom and Jerry. The cat, Tom, and his mouse sidekick/foil made their debut in 1940 in the cartoon *Puss Gets the Boot*. Another noted film feline is Felix, who appeared in his first film, *Felix Saves the Day*, in 1922. He has more recently been showing up on Saturday morning "'toon shows" and has some new videos out as well. Welcome back, cat.

Videos are about $20 or so, and you can find them advertised in cat magazines, in mail-order catalogs, and sometimes at video stores. Give your library's video collection a look too.

The Least You Need to Know

➤ New cat-related features are cropping up regularly as part of computer online services.

➤ There are books to help you raise your cat, others with just plain heartwarming stories about cats, and several mysteries featuring or starring cats.

➤ Look to your public library to borrow video- and audiocassettes for free.

➤ Your cat might like his own video, and there are quite a few of them being produced these days.

Part 4
Caring For Your Cat

Whether we choose Cleopatra and Socrates or Fluffy and Tom, when we name our cats we accept them into our lives. Once they are "domestic cats" (although they don't always remember that), we take responsibility for the mental and physical health concerns that will make the shared human/feline life better for both of us.

Some of what you'll read in this section is about adapting a "wild" creature to the constraints of human civilization. Some of it is about adapting "civilized" humans to the drives and instincts of the essential feline spirit. And most of it is about how to keep both species healthy and happy.

brush
brush

Everyday Concerns

In This Chapter

➤ Grooming for good health

➤ Hair balls

➤ Coping with parasites

➤ Sleep secrets

Everyone knows that cats are survivors. They are, in fact, one of those species that seem to have undergone little or no change over the past 8,000 or more years. So why can't we leave them alone?

Let's look at the question in human terms. Why do we shower, brush our teeth, shave, shampoo, and blow-dry our hair? Certainly the human race could survive without all that. (And save some time too!) Why do we take vitamins? Why do we go on vacation, celebrate important dates, and decorate our homes? Most of us could keep going without that stuff.

The answer? Because we don't want just *life*, we want a better life. And we want a better life for our feline companions also. To significantly improve your cat's lifestyle takes only a small human commitment to some of its everyday concerns.

Why Do Cats Need Combs?

Most cats spend almost as much time grooming as Tammy Faye Bakker. Grooming is more than instinct for a cat, it's an art form! So why do we have cat combs, double-sided cat combs, undercoat rakes, slicker brushes, curry brushes, and cat grooming gloves? It all boils down to three human goals:

➤ Optimum health for the cat

➤ Optimum comfort for the humans who share their living quarters with the cat

➤ Beauty

It's Been Said

MEOW!

"Cats are *always* elegant."

—John Weitz, American fashion designer

When cats groom themselves by licking their fur, they remove dead hair and debris and aerate their coats. For many shorthaired cats, self-grooming is sufficient for everyday cleanliness so that humans need to step in only occasionally. Longhaired cats, however, need considerably more attention.

Most experts recommend grooming longhaired cats for at least 15 minutes a day to prevent coat tangling and matting. The most common places for mat formation are behind a cat's ears, under the legs, and on the belly. Fine hair in these areas can begin tangling and matting within hours of grooming. Once mats become established, they spread like mold on bread. They become a hiding place for fleas and a breeding area for both bacterial and fungal infections.

Sayings and Superstitions

Folklore has attached many meanings to touching the cat. Back in the days when humans grooming cats was unthinkable, it was said: If you rub a cat's fur backwards, you'll soon get into a fight.

A newly-formed mat can be carefully separated and untangled using a gentle spreading motion of your fingers. A small but somewhat more established mat can be cut out with blunt-nosed scissors. A cat that is severely matted, however, may need to be anesthetized by a veterinarian to have the mats removed surgically. Occasionally, a severely matted cat is shaved by a groomer. The coat will grow in again in three to four months.

From a human comfort point of view, grooming your cat will keep down the amount of shed hair that is deposited on your furniture and clothing. It will also keep down the amount of cat dander in the air, which might allow people with allergies to visit you!

And finally, beauty. If cats are living sculptures, if their movements are music, if their very presence improves the look of a room, then it follows that we humans should groom them to "be all they can be," both for them and for ourselves.

Ears, Eyes, Nose, Teeth, and Claws

Most cats do a fine job of keeping their own ears clean. Earwax (a yellow-brown substance often found at the base of a cat's ears) is produced by the cerumen glands and is perfectly normal. If it builds up excessively or if your cat's ears become dirty from his or her outdoor adventures, you can clean them with cotton balls dipped in warm olive or mineral oil. Do not put cotton swabs down into your cat's ear canals.

Unlike humans, cats do not cry by shedding tears. Excessive tearing usually indicates a medical problem and should be reported to your veterinarian. Sometimes small scraps of debris will collect at the corners of a cat's eyes. These can be gently removed with a moist cotton ball. Some cats of Persian descent with flat faces are prone to tearing and may develop tear stains from their eyes. These can be washed with a moist cotton ball or soft cloth.

A cat's nose is extremely sensitive, generally needs no special care, and should not be tampered with by humans. A runny nose or a particularly dry nose are both signs that something is wrong.

Many cat owners, even the devoted ones, object to the idea of cleaning a cat's teeth. But unattended problems with teeth and gums can cause cat halitosis, which is something you do not want! Cat halitosis produces a horrible, urine-like smell from the mouth. It is a metaphoric red flag telling you that your cat's health has been endangered.

Experts suggest brushing the teeth with a soft child-size toothbrush. You can use plain water or a specially formulated cat toothpaste. *Do not use human toothpaste since some brands contain detergents that could be harmful to cats.*

Some outdoor cats and all indoor cats will need to have their claws clipped from time to time. Once a month is usually a good routine. Unless your cat is particularly docile, it is generally best to clip only a few claws at a time. If you're just beginning this grooming activity or if you're worried about clipping too much, it's better to err on the conservative side and clip more often.

To clip the claws, press gently on the top of the cat's foot so that the claw comes forward and is exposed. Except when cutting black claws, you will be able to see a pink area called the quick. Cut the nail just up to the quick. Do not cut through the quick because it will bleed and be painful for the cat. (See the following drawing.) With black claws you will need to learn by experience approximately where the quick is. Begin conservatively by cutting only the tip of the claw.

Where to trim your cat's claws.

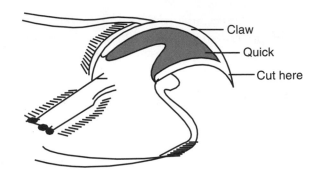

It's Bath Time—Or Is It?

Most cats are quite certain that water is intended only for drinking, and they can't understand why any self-respecting animal would want to douse its fur with it. So why should we put them through a bath?

Some cats (notably toms who are allowed outdoors) don't do quite as thorough a job at self-grooming and hygiene as others. Most humans find it more pleasant to have them a little cleaner while they are in the house. Baths are also a means of controlling fleas and are necessary for some skin problems.

Your cat may not like having a bath!

Unless your cat was introduced to baths as a kitten, he or she may object (with various degrees of force and fury) to the idea of being bathed. The bathing procedure, therefore, may require two people at first, one to hold the cat and one to do the washing. Try to talk reassuringly to your cat, keeping it as calm as possible. If the cat objects fiercely, do not hold tighter and force the animal down. This will make an issue out of baths that may never get resolved. Instead, let the cat go and try again later.

When preparing for the bath, place a rubber mat or a cloth bath mat at the bottom of the sink or tub. This will give the cat something to dig its claws into if he or she should feel the need to hold on. About four inches of water will be adequate for most baths, but be sure the water is warm enough. A cat's body temperature is higher than ours, so the water should feel quite warm to your touch. (About 90 to 95 degrees Fahrenheit is okay.)

Be especially careful when soaping the cat to avoid its sensitive eyes, ears, and nose. Rinse thoroughly after the shampoo and then towel dry. Many professional groomers suggest using a hair dryer set at a low speed to dry the coat before releasing the cat. Most cats won't object to the hair dryer.

It's Been Said

"A cat's rage is beautiful, burning with pure cat flame, all its hair standing up and crackling blue sparks, eyes blazing and sputtering."

—William S. Burroughs, American novelist

Some Helpful Information

A cat's skin is very sensitive! Be sure to use a shampoo made for cats or recommended by a veterinarian. The residues from some human shampoos could prove toxic to the cat when licked. If you can't get cat shampoo and the bath *must* be done immediately or sooner, use baby shampoo.

Some Helpful Information

If Your Cat Gets Sprayed by a Skunk

Oh, agony! Quick, get the cat shampoo and some old towels. After the bath, start the soak. Milk or tomato juice usually work best. Pour either the milk or the juice straight onto the cat, rub it in, and then talk gently to your cat, holding her for about 10 minutes. Rinse thoroughly.

If you believe in the Boy Scout motto (Be Prepared), you can buy commercial skunk odor removal products in many pet stores.

How to Find a Professional Groomer

Some loving cat owners get squeamish about cutting claws, combing fur, and giving baths. Others simply don't have the time. So who do you call? The professional cat groomer, of course. If you can find one!

No license is required to become a pet groomer, and there are an estimated 30 to 40 thousand groomers currently in business across the nation. Unfortunately, not all of them will do cats. In fact, the national trade association is called the National Dog Groomers Association of America, Inc.

So how does one go about finding a good cat groomer? Here are some suggestions:

➤ *Ask your vet:* Most veterinarians who recommend frequent baths or special grooming know people who will do the job.

➤ *Ask your cat-owning friends:* Friends who have their cats groomed will also be able to tell you if the groomer does a good job.

➤ *Look under Pet Grooming in the Yellow Pages:* Most of the ads will be for dog groomers, but those that take cats will usually indicate this with a line or two in their ad. If you don't find any cat notices, call all the groomers who advertise and ask them if they groom cats. Ask also for references—the names of people who have their cats groomed at the establishment. You don't want your cat to be the first one they ever tried to do!

➤ *Call some of the national cat organizations:* These friendly people will usually refer you to local groups or breeders who can put you in touch with groomers near you. There's a list of cat associations in Chapter 22.

Shedding and the Healthy Coat

Shedding is a normal process for cats. When cats are allowed to go outdoors, a molting or "blowing of coat" usually occurs twice a year (spring and fall). Among indoor cats, shedding is often a more continuous process with some extra emphasis in the spring and fall. Unusually heavy shedding, shedding at unexpected times, or shedding confined to certain areas of the body can all be signs of illness.

The cat's self-grooming during periods of shedding increases the formation of hair balls since more hair is loose and therefore more is ingested. This is a process you want to minimize as much as possible by extra grooming. Even if you don't ordinarily groom your cat, you should make a valiant attempt to do some grooming during shedding season. It will keep your house cleaner and your cat healthier.

Hair Balls

If you see your healthy cat vomiting, don't panic. It's probably a hair ball.

Hair balls occur when ingested hair collects in the stomach. They are normal in cats, but they can sometimes lead to serious obstructions requiring surgery. The best prevention methods are regular grooming, adding some insoluble fiber (grass or rye grass, for example) to the diet, and administering a hair ball prevention product, such as mineral oil, to the cat. For a choice of products and advice on how much to use, consult your veterinarian. Do not rely on printed product labels.

When a cat coughs up a hair ball, it is usually a brown mass, often tubular, that comes up alone or along with some clear, sometimes foamy fluid. Hair balls are also sometimes evacuated with the stools. Lack of appetite and/or constipation can be symptoms of a hair ball problem.

About Those Skin Bugs

Flea

Cat louse

What is that?

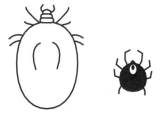

Tick (engorged and not engorged)

Mite

Fleas, lice, ticks, and mites all attack the skin of the cat. Their bites cause itching, sometimes inflammation and eczema, and sometimes diseases such as Lyme disease and mange. Cat fleas are also intermediary hosts for tapeworms.

There are many over-the-counter products available to control fleas, lice, and ticks. These include a variety of collars, powders, and shampoos. Most of them work quite well for moderate infestations, but advanced cases will need medical attention. Be careful to choose only products made for cats because dog products can cause allergic reactions and serious irritations. In some cases, the reactions are so severe that they cause toxicity and even death. Even some flea collars made for cats may cause a skin reaction on some cats, so check the neck area carefully for a few days after putting on the collar.

The newest product for flea control does not kill fleas. Instead it sterilizes the fleas that bite your cat so that they cannot reproduce. It is available through your veterinarian under the trade names PROGRAM and Advantage. Administered once a month in pill form, this product is most effective on indoor cats who do not bring new fleas into the house.

Bet You Didn't Know

Most of the life cycle of the flea occurs off the body of your cat. Flea eggs and larvae are usually found in pet bedding, at the base of carpet fibers, under rugs, in cracks in the floorboards, and in upholstered furniture. Commercial products are available for ridding your home of fleas. For extra heavy infestation, you can call a professional exterminator.

There are several kinds of mites that infest cats and cause different diseases. They are minute, almost invisible, and more difficult to eradicate than fleas or lice. In most cases, you'll need veterinary help.

Engorged ticks, on the other hand, are easily seen and need to be removed from the skin as soon as possible. Wet the head of the tick with alcohol, wait two minutes, and then remove the entire tick by pulling evenly with tweezers.

To guard against an infestation that grows and gets out of hand, be aware of changes in your cat's behavior patterns. Itching and scratching, rubbing the head on the floor (especially the ears), persistent shaking of the head, and agitated restlessness can all indicate a worsening situation with external parasites. If you suspect that the methods you are using are not working adequately, don't put off an appointment with the vet. The longer you wait, the more difficult the cure will be.

What No One Wants to Talk About: Worms

A cat dragging her bottom could have worms.

The majority of cats have worms at some point in their lives. Common symptoms requiring immediate attention are: a distended abdomen (potbelly) accompanied by loss of weight, restless and uncomfortable behavior, loss of appetite, and rubbing of the anal area on carpets or floors.

Cats are susceptible to several kinds of intestinal parasites including roundworms, tapeworms, hookworms, coccidiae, and trichinellae. It is essential that your veterinarian identify the parasite infestation in order to prescribe the proper medication. You'll need to gather stool samples, sometimes more than once.

Sayings and Superstitions Many cat owners believe that regularly adding fresh shredded carrots or small amounts of garlic to a cat's food will keep him or her free of worms. Don't count on it.

To Sleep, Perchance to Dream

Sleep. There are those who say it's what cats do best. Most healthy adult cats sleep away 50 to 60 percent of each day, while some manage 70 percent. Senior cats and very young kittens can get that figure up to 80 percent easily. How do they do it?

In the first place, they have different body rhythms than we do. Cats are naturally nocturnal animals, but they don't stay up all night nor sleep all day. They prefer many short periods of light sleep and a few periods of deep sleep over the human pattern of one long sleep per 24-hour day.

It's Been Said "Cats are rather delicate creatures and they are subject to a good many ailments, but I never heard of one who suffered from insomnia."

—Joseph Wood Krutch, American critic and essayist (1893–1970)

161

During periods of light sleep, cats are pretty much aware of what's going on around them. In fact, the British say, "The cat sees through shut lids." Cats can either move from light sleep into deep sleep or from light sleep into instant awareness and action.

Like humans, cats have at least two different types of sleep as measured by brain waves: slow-wave or quiet sleep, and REM (rapid eye movement) sleep. During slow-wave sleep, the cat relaxes its muscles, and brain activity slows to a rhythmic pattern. The cat, however, can be easily awakened and maintains enough muscle tone for her to hold her head up in the "sleeping sphinx" position if she wants to.

MEOW!

It's Been Said

"Drowsing, they take the noble attitude/ Of a Sphinx in deep solitude/ Sleeping ever in a desert land/ Dreaming dreams that have no end."

—Charles Baudelaire, French poet (1821–1867)

REM sleep is deeper but lasts considerably less time. In humans, it's usually the time during which we dream. Most experts believe that it is also the time that cats dream. Many cat people have seen their "sound asleep" pet suddenly begin to twitch its tail, move its feet, or sometimes even make aggressive sounds. It's probably a dream that would rival a movie chase scene!

Cats Who Sleep on Your Bed

Because cat body rhythms are different from human body rhythms, many owners get pounced upon or sandpaper-tongued at odd hours of the night or just before dawn. No loving talks or gentle caresses will stop this instinctual behavior. A little imposed training is needed. You might try keeping a filled squirt gun on the nightstand.

The Least You Need to Know

➤ Grooming improves not only cat health and beauty but also hair and dander control in the cat owner's living quarters.

➤ Teeth and claws also need regular attention.

➤ Do not use human toothpaste or shampoo on cats.

➤ External and internal parasites such as fleas and worms must be controlled or eradicated.

➤ Sleeping away two-thirds of each day is normal for a cat.

Chapter 16

Professional Health Care

In This Chapter

➤ About vets

➤ Weight watching

➤ Common cat diseases

➤ That old cat!

Being a small animal veterinarian is a lot like being a pediatrician. Your patients can't tell you where it hurts, how much it hurts, or when it hurts. Instead, communication and interpretation of the symptoms come from a loving caregiver who is always anxious, who doesn't always trust that you're doing the right thing, who pays the bill, and who doesn't always listen to your advice.

But like it or not, most pet owners admit that the vet knows more than they do—about some things. The vet also has the tools to prevent some diseases and cure many others. About making a cat more comfortable, however.... Well, maybe that's a joint effort, 50 percent caregiver and 50 percent veterinarian.

How to Select a Vet

Should you just drive to the vet's office nearest you? Should you check the phone book for names and pick one? It's risky. Having read this far, you certainly know that cats are different from other animals. They have some unusual sensitivities and reactions to chemicals, and they have some instinctual drives that prompt them to hide their infirmities. You need a vet who knows cats well.

Cat people seem to find each other wherever they are and you should seek them out when you begin vet hunting. Talk with cat owners or cat groomers who have used the veterinarians you are considering. You can also call and ask for the names of cat specialists from a veterinary college near you (see the appendix at the end of this book) or from your local animal shelter.

The American Animal Hospital Association in Denver, Colorado is a national trade association for veterinarians. If you call them at (800) 883-6305 and give them your zip code, they will provide you with a list of member veterinarians in your area. You can even get professional bios on the vets you are considering as well as order a number of health care pamphlets. If you prefer a referral to a cats-only vet, you can call the American Association of Feline Practitioners at (505) 343-0088.

You can get cat tips and veterinary advice from the American Animal Hospital Association's World Wide Web site.

Bet You Didn't Know

HEY!

Veterinarians are not trained down on the farm! Entering this profession requires four years of undergraduate work and an additional four years in a veterinary graduate program to earn the Doctor of Veterinary Medicine (DVM) degree. Your general practice neighborhood vet has training in 21 medical specialties. Some vets go on to specialize further in such fields as dermatology, oncology, geriatrics, and so on, while others specialize in treating one type of animal only, cats for instance.

Tales

James Herriot is perhaps the most widely recognized veterinarian's name in the world. Yet there has never been a veterinarian named James Herriot; it was the pen name of a Glasgow-born Scotsman named James Alfred Wight (1916–1995). After graduating from Glasgow Veterinary College in 1940, Dr. Wight set up practice in rural Yorkshire, England and kept careful notes for 50 years on every patient he saw. His first book as James Herriot, *All Creatures Great and Small,* was published in 1972, followed by 17 other titles and a BBC television series. In 1994 St. Martin's Press published *James Herriot's Cat Stories,* a collection of 10 tales illustrated with watercolor paintings by Lesley Holmes.

What to Expect at the Annual Checkup

Most people take their cats to the vet once a year as a preventative measure.

"That means shots, doesn't it?" you ask.

Yes, vaccinations are extremely important and we'll get to them in just a minute. But there's more. A lot can happen in a year in the life of a cat. At an annual physical, body systems and overall health should be checked and recorded for future comparison against a time when there might be trouble developing.

Just like a human doctor, your veterinarian will listen to the heart and lungs and palpate the organs in the cat's abdomen. He or she will examine the condition of the ears and check both the ears and skin for external parasites. Teeth and gums are inspected for damage or infection. The veterinarian will also check the eyes and nose for unusual discharges. Anal glands are checked for proper function and to be sure they are not impacted. A stool sample may be needed to inspect for worms, or a routine worming may be carried out.

Cats in Our Language

Despite the name, *catgut* does not come from cats. It is a tough cord usually made from the intestines of sheep and sometimes from pigs or horses, but never from cats. The intestines are first cleaned and cured, then woven into cords of various thickness. For centuries, these cords were used for surgical sutures and the strings of musical instruments and tennis rackets. Today, plastics and other synthetics have pretty much replaced catgut.

Do I Have to Get on the Scale?

What do humans hate most in a doctor's office? The scale! But fat cats are not nearly so self-conscious as fat humans. In fact, they rather like themselves the way they are and will proceed quite happily through life. Studies show that added weight has little effect upon a cat's life span. Hey, maybe we humans should take a cue!

Some cats are naturally lean and some are not. Diet and exercise can help maintain the cat at its optimum weight, but that weight is determined in the genes and cannot be changed much. You just can't change a cuddly, pudgy Persian into a sleek, scintillating Abyssinian. The moral of the story is to love the cat you have.

Cats in Our Language

Fat cat is American slang for a person who is obviously (and sometimes ostentatiously) prosperous, regardless of body size and shape. In fact, *fat cats* has been used in the press to refer to sleek stockbrokers!

That does not mean, however, that your cat's weight should not be monitored and charted by the vet. Sudden weight gains or losses are often indicative of disease. Fat cats are more prone to urinary problems than lean cats. They can also injure their joints more easily.

A genuinely overweight cat (this is only about 10 percent of the cat population) can be encouraged to slim down a bit for health and comfort. However, you should put your cat on a reducing diet only with the advice and assistance of your veterinarian since proper nutritional balance is extremely important to success. Never try to reduce your cat's weight with a forced fast. Fasting by overweight cats can bring on fatty liver disease (hepatic lipidosis), which can be fatal.

You want to give me a shot?

Oh, No! Shots!

Many serious diseases in cats can now be prevented through immunization. The program for kittens will be discussed in Chapter 19. In each of the following diseases, once the initial immunization is established, the adult cat needs only boosters to maintain its immunity. The frequency of required booster shots depends upon the disease and the product used to establish immunity. Your veterinarian will give you a schedule of the common annual boosters.

Here is a list of the most common:

➤ *Feline distemper:* A very infectious and potentially fatal viral disease that can be spread from cat to cat or brought into the house on human hands and even shoes that have touched an infected cat. Also called feline panleukopenia, feline infectious enteritis, show fever, and cat plague. Not related to canine distemper.

➤ *Rabies:* A fatal disease that can be transmitted from animals to humans. All cats should be inoculated, many states require it.

➤ *Feline leukemia virus:* Similar in some ways to the human HIV virus, but not exactly the same. It is diagnosed by a blood test and is transmitted from cat to cat by long exposure to saliva and/or blood, usually while mating. *It cannot be transmitted to humans.* FeLV-negative queens (breeding females) should be inoculated before mating. Pregnant cats should not be inoculated. Many stud cat owners insist that visiting queens be tested before mating.

➤ *Cat flu:* Actually two viruses with similar symptoms that a combined vaccine usually inoculates against. The symptoms of both viruses include coughing, sneezing, and a runny nose and runny eyes. The viruses are a special threat to the very young and the very old. A cat who has the disease and recovers can become a carrier.

MEOW!

It's Been Said

"I can look back with fondness on a life spent tending to cats.... And if it is not their way to show a little appreciation, I can understand that...I'm a pretty crusty old bird....

"There have been many a time when I've choked up at an unexpected kindness and said nothing. Later on, I wanted to kick myself. Well, maybe there are cats walking around today wanting to kick themselves for hissing and spitting at Camuti when he was only trying to help them. I hope so."

—Dr. Louis J. Camuti, legendary cat specialist, from his book *All My Patients Are Under the Bed* (with Marilyn & Haskel Frankel), Simon & Schuster, 1980.

Two Nasty Virus Diseases

Effective and reliable vaccines have not yet been found for two life-threatening viral diseases. Experts believe, however, that current work will lead to solutions that will conquer them.

Feline immuno-deficiency virus (FIV) has frightened many pet owners because it resembles AIDS even more than FeLV. This virus attacks and breaks down the cat's immune system. It cannot be transmitted to humans, nor can cats get the HIV virus. Like HIV, however, many cats infected with FIV enjoy long periods of good health before secondary infections take their lives. It is usually diagnosed by a blood test. If your cat is FIV positive, you should keep him or her away from other cats.

Feline infectious peritonitis (FIP) can appear in two forms: wet and dry. Symptoms of the wet form are a swollen abdomen, diarrhea, vomiting, and weight loss. The dry form affects the central nervous system with symptoms that include jaundice, respiratory problems, loss of coordination, and, near the end, seizures. FIP was a rare disease but is becoming more common. When contracted, it is virtually always fatal. A vaccine has been in use for five plus years now, but there are still questions surrounding it.

Bet You Didn't Know

In the United States, there are a number of large, specialized pet hospitals that might remind you of the Mayo Clinic. Among them is the Animal Medical Center in Manhattan, one of the largest private animal hospitals in the world. With a nine-story building, a caseload of approximately 65,000 dogs, cats, and other pets each year, and specialists in every field, it is a source for consultations and expert care to a huge population of pet owners.

Some of the nation's other regional pet hospitals are associated with veterinary schools, such as the one at Tufts University. Others are associated with major city animal shelters, such as the one in San Francisco.

Signs that Your Cat Might Be Sick

Since your cat can't tell you he's sick, and will in fact often try to hide it from you, you must become aware of the behavior clues that should signal a vet visit. The following is an alphabetical list of symptoms and behaviors, along with some of the illnesses they might indicate:

➤ *Breathing difficulties:* Foreign bodies, head cold, leukemia, upper respiratory system disorder

➤ *Changes in the skin:* Allergies, external parasites, fungus infection, improper diet

➤ *Constipation:* Blockage of the intestine, foreign bodies, infectious peritonitis, head cold, kidney stones, uterine infection, worms

➤ *Coughing and sneezing:* Cat flu, head cold, upper respiratory system disorder

➤ *Diarrhea:* Hair balls, improper diet, infectious peritonitis, kidney problems, leukemia, poisoning, worms

Some Helpful Information
Animal health insurance is available throughout Canada, the European Community, and Australia, but has still not found its way everywhere in the United States. Ask your veterinarian if a health care plan is available where you live. Small monthly or annual payments may ensure that your cat will get all the care it needs in an emergency without putting a burden on your budget.

➤ *Fever:* Bacterial infection, flea infestation, hair balls, kidney problems, upper respiratory system disorder, viral infection

➤ *Increased thirst:* Diabetes, flea infestation, kidney problems, liver disease, leukemia, poisoning, uterine infection

➤ *Running eyes and nose:* Cat flu, feline pneumonitis, injury, upper respiratory system disorder

➤ *Scratching ears and shaking head:* Ear infection, ear mites

➤ *Swollen body:* Distemper, fleas, foreign bodies, infectious peritonitis, leukemia, worms

➤ *Vomiting:* Foreign bodies, hair balls, improper diet, infectious peritonitis, poisoning, worms

Some Helpful Information

Never give your cat aspirin. No, not even baby aspirin! Aspirin is likely to cause hemorrhaging in the cat's gastrointestinal tract. It also depresses bone marrow activity, which makes replacement red blood cells, and it can be harmful to the kidneys. One of the most common reasons cats are brought to animal emergency clinics is aspirin intake! Acetaminophen (Tylenol and other brands) also causes problems, but for other reasons. Remember: *cats are sensitive and small, use only cat medications.*

How to Give a Cat a Pill

The incredible resistance and agility of the cat is again demonstrated whenever it takes two people to give an eight-pound animal a pill! (And that seems to be more often than not!) Like children, cats do not like to be told "You *have* to...." Unlike children, they cannot be "reasoned with" (read as "ordered to").

In the two-person method, one person holds the cat while the other pries open the cat's mouth by placing the thumb and forefinger on either side of the jaws and pushing firmly but gently. The pill is popped in as far back on the tongue as possible. The cat's mouth is then shut and held closed while the nostrils are covered with a finger. This forces the cat to swallow. Some pet owners also stroke the cat's throat at this time. Be sure that the cat does swallow. Some wily cats will hide the pill in their mouth and then spit it out when the pill administrator is not looking.

If two people are not available, you can get some added restraining power (and protection from claws) by wrapping the cat in a bath towel leaving only its head showing. Then follow the steps in the two-person method.

Plastic "pill poppers" are also now available in the marketplace. They look a little like fat, long syringes. The pill is loaded inside, the cat's mouth is forced open, the popper is placed with the end near the back of the cat's mouth, and the human pushes the plunger. If you choose to use this method, be absolutely certain that the pill popper has a soft tip to prevent injury to the cat's throat. Also watch to be sure that the pill does not miss its mark or get spit out by the cat.

It's Been Said

"He seems the incarnation of everything soft and silky and velvety, without a sharp edge in his composition...."

—SAKI (Hector Munro), British novelist (1870–1916)

One wonders: did he ever give a cat a pill?

Some owners try concealing the pill in a favorite treat. Sometimes this works, but sometimes the cat manages to eat all of the treat and then spit out the pill. A more reliable method is to pulverize the pill and mix it with a favorite treat (tuna or liverwurst usually works), then roll up a bite or two, each the size of a nut. If your cat loves butter, you can mix the pulverized pill with a small amount and then put it on your cat's paws. He or she will usually lick it off. Before choosing any of these food-associated methods, however, be sure to check with your vet because some medications lose efficacy when mixed with food.

Ancient Wisdom—How to Cure with a Cat

Despite the cat's bad rep for hanging around with the wrong people (witches and devils), recorded recipes for healing with the help of a cat go back as far as 1602. Here's a sample of some of the less repulsive:

1607   For the paine and blindnesse in the eye….Take the head of a blacke Cat, which hath not a spot of another colour in it, and burne it to pouder…then take this poulder [*sic*] and through a quill blow it thrice a day into thy eie.

1684   For the Shingles: Take a Cat, and cut off her Ears, or her Tail, and mix the Bloud thereof with a little new-Milk, and anoint the grieved place with it Morning and Evening for three days.

1721   Scottish proverb: *Cast the cat o'er him.* It is believed that when a Man is raving in a Fever, the Cat cast over him will cure him.

1883   For a sty: Brush the sty seven times with the tail of a black cat, and the sty will be gone by the next morning.

1887   For whooping cough (an Irish cure): Nine hairs from the tail of a black cat, chopped up and soaked in water, which is then swallowed, and the cough will be relieved.

1923   Advice from England: To get a bad place well, let a cat lick it.

Alternative Medicine

Human interest in "natural healing" using clinical nutrition and herbal remedies is growing rapidly with more and more people using these methods to supplement traditional medical care. More humans are also using acupuncture, homeopathy, and chiropractic medicine. What has this got to do with cats? Well, there is a movement among veterinarians to recognize and include these healing methods in their practices.

The American Holistic Veterinary Medical Association (AHVMA) was founded in 1982 and has grown to a membership of over 500 veterinarians and other health care practitioners. If you want to include alternative medicine in your cat's care, you can get the names of practitioners near you by sending a self-addressed stamped envelope to AHVMA, 2214 Old Emmorton Rd., Bel Air, MD 21015. You can also ask your veterinarian and local animal protection agencies for referrals.

What Humans Can Catch

There are only a few diseases that can be transmitted between cats and humans. It is important that you know what they are and how to avoid them:

➤ *Rabies:* Even indoor cats should be immunized, just in case they get out into the world on occasion.

➤ *Fleas:* Cat fleas prefer cats, then dogs. But if there's nothing else, they'll jump on humans.

➤ *Ringworm and other skin fungus:* Cats, especially longhaired varieties, can bring the spores (which are often picked up from the soil around a house) indoors on their coats. Humans can get ringworm by petting the cat or from shed hair in the house, even though the cat does not get the disease. When humans have ringworm, the cat should be treated also, and the house, particularly the carpets, should be cleaned with anti-fungal solution wherever possible.

➤ *Toxoplasmosis:* Toxoplasma is a microscopic parasite that can be ingested by the cat from undercooked or uncooked meat (field prey). It does not usually make the cat ill, but it is passed in the feces. Its danger to humans is primarily to pregnant women because it can cause severe damage to the brain and eyes of the fetus. It is recommended, therefore, that pregnant women do not clean litter boxes. Toddlers and young children should also be kept away.

Common Problems of the Older Cat

There have been reports of cats living 30 years, with one claiming the record at 36, but that is very, very unusual. A 12-year-old cat would be paid Social Security benefits, according to our government's current age guidelines (if cats could collect that is). A 20-year-old cat should have already gotten a Happy Birthday letter from our president like every American who lives a whole century.

How Old Is a Cat in People Years?

Each cat ages as an individual just as each human does, but here are the generally accepted aging comparisons:

Cat years	1	2	7	10	15	20
Human years	15	25	50	60	75	105

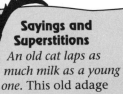

Sayings and Superstitions
An old cat laps as much milk as a young one. This old adage might just be the secret motto of the downsizing corporations of the '90s, with the unspoken thought added, of course, that the old cat, with an ever growing likelihood of medical problems, costs more to keep!

With age comes some changes. Older cats are less adaptable to stress and sudden changes in day-to-day routines than younger animals. As they age, cats are prone to gradual deafness and the development of many of the same diseases that older humans endure, such as diabetes, heart disease, arthritis, kidney disease, tumors, and constipation.

Unlike humans, many older cats develop hyperthyroidism, a condition in which the thyroid gland overproduces. If your cat is eating normally but losing weight, you should check with your veterinarian since this condition is treatable with medication or surgery.

Just like kittens, older cats are sometimes a problem and often a joy. They are usually more affectionate and attentive than their "prime-of-life" cousins, they sleep a lot, and they like their comfort. But then again, don't we all!

The Least You Need to Know

➤ Annual checkups and booster vaccinations are essential to a cat's good health and long life.

➤ Since most cats try to hide illness, it's important to recognize and note symptoms or changes in behavior.

➤ Never give a cat aspirin, it could be fatal.

➤ Most cat diseases cannot be transmitted to humans. Rabies, fleas, skin fungi, and toxoplasmosis are exceptions.

➤ Aging cats develop many problems similar to aging humans, but are almost always pleasant company.

No Bad Cats

One of the unwritten rules for writing a book like this one includes: *Don't start the chapter on a down note*. But sometimes a down note is needed to make the high notes brighter, clearer, and stronger. So begging the pardon of the book-writing rule keeper, let's start with a definite down note.

Behavior problems are by far the most common reason that cats are brought to a veterinarian or a shelter to be euthanized. More than eight million cats are put to death each year in the United States. And that's not the whole of it. Those statistics recognize only the cats owned by the kinder, gentler people and do not include the millions of cats that are pushed out of car doors into neighborhoods or wooded areas far from their homes.

Cats Will Be Cats

Unlike dogs, who have lost most of their ancestral wolf traits through their long association with humans, cats are still "wild things" in many of their behaviors. Not only are their ancient instincts strong, but the cat as a species does not seem to want to give them up or adapt them to the needs and desires of their human companions.

Many of the so-called problem behaviors of cats are really just cats doing what comes naturally. The real problem is that many humans don't know what is natural for a cat. Such people attribute human thoughts and emotions to a cat's activities.

A young male cat scratches the leg of the brand-new dining room table, for example, and the distraught owner cries out to her husband that the cat was mad at them because they were late coming home and didn't leave any food out. More likely, the cat was declaring that the table was one of his possessions. Because he is a cat, he makes no association

It's Been Said

"The phrase 'domestic cat' is an oxymoron."

—George F. Will, American journalist

between the scratched table leg and the belt that is lashed, whip-like, across his back. But he learns that the man who did the whipping can be an enemy.

There's no doubt about it: Cats are loving companions who bring joy, laughter, and comfort to millions of people; but they are cats. If we accept them into our homes, we must understand their drives and motivations and provide acceptable outlets for the resulting behaviors. If we must train them, we must use methods that cats understand, not human rules and human punishment techniques.

I Couldn't Help It, Ma! Honest!!

As a primer, let's look at four of the most common types of cat behavior that humans often find objectionable. Each category includes several normal cat activities that make people scream "Bad cat!" Understanding the underlying drives behind these activities may not make them any more pleasant to us, but it may help us provide for acceptable alternative behaviors, take steps to diminish the drive, and accept and love the cat as a cat.

Aggressive Behavior

You are calmly stroking your cat when suddenly his front feet are wrapped around your hand, claws out. Maybe there's even a little bite before your cat jumps from your lap and runs under the couch. What happened? What did you do wrong?

Usually nothing. Experts don't really know why cats suddenly scratch. They do know, however, that some degree of aggression is natural in all cats, probably coming from their instinctual survival behaviors. Most cats do a good job controlling this behavior indoors. Their bites and scratches are really just "see what I can do" statements.

Some cats, however, take aggression a few steps farther indoors. Sometimes, for example, they will dash out from a hiding place, dig their claws into your ankle, and dash away again. This is unacceptable behavior that can become a ritualized daily occurrence if allowed to go on. Your cat must be made to understand that clawing is not a game and that you, the dominant cat in the house, will not allow it. When the cat attacks, stamp your feet hard, clap your hands, and shout "Bad cat!" or something that makes a challenging sound. If you have one handy, squirt the cat with a water gun.

The best prevention of aggressive behavior in a grown cat starts in kittenhood. It's important that you don't encourage biting, scratching, and attack-the-human-hand games with your kitten. Like the human, what the cat learns in childhood usually stays, either consciously or subconsciously, in its mind.

It's Been Said
"Those who'll play with cats must expect to be scratched."

—from *Don Quixote* by Miguel de Cervantes, Spanish writer (1547–1616)

Aggression between cats in a multi-cat household is more difficult to control. Cats have their own social structure, and most experts advise that cat owners let the cats work it out. If the aggression continues longer than a few weeks, if it becomes more than you can tolerate, or if a cat becomes injured, however, step in and then try to find another home for one of the fighting cats.

Beyond the Litter Box

Cats are clean animals and are so easily trained to use a litter box that many people forget that they can, and sometimes do, use other places to relieve themselves. Once a new "place" for a cat to relieve itself is established, the habit may be hard to break. When you come upon the initial deviation, try to find the cause.

When cats deposit feces just outside the litter box, it often means that the box has not been cleaned recently and is too dirty to the cat. Frequent switching from one type or brand of litter to another can also cause rejection by some cats, especially older cats who do not like change. Find a type of litter that you and the cat like and stick with it.

Frequent urinating outside the litter box, sometimes referred to as FUS (frequent urinating syndrome), is a very common problem. It can be a sign of kidney disease, bladder infection, diabetes, emotional stress, or another disease. Rubbing your cat's nose in the soiled place and spanking, as is often done with dogs, will not have any effect on the cat's behavior. Your first step in correcting this type of behavior is to have the cat checked by a vet to be sure there is no underlying physical cause. Then you must look for the behavioral cause.

Cat spraying (urinating for scent marking) is instinctual behavior used to establish territory, and sometimes this outdoor trait is moved indoors. It might occur when a new cat (or even a new person such as a baby or a new husband, wife, or roommate) is introduced to the household. It might occur when a cat is moved to a new house or apartment. Or it might occur when a cat sees other cats through the window or perhaps hears or smells them outside the apartment door.

While working on this problem and trying to make your cat feel comfortable again, it is often a good idea to make the places your cat has already used as inaccessible as possible. Some cat owners block off such places, others even put the food bowls there. Keeping a cat away from a place that still carries the odor of urine (even if humans can't smell it) will make the formation of a new habit less likely. Some owners also add another litter box in the house, giving the cat a choice of more than one location. More about spraying in just a bit.

A tomcat spraying.

Destructive Behavior

Scratching furniture and woodwork is another residual behavior of the instinct of cats in the wild to mark their territories by leaving scratch marks on trees. All kittens will try out their scratch marking ability, so kittenhood is the time to teach them to use a scratching post. If you bring an adult cat into your house, it may take a bit longer to discourage scratching, but it can usually be done. Spend time each day playing with your cat near the scratching post and encouraging him to use it.

Some cats left home alone all day become bored and use territorial scratching as an amusement. It's important, therefore, to have plenty of cat toys about and (many people say) more than one cat, since they do amuse each other once they decide to get along.

Some cats suck on yarn and woolen fabrics, and some even eat holes in their owners' clothes. No one knows exactly why they do this—one theory is that it reminds them of suckling, but that's only a theory. When wool or other fabric is actually eaten, it is usually passed without harm through the cat, but it does sometimes cause digestive problems and even blockages that require surgery. If you notice your cat eating or sucking on wool, it is best to keep all fabrics out of its reach. Siamese and Burmese cats are often wool suckers.

Some cats eat houseplants. While the cat is primarily a carnivore, most cats like a little salad now and then. Houseplants, therefore, are tempting. Some of them are poisonous (there's a list in Chapter 9), while others just taste good.

What to do? Well, you have three choices. You can avoid battle with your cat by trying to keep your favorite plants out of reach, you can provide plenty of plants that are edible and tasty for the cat to eat at floor level, or you can opt for silk plants or no plants in your home.

Fear

Fear of humans is instinctual in the tiger. Sometimes a vestige of that instinct appears in the cat. It can be a good thing if it helps your cat recognize you as the dominant being in the household and worthy of due respect. Fear can bring about a behavior problem, however, when a cat will not come out of hiding as long as a stranger is in the house or, worse yet, when a cat hisses, spits, and attacks a stranger. This is a problem that takes both patience and perseverance on the part of the owner and sometimes requires professional help.

Learned fear, such as the fear of getting a shot or a bath, can cause aggressive self-preservation behavior such as scratching, biting, or trying to escape, but it can often be calmed with patient handling. If your cat shows aggressive fear, proceed very slowly or, if possible, put the activity aside for another time.

Some Helpful Information

What does it mean when your cat starts racing about the room like a dervish? Is she afraid? Has she gone temporarily mad? Hardly ever. Such behavior is perfectly normal for the cat. Most experts believe it is a release of tension, something like the jumping and dancing that football players do after a touchdown run or a big win. It occurs most often near sunset—the cat's natural hunting time. Don't worry. It's unlikely she'll bash into a wall, and she'll be her own normal self in just a few minutes.

Tales

There are folktales from all over the world to remind people that a cat will always act like a cat. In a tale from Syria, *The Cat Who Went to Mecca,* the king of cats makes a pilgrimage to Mecca, the most holy place in his world. When he returns, the king of mice feels obligated to pay him the traditional visit of congratulations. The king of mice's advisors object, saying that the cat is their natural enemy.

But the king of mice has seen the king of cats at prayer, and he is certain that the pilgrimage has changed him. Despite the protests of his people, the king of mice ventures out to pay his respects to the king of cats.

The moment the king of cats catches sight of the king of mice, he interrupts his prayers and pounces. The king of mice barely escapes and rushes back to his subjects. When they gather round him and ask how the greeting ceremony went, the king of mice replies, "He is the same. He may pray like a pilgrim, but he still pounces like a cat."

Mind Games

Despite the many written testimonials on the similarity of the cat mind and the human mind, there is still a great deal of mystery about the cat. We just don't always know why cats do what they do. We do know, however, that it is usually non-productive and sometimes actually destructive to attribute human motivations to cat activities.

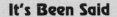

It's Been Said

"Most of us rather like our cats to have a streak of wickedness. I should not feel quite easy in the company of any cat that walked about the house with a saintly expression."

—Beverly Nichols, British novelist (1899–1983)

He Did It For Spite

One woman was trying to complete the knitting of a baby afghan while her son, his wife, and their new baby were visiting. When Clarance the cat curled up next to her (on top of the already finished portion of the afghan) she shooed him away briskly. That evening, the whole family went out to dinner. When they returned home, Clarance had pulled the afghan out of the knitting bag, pulled the circular needle out of the work, and unraveled and tangled several inches of the intricate pattern.

The poor grandmother was bombarded with conflicting emotions: "He did it for spite! He was jealous of the baby! He wanted more attention!" she cried as she scooped up Clarance and pushed him down the cellar stairs.

What really happened? Maybe Clarance liked the feel of the soft wool and was trying to make a comfortable bed for himself. Maybe he was fascinated with the regular movement of the knitting needles and wanted to play with them. Maybe he considered the baby a rival in the household and wanted more attention for himself. Who knows? But the human emotion of spite was probably *not* the motivator.

She Manipulates Us Horridly

"Jezebel gets what she wants, one way or another," says a Kansas man. "If I'm trying to read the newspaper, she'll rub around my legs, walk over my shoulders, bat the newspaper with her claws, whatever it takes to make me stop and do what *she* wants to do. She's better at getting attention than most of the humans I know!"

Getting human attention seems to be a natural talent of most household cats, but some subtle creatures seem to go even further and try to manipulate human behavior. Faked injuries are commonly reported. For example, a couple who frequently travel noticed their cat limping badly and holding up a front paw as they were packing their suitcases. With non-refundable flight tickets in hand, they called a relative who agreed to take the cat to the vet. Nothing could be found despite almost $200 in bills for x-rays, testing, boarding, and observation. The cat was fine when the couple returned home. Two months later when packing for another trip, the limp developed again. But this time it was the other leg!

181

Certainly some of the joy of living with a cat is the intimate contact with a mind that thinks! Cats are neither leaders nor followers, but very independent beings. They are always something of a puzzle and something of a challenge. Maybe that's why we love them so much.

The "Not-so-Nice" Image of the Cat

People not only impose human emotions and motivations on the cat, they also describe some not very nice human behaviors as cat-like. Here are some commonly used expressions and slang in English:

Cat: A malicious woman.

Cat-farting about: Fussy actions that have the effect of being irritating.

Cat-fight: An intense fight or argument between two women.

Cat-fit: A fit of anger or an emotional outburst.

Cat-house: A brothel.

Catty: Slyly spiteful or malicious.

Cat-witted: Unteachable and spiteful.

Have kittens: Become nervous, agitated, or "all hot and bothered."

Sourpuss: Grouch.

Tabby: A spiteful woman.

Raging Hormones

Many of the cat behaviors that humans find undesirable, such as scratching and indoor spraying, are greatly intensified by sex-related hormones. Even though he is never allowed outdoors, a tomcat will become agitated when there is a female in season in the neighborhood. He will also react intensely if he sees another cat through the window by spraying, scratching, and sometimes displaying bad temper.

Outdoor toms are also usually the culprits in the objectionable caterwauling that occurs during the night. These cries and the frequent fights among toms are usually related to territorial disputes (as are most human wars).

Females are not quite as territorial as male cats, but they too will fight to keep out an unwanted visitor, and they will also mark their possessions. Females in season want to go out looking for a mate, and a female cat will stay in season until she finds one or the weather turns colder. Owners often report personality changes that include impatience, restlessness, and verbal complaining.

For those people who don't want to handle hormone-intensified cat behaviors, there is really only one option: spaying or neutering all cats in the household. No amount of training will help. These behaviors are stimulated by sexual hormones that create drives necessary for procreation and the preservation of the species. These drives are just as intense as the drives to eat, drink, and sleep.

When Your Cat Makes You Angry

It would be a rare couple and a rare family that never had a fight. And it would be a rare cat that never made its owner angry. But for families and for cats, research shows that physical punishment and abuse do not work.

If your cat makes you angry, express your anger with shouts or by punching a pillow. After you cool down, try to understand the cause of the behavior that made you angry. Then try to think of a way to prevent it, preferably something that makes the act undesirable to the cat.

Let's say, for example, that you leave your Thanksgiving turkey on the countertop to cool a bit before carving and go into the living room to join your guests for some hors d'oeuvres. While you are there, Henry VIII jumps up on the counter and begins his feast. Don't throw Henry against the wall when you discover him calmly washing his face. In his mind, the turkey was left there just for him.

Sayings and Superstitions
In a cat's eyes, all things belong to cats.

—English proverb

Instead, try to make him understand (ahead of time, of course) that jumping up to the countertop is always unpleasant. One man put double-sided carpet tape on the counters. His cats did not like getting their feet stuck. Because cats are intelligent and don't repeat behaviors that cause them discomfort, it took only a few days to train them not to jump up.

Cats Under Stress

Many of life's stressful situations for humans are also stressors for cats. Like humans, cats usually respond to stress with changes in their behavior patterns. Some common changes are over-eating or under-eating, over-grooming to the point of licking a spot to baldness, restlessness, and not using the litter box.

Among the most common cat stressors are:

Sayings and Superstitions
Cat got your tongue? Children and even some adults who feel stressed or intimidated often can't speak a word when questioned. This old saying blames it on the cat!

➤ Extended absence of a loved family member

➤ Introduction of a new human into the household

➤ Introduction of a new cat into the household

➤ Long hours of being left home alone

➤ Human stress that changes the behavior of a loved human

➤ Moving to a new home

➤ Loss of a companion cat in the household

Depression Is Real

Some cats, like some humans, suffer from depression, but the cat can't declare, "I'm depressed." It's almost eerie that common symptoms of cat depression are so similar to the symptoms of human clinical depression:

➤ Listlessness

➤ A lack of interest in life

➤ Ungroomed, uncared for appearance

➤ Changes in eating habits—either refusing food or binge behavior

➤ Changes in sleep patterns

➤ Personality changes

Before assuming that your cat is depressed, it's essential that you take him or her to the vet for a complete examination. Many of these symptoms can also be caused by a physical illness, such as an infection. If nothing shows up in the exam or the tests, you should try giving the depressed cat extra attention. Besides playing and petting, this includes the grooming that the cat is not doing and perhaps some tempting food if anorexia is a symptom.

Most cats come out of depression with a little help from their humans. But if the condition persists, there are cat-sized doses of anti-depressant drugs available from veterinarians.

Animal Behavior Therapists

There are now efforts under way within the American Veterinary Medical Association to make animal behavior therapy a specialty, but there are still few course programs available in veterinary colleges. Some veterinarians have pursued study on their own; others have sought out individuals who work successfully with cats and other animals to refer their patients to.

Some veterinary colleges do have behavior advisors associated with their clinics. Often, they have help lines you can call for advice by phone. There are fees, however, that vary, so ask how much it will be before you start talking.

There has also been some effort made to establish requirements for "certification" in animal behavior therapy, but to date there are no license requirements anywhere in the United States. That's right, anyone who thinks they understand animals can hang out a shingle that reads "Animal Behavior Therapist."

It's Been Said

"Genius is patience."

—Georges Louis Leclerc, Comte de Buffon, French naturalist and writer (1707–1788)

The lack of licensing standards, however, does not mean that a person without formal education can not be a good, or even an excellent, cat therapist. Trying to understand the behavior of an animal that does not speak our language and trying to help that animal and its human owner adapt to life together takes love and tremendous patience. We must remember that we cannot get into the cat's mind because we are not cats. So let's take our "hats off" to the dedicated individuals who make contributions in this field.

The Least You Need to Know

➤ Most problem behaviors are actually the result of cats following their natural instincts.

➤ Hitting or otherwise physically punishing a cat will not correct its behavior.

➤ To change a cat's behavior, you must understand what is causing the behavior and address that root cause as the problem.

➤ Like humans, cats can become stressed, and they sometimes become depressed.

➤ Although a new field, there is research being done in cat behavior therapy, and the field should continue to grow.

Sex!

Cats are soooo sexy! In the wild, sex and survival drives determine nearly all of their activities. Yet in many of their sexual behaviors, cats are different from other species, even most other mammals.

Perhaps this chapter should be called "Sex and the Single Cat," because cats do not take lifelong mates. That's not to say that two cats cannot be lifelong friends within your home, but the friendship has nothing to do with sex.

Sexual activity among cats is motivated by powerful hormones that seem to overrule everything else. Unlike the human sex act, however, there seems to be little pleasure for either partner in cat sex.

Let's play voyeur for just a bit and find out what's going on here.

Tomming Around

The seasons affect the sexual behavior of cats. Male cats are ready anytime, but they will mate only with a queen who is in season, and the season of the queen is dependent upon the amount of daylight and warm weather.

It's Been Said

"In the spring a young man's fancy lightly turns to thoughts of love."

—Alfred, Lord Tennyson, British poet (1809–1892)

Cats in Our Language

When the word *tomcat* is applied to males of the human species, it is usually slang for a promiscuous woman-chaser or sometimes for a man lacking a sense of responsibility for his offspring.

As the days grow longer, starting in late January in the northern hemisphere and late July in the southern, more and more queens come into season and more and more toms are stimulated to seek them out and fight over them. All this activity winds down in the fall as the days become shorter and cold weather approaches. Whoever said, "There is but little caterwauling on cold winter nights," was observant indeed.

A male cat with his sexual organs intact (commonly called an unaltered male or a tom) will mate whenever he can with any female cat who will have him. His sex drive stimulates him to mark out his territory by spraying and scratching, to roam quite far from home, to fight with any other cats (usually but not always males) who come into what he feels is his territory or whose territory he crosses, and sometimes to become aggressive toward people and other animals.

Tomcats rarely show any interest in their kittens, in fact they usually don't recognize them as their own. Queens will almost always keep toms as far away from their nests as possible. And rightly so, because some toms have been known to kill kittens. This behavior probably goes back to an instinctual behavior of the new stud lion who routinely kills off all the cubs of the predecessor he just ousted.

What Makes the Male Cat Male

Growth toward sexual maturity is first triggered by hormones released from the pituitary gland (a small gland at the base of the brain). The process takes longer to reach fulfillment in male cats than in females.

Most male kittens are able to produce reproductive cells (sperm) by the time they are 5 months old. They do not usually mate, however, until they reach a minimal body weight of seven to eight pounds, which generally happens between 9 and 12 months of age.

Some young toms.

Testosterone, a hormone produced primarily in the testes, influences the development of masculine characteristics. As male kittens reach puberty, they develop thicker skin on their necks to protect them in fights with other cats. Their cheek ruffs (hair on the outer parts of their faces) grow to make their faces look larger, and their bodies grow larger than those of female cats. The most easily recognizable sign of male sexual maturity, however, is the change in the odor of the urine. No one knows exactly what causes this unusual and pungent smell.

Sayings and Superstitions
Useless as tits on a tomcat!

—rural North American folk saying

189

Seasons of the Undeniable Urge

Most female cats reach sexual maturity between 5 and 8 months of age, but a few get there as early as 3 1/2 months. You'll know exactly when your kitten comes of age because her behavior will change dramatically as she becomes a sexual animal in season. Siamese, Orientals, and Burmese kittens tend to mature early. Persians mature later than most cats, usually at about 12 months, but sometimes even later.

Sexual behavior in a female cat is governed by the stages of her cycle:

➤ *Anestrus:* She has no interest in sex and her body is sexually inactive.

➤ *Proestrus:* A period of about two days when she is acting strangely and seeming to look for a mate, but she is not yet ready to have sex.

➤ *Estrus:* A period of usually 5 to 8 days when she will mate willingly with any male cat. (Estrus can actually last from 3 to 20 days.)

➤ *Diestrus:* An intermission between cycles. During this period that usually lasts 2 to 14 days but can last as long as 30 days, ovulation will not occur and the female cat is not interested in sex.

The female cat's cycle.

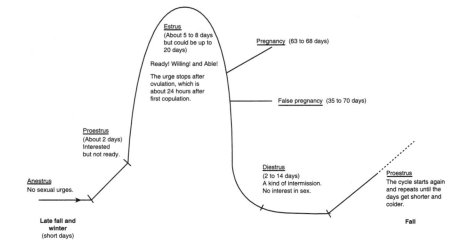

The estrus stage is often referred to as the *heat*. During this time, a female cat becomes agitated and sometimes nervous. Often, she will call almost constantly in a curiously drawn out meow/moan, and she will rub her body against anything she can find, including humans. Sometimes she will roll about on the floor and throw herself into sensuous (she thinks) poses. She may even present her posterior to anyone and anything with her tail up and to the side and her front feet and head low. She will also try every wily trick she can think of to get out of the house.

You will certainly know when Annabelle is in heat, but you won't see any red stains on the carpet or furniture because there is no discharge associated with a cat's estrus. Female cats often do, however, have spotty urination that is uncontrolled.

Unlike every other mammal, cats do not ovulate until copulation occurs. In fact, the sex act actually stimulates ovulation so the sperm are there waiting when the eggs explode from the ovaries. Needless to say, there are few infertility problems in the feline population.

If a cat is not bred during the estrus stage of her cycle, there is a brief between-cycle interval called diestrus when ovulation will not occur. Then the cycle begins again. These four stages repeat until the cat is bred, has a false pregnancy, or the days get shorter and the weather colder. Then the cat enters the anestrus stage and has a quiet autumn and winter until the days begin to get longer again. Some indoor cats and some cats in warmer climates, however, cycle throughout the year.

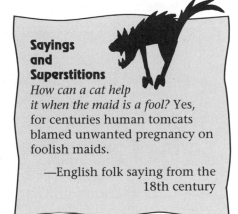

Sayings and Superstitions
How can a cat help it when the maid is a fool? Yes, for centuries human tomcats blamed unwanted pregnancy on foolish maids.

—English folk saying from the 18th century

How Kittens Get Made

A mating between two cats doesn't take long and doesn't look like much fun from the human perspective. The whole thing lasts about 10 seconds! It always starts with the tom sniffing the queen's genitals while she crouches in ready position. He then mounts her, often biting the loose neck fur. Penetration can last as little as 3 seconds, during which time the queen screams the dramatic copulation scream and then turns immediately to scratch and swat the tom and break his hold. Both cats then clean their genitals.

Why the dramatic scream? It's not from pleasure. The penis of an unaltered cat is covered with backward pointing barbs (like the ones on fishhooks). It slides in easily enough, but once it moves around or begins to withdraw, the barbs cut up the lining of the vagina, which probably hurts like hell! But don't waste your sympathy on poor kitty because the queen will be ready to do it again in a matter of minutes, not hours. And if her first lover is a little indisposed, she'll find another.

MEOW!

It's Been Said
"No matter how much cats fight, there always seem to be plenty of kittens."

—Abraham Lincoln, 16th President of the United States (1809–1865)

It's not at all unusual for a female cat to mate with five or six toms during one estrus cycle. Her

191

promiscuity is often quite vividly demonstrated between 63 and 68 days later by the appearance of littermates obviously fathered by very different cats.

Some Helpful Information

Many people believe a female cat should be allowed one litter to develop her personality to the fullest with the experience of motherhood. Wow! This is another great example of our tendency to impose human values on the feline soul. Research has shown again and again that *breeding has no permanent effect on the personality of a cat.*

Caring For the Pregnant Cat

Pregnant cats get along rather well in the wild, remaining quite fast and agile until the final weeks before delivery. There are few noticeable changes in the early days of pregnancy, but as time goes by, your cat might stay closer to home, rest more, and become a little quieter. Somewhere in the second or third week of the pregnancy, you may notice that her nipples have become enlarged and have changed from pink to rose-colored. By the fourth week, a veterinarian can usually feel the fetuses.

Bet You Didn't Know

Cat menopause? Hardly! Cats proclaim "You're NEVER too old!" Although litter size may diminish, cats can continue to give birth right through their teens. There have even been reports of healthy litters delivered by 25-year-old queens. Now those cats *deserve* the name queen.

A normal diet is usually adequate for the first few weeks of pregnancy, but your cat's appetite will probably increase after the fourth week until she is eating almost double her normal amount of food just before delivery. She will need extra high-quality protein and some extra minerals, such as iron and calcium. Since there are many excellent commercial foods available for the pregnant cat, you might want to consult your veterinarian for suggestions.

False Pregnancies

Sometimes when a cat does not mate during estrus or when a mating does occur but is sterile, a false pregnancy will occur. In this case, the hormones of pregnancy will make your cat act and feel as though she is pregnant. This condition will last from 35 to 70 days, with some cats even going through milk production and false labor.

False pregnancies usually end of their own accord and the cat resumes her normal cycle. When they recur again and again, however, you should consult a veterinarian. Although there is hormone therapy available to relieve the uncomfortable symptoms of repeated false pregnancies, many owners prefer to have their cats spayed.

The Importance of Spaying and Neutering

There are three reasons why spaying or neutering a cat benefits both cats and humans:

➤ Population control

➤ Behavior modification

➤ Improved health

Many people, however, hesitate to spay their female cat or neuter their male cat because they feel it is somehow unkind. But is it kind to allow the queen to bear litter after litter in endless repetition? Is it kind to let the tom roam to fight and fight again until he contracts a fatal disease or is killed by a car? Or is it more kind to remove the sex drive that rules cats' lives, thus allowing them to live fuller and longer lives as human companions. Let's look at the three reasons to spay or neuter.

Bet You Didn't Know Statistically speaking, a cat and her offspring can produce 420,000 kittens in seven years.

Population Control

The cat population is increasing around the world and particularly in North America. This is fine if it means that more and more people are making cats their pet of choice. But there's more to the statistics. The number of feral cats in our cities and our suburban residential areas is also growing rapidly.

Cats without a home are cats struggling to survive by eating from garbage cans and sleeping in the dug-out areas around basement windows. They fight, they are prone to abscesses and other diseases, they transmit fatal viral diseases from one to another, and they often get hit by cars. Other cats are put to death simply because a home cannot be found.

Municipalities and animal protection agencies are struggling to get the cat population explosion under control. Many cities have programs to capture and euthanize abandoned or feral cats. Animal protection agencies, with the help of volunteer veterinarians and concerned citizens, have organized spay and neuter programs in an effort to cut down on the number of cats being put to death. And many shelters are now spaying or neutering kittens before they are released to homes since studies have shown that these procedures can be done on kittens as young as six weeks without harm.

Some Helpful Information

If you are interested in establishing a spay and neuter program in your community, you can get advice and information from:

➤ Animal Protection Institute of America

➤ The Humane Society of the United States

➤ The Pet Savers Foundation/Spay USA

Addresses and phone numbers for these organizations are in Chapter 25.

Tales

A restaurant owner on British Virgin Gorda was amazed at the efficiency of a young group of veterinary students from Tufts University who came to the island to help control the cat overpopulation problem. At night they captured almost one hundred cats in humane traps. Then they tested for infectious diseases, inoculated all the healthy ones, and spayed or neutered them. Within a week, the cats were freed again to the location from which they were taken. "This doesn't solve the problem," said the restaurateur, "but it sure helps. I found out they've been coming to the island just about every year since 1986!"

Behavior Modification

How does spaying or neutering change the behavior of cats? In females it stops the heat seasons from occurring. The queen no longer vocalizes her need throughout the day and night. Her rubbing, rolling, and posing stops, as well as the spraying that some female cats take up during their seasons. Spayed females no longer feel the need to escape outdoors to find a mate, and they develop a keener interest in and attachment to their owners. And not least important, there are no new kittens twice a year.

Neutering a male cat usually stops his fights and his roaming, especially if the neutering is done early in his life. In most cases, neutering will also stop the urine spraying that can leave a seemingly permanent scent in your home. The neutered male is less aggressive and more companionable. He is interested in his owner and what is happening in the house, and he likes to play. Neutering does not make him fat, but overfeeding and boredom will.

Improved Health

Spaying reduces the risk of mammary (breast) cancer in female cats, especially if it is done before the first heat. Sexually intact queens have a seven times higher risk of developing mammary tumors. This statistic is especially important because 85 percent of breast tumors in cats are malignant.

Because the uterus is removed in spaying, the procedure also eliminates all the potential diseases of that organ. These include *pyometra* (a pus-filled uterus), *metritis* (an inflammation of the uterus), and *endometritis* (inflammation of the lining of the uterus).

Neutered male cats live longer than their intact brothers because they get into far fewer fights. With fewer fights, they have a lower risk of abscesses and irreparable wounds. They also roam less and are therefore at lower risk for becoming highway fatalities.

Should You Do It?

Yes! Veterinarians and animal protection groups are in total agreement. There are no negatives to the spay and neuter question. Removing the sex drive in cats improves their behavior in your home, makes them more comfortable in their own lives, and helps control the overpopulation problem in your community.

Purebred cats are, of course, the exception to that recommendation. We'll talk more about breeding and showing purebreds in Part 5. For now, however, just remember that breeding and showing are very different activities from living with your cat.

The Least You Need to Know

> ➤ Unaltered male cats roam, fight, spray urine, and protect their territories. They will mate with any available female at any time.

> ➤ Unaltered female cats usually come into season when the days begin to get longer in late winter and continue to cycle until they are bred or until the days begin to get

shorter again in early fall. They can and often will mate with several toms during one heat, producing a mixed litter.

➤ Pregnancy lasts between 63 and 68 days. During the latter part of that gestation period, the pregnant cat needs extra protein and minerals.

➤ Spaying or neutering is universally recommended by veterinarians and animal protection groups. It improves in-home behavior, increases life expectancy, and helps to control cat overpopulation.

meow meow meow meow meow...

Chapter 19

Raising Kittens

In This Chapter

➤ The miracle of birth

➤ From newborn to one of the kids

➤ A place to call home

The great American poet Carl Sandburg once said, "A baby is God's opinion that the world should go on." We might say the same of a kitten. Or, for that matter, of a puppy, a foal, baby birds, and all new life.

The miracle of birth is the very essence of creation. Think about it: *where there was nothing, there is suddenly a new being.* A cat giving birth almost always means new *beings.*

When you watch your cat participating in this miracle, you'll be both anxious and proud. But your overwhelming emotion will almost certainly be awe. You can't help but wonder that she can know just how to do everything so well.

Getting Ready

During the 63 to 68 days of pregnancy, there really isn't much for owners to do. But if you really want to help, you can prepare a birthing box.

Cats like a quiet, out-of-the-way place to give birth. They usually choose darkness, and they seem to prefer a sense of overhead covering. Your cat might choose a closet, a corner cluttered with discarded toys, under the bed, or sometimes on top of the bed (among your cherished, hand-embroidered throw pillows, naturally). Or she might choose a pile of car-washing rags in the corner of the garage. Sometimes an indoor cat will try to get outdoors just before delivery to find her own secret place. Rather than take a chance on such inappropriate (from a human point of view) places, it's far better to try to persuade your cat that a birthing box is the ideal place to have kittens.

You don't have to be a carpenter to create a birthing box. In fact, an ordinary cardboard box will do nicely. Cut a hole in one side that is six to eight inches long by six or so inches high. Be sure this entryway is up about four inches from the floor of the box to prevent the kittens from falling out. The flaps from the top of the box can be folded closed for privacy and security for the queen, or they can be allowed to fall open for cleaning and extra care of the kittens. Or you can fabricate a lid (cut from another slightly larger box) that can be easily removed when necessary.

A simple birthing box (decorations optional, of course).

You can use several layers of newspapers to line the bottom of the box before delivery. Or you can use old towels or sheets. Just be sure that they are clean and dry.

Introduce your cat to the birthing box at least a week before the kittens are expected. If she seems to be choosing another spot such as a closet, however, you might put the box close to her place of choice and encourage her to sleep in it by lining it with soft towels.

Cats in Our Language

In British public houses, the large and small pewter pots in which beer was served were called *cat and kittens.* The theft of these pots (which occurred quite regularly) was called "cat and kitten sneaking."

When the Time Has Come

Your cat's mammary glands will enlarge during the week before delivery, and colostrum (milk) can usually be expressed from the nipples about 48 hours before delivery. But the real sign of impending birth is your cat's behavior. Watch for these signs:

➤ *One or two days before delivery:* Loss of appetite, anxiety, vocalizing, and shredding the newspapers or other materials in the birthing box.

➤ *Hours before delivery:* Frequent licking of the genital and abdominal areas.

➤ *During the first stage of labor:* Kneading and rearranging the nesting material, rapid breathing, panting or purring, some discharge from the nipples, and sometimes some bloody discharge from the vaginal opening. Many cats move about frequently, changing position as though trying to get comfortable. This stage can last up to six hours.

➤ *During the second stage of labor:* Straining and pushing, sometimes in the same position as a bowel movement or on her side or chest. This stage may last an hour before the first kitten is born. The time between kittens can vary considerably. It might be five minutes or two hours.

The Birthing Process

The head and paws of a kitten appear first from the birth canal. Once you can see them, the kitten should be born within 15 minutes. If gradual progress is not being made, you should call your veterinarian.

Some kittens are born rear feet first. If you see this happening, don't panic. It rarely presents a problem. You should call your veterinarian, however, if a kitten seems stuck rather than gradually moving outward.

As soon as the kitten is born, the queen will tear off the amniotic sac and lick the kitten clean. She will also bite away the umbilical chord. When the placenta is delivered, she will eat it, the sac, and the chord. This afterbirth material contains many valuable nutrients.

Some Helpful Information

Cats usually do better giving birth without intervention from their owners. A watchful eye is most often the best assistance. Call your veterinarian if your cat fails to deliver a kitten after two hours of bearing down (second stage labor) or if she stops bearing down completely even though she has obviously not yet delivered all her kittens.

Some Helpful Information

Avoid bathing a mother cat both immediately before and for some time (usually until weaning) after she has given birth. You do *not* want to wash away the particular scent associated with each teat. When each kitten cannot find its own teat through scent, the littermates become confused. Older kittens will even fight.

The First Days

The average kitten weighs about 3 1/2 ounces at birth. It is both deaf and blind, but it is sensitive to touch. It has a limited sense of taste and smell.

Newborn kittens are neither strong nor mobile. They sleep 90 percent of their day. When not sleeping, they are eating. After each nursing session, the queen will lick each kitten to stimulate elimination. She usually then eats this waste matter in order to keep the nest clean. It is essential that newborn kittens spend most of their time close to their mother since they are extremely sensitive to cold and cannot regulate their body temperatures.

Tales

Satoshi was a 16-year-old Japanese exchange student living in an American household when Belinda gave birth to her kittens. He had never before witnessed a birth. Belinda, on the other hand, was an experienced mother and her labor and delivery were easy.

Satoshi sat as a silent observer as the kittens emerged into the world, and he sat stone still, intent and silent, as Belinda tore open the sacs and cleaned each tiny, blind, and deaf kitten. Then, suddenly, he jumped up and began to point toward the kittens saying, "Oh, Oh, how they know to do that? How they know?" Each kitten had wriggled its way to its mother and had chosen the particular teat it would use until weaned.

Satoshi had been interested in the birthing process, but he saw an awesome miracle elsewhere. How did these tiny, helpless creatures know how to move themselves toward a nipple and begin to suck? What incredible knowledge drives new life?

The First Weeks

Hearing begins to develop in the newborn kitten at about the fourth day, when the auditory canals begin to open. By day 14, these canals are fully open, but the full adult hearing capability is not fully developed until about three months of age.

The process of sight development is similar. The eyes open between the seventh and tenth day. By the end of the third week, a kitten has enough depth perception to understand that a table has an edge. That same kitten, however, does not yet have the intelligence not to fall off. Sight, especially tracking ability, is not fully developed until about three months.

Most cats are good mothers.

What very young kittens do best is eat and sleep. Most kittens will double their birth weight by the end of the second week. From birth, they can purr and meow, and they can move themselves about for very short distances with a kind of swimming motion.

By the end of the third week, kittens approach four times their birth weight. They usually try standing on their feet and taking their first wobbly steps. Some owners begin to offer solid food (usually strained baby foods) at this time.

By the fourth week, the queen usually moves her kittens to another nest. They begin to play with each other (cuffing and swatting) and some of them will climb out of the nest. Some owners make a kitten-sized litter box available at this time.

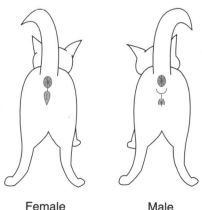

Female   Male

Boys or girls? Distance is the key to differentiating sexes in young kittens. The two openings are farther apart in a young male.

Foundlings

With so much responsibility on the mother cat, how can kittens who are orphaned or cruelly dumped into the bushes near a house or under the lights at a parking lot survive? It takes a lot of help from caring humans.

If you find such kittens and know of a nursing mother cat with kittens of about the same age, you can try an adoption. Many nursing cats will readily accept new kittens. (Of course, it is essential that you have the foundling checked by a vet first or you might endanger an entire litter and the mother too!) Also watch the nursing process for a while to be sure everyone is getting enough milk.

Sayings and Superstitions
He takes to it like a kitten to a hot brick.

—American folk saying

If an adoption is not possible, your first job will be to keep the kitten warm. At about a week old, a kitten's body temperature is usually around 100 degrees Fahrenheit, and that temperature must be maintained despite the kitten's inability to do so naturally. It is usually recommended that the room or kitten-box temperature be kept at 80 degrees Fahrenheit for about 20 days. After that, it can gradually be lowered to about 70 degrees Fahrenheit.

There are special incubators available, and your vet may have one that you can use or rent. If not, you might want to try using a water circulating heating pad. (Do not use heating pads with electrical wires because they can cause burns.) Cover the pad with towels or old sheet pieces and lay it on only half the floor of the box so that the kittens can get away in case it becomes too hot. For very young kittens who are unable to move themselves, drape the pad on the sides of the box. Be sure to check the temperature setting and the heat inside the box often. If no heating pad is available, an old-fashioned hot water bottle wrapped in cloth will add some warmth.

Cow milk does not adequately substitute for cat milk, and many kittens cannot tolerate it, so you will do best to purchase orphaned kitten formula (Borden's KMR, for example) at your pet supply store or from your veterinarian. If you cannot get kitten formula but live on or near a farm, sheep milk can be used. You can also purchase the necessary bottles and nipples in most pet supply stores. Very small kittens will need to be fed at four to six hour intervals. Kittens over five ounces can usually do well at six to eight hour intervals.

Weaning

Mom cat will usually complete the weaning of her kittens by week eight. Most authorities recommend introducing solid food by the end of week three, however. The first offerings can be a teaspoon or so of jarred baby meats (veal is a good starter) softened and diluted with a little water.

In weeks five and six, the consistency of the solid foods can be thicker and other foods can be introduced. Specialty products are available from pet food suppliers and veterinarians. Many owners, however, use cottage cheese or well-scrambled hamburger.

From weeks five to eight, the mother cat may leave her kittens for longer and longer periods of time. She may want to go outdoors if she had that privilege before giving birth. Be extra careful if you choose to allow this freedom because a female cat, unlike most other mammals, can come into her estrus cycle while she is still nursing a litter. And that could mean another litter without adequate recovery time for her body.

MEOW!

It's Been Said

"A kitten is the most irresistible comedian in the world. Its wide-open eyes gleam with wonder and mirth. It darts madly at nothing at all, and then, as though suddenly checked in the pursuit, prances sideways on its hind legs with ridiculous agility and zeal."

—Agnes Repplier, American writer (1855–1950)

Growing Up

Who could not love a kitten? Cute and cuddly, fierce and fiery, they are comic miniatures. But growing up has its responsibilities.

Kittens should be introduced to the litter box by six weeks of age, and most kittens are fully trained by two months. At that same two-month stage, they will be exploring your house. You'll soon find out how well they can climb! If you don't want open season on your draperies and furniture, you may want to confine them to one room.

But do play with them! Just about all authorities agree that kittens who are lovingly handled during the early weeks make better companions. They also handle stress better throughout their lives! (Sort of like humans, huh?)

If you keep the litter together, you'll find yourself laughing as you observe such games as cuffing, chasing, rolling, pouncing on each other's tails, and some roughhouse biting and scratching. This play activity, which starts out tentatively at four weeks, will increase with each passing week to a peak at about 11 weeks.

During this cat childhood, even the solitary kitten will play. She will chase shadows and her own tail, she will pounce at nothing, and she will run for sheer joy.

> MEOW!
>
> ### It's Been Said
>
> "A kitten is so flexible that she is almost double; the hind parts are equivalent to another kitten with which the forepart plays. She does not discover that her tail belongs to her until you tread on it."
>
> —Henry David Thoreau, American essayist (1817–1862)

Kitten Health Care

A healthy litter need not be seen by a veterinarian until the first shots are needed for feline distemper at about six to eight weeks. Feline leukemia virus vaccinations are usually started at about nine weeks. Rabies and other vaccines can be given at other intervals as required by state law or as thought necessary by your veterinarian.

Since the timing of the first shots and the intervals and number of required boosters are so dependent upon the procedures used by the individual veterinarian and the recommendations from the manufacturers of the various brands of vaccines, it's impossible to give a hard and fast schedule for vaccinating your litter. You should talk with your veterinarian as soon as the kittens are born about which vaccines will be used in order to schedule optimum protection.

And finally, a word about *guilt*. Try not to feel guilty if one of the kittens dies. Kittens have a high mortality rate. Including stillborns, expert estimates set the rate at over 20 percent even with in-home deliveries. Among feral cats, it is considerably higher.

Signs of a kitten in distress are:

➤ Not nursing

➤ Mewing

➤ Listlessness and not trying to get close to the queen

➤ Not gaining weight

If you see a kitten in trouble, you should call your veterinarian. But do remember that some problems simply cannot be fixed.

When You Keep Kittens

So you've fallen in love. You just can't bear to part with one of the kittens, or all of them. It happens, and for most people and most cats, it's great. But there's a thought or two you should keep in mind.

Sexual maturity comes early to cats, even before they are four months old for some females. Males mature a little later and do not usually become sexually active until they reach at least seven pounds. Therefore, if you plan on spaying or neutering, it is important not to let time pass unheeded. That six-month-old, five-pound bundle of joy *could* produce a litter!

Some cats play like kittens throughout most of their lives and are a joy to their owners. Most cats, however, become adults psychologically as well as physically before they reach their first birthday. They will develop a routine of sleeping and eating, and you will soon know their preferences for everything. They will also take a position in the cat or pet hierarchy in your home. And it isn't always the biggest or oldest who has the most power.

Bet You Didn't Know

HEY!

There's a species of wild cat that is smaller than your average adolescent house cat! The black-footed cat (Felis nigripes) reaches a top weight of less than 5.5 pounds (2.5 kg). Loners most of the time, they have extraordinarily strong voices that they use to roar when seeking a mate. They survive quite well in the Namib, the Kalahari, and the Great Karroo deserts of Namibia, Botswana, and South Africa respectively.

Finding Homes

Most breeders will not release a kitten to a new owner until it is at least three months old. Many wait until four months. Why? It is believed that kittens learn many socialization skills from their mothers and their littermates. Generally, cats who stay with their families longer make better companions.

However, many home-bred kittens are given away as young as six weeks. These kittens usually survive and most of them do quite well in families. But if you have a choice, try to give your kittens a little extra time to be kittens-with-a-family.

MEOW! **It's Been Said**

"My love she is a kitten, And my heart's a ball of string."

—Henry S. Leigh, British poet (1837–1883)

The Least You Need to Know

➤ Cats will choose to give birth in a place that is quiet, out-of-the-way, usually somewhat dark, and often with a sense of covering overhead.

➤ There are behavioral signs that indicate the approach of labor and its progress.

➤ Most cats manage the birthing process without human help.

➤ The development of a kitten is predictable week by week.

➤ A house full of kittens is a house full of laughter.

MEOW MEOW MEOW MEOW MEOW MEOW MEOW MEOW MEOW MEOW *

CAT CARRIER

* TRANSLATION: LET ME OUT, LET ME OUT, LET ME OUT, LET ME OUT.

Chapter 20

Travel Time

In This Chapter

➤ Leaving your cat at home

➤ Boarding your cat

➤ Traveling cats

➤ When you move

Cleveland Amory's best-selling book, *The Cat Who Came For Christmas,* made the name Polar Bear almost as widely recognized as Morris or Garfield. But to his credit as one of the world's leading respect-for-animals advocates, Mr. Amory did not ask Polar Bear to help promote the book by going along on the publicity tour. Although he had been told that the traveling cat would increase the publisher's profits and his own royalties, he knew the experience would be excruciating both for himself and for Polar Bear.

Polar Bear's preference to stay put is the rule, not the exception, in the cat world. The fact is, *most cats do not travel well.* Essentially, cats are very territorial and they either want to stay home or go home. So why a chapter titled "Travel Time"?

Because at the turn of the 20th century, travel for humans is almost inevitable. This can cause problems for both the cat who stays at home and for the cat who must go along. Let's look at some ways to make the going easier.

Long Weekends

Although it's always safest to have someone look in on a cat each day to prevent or discover any accidents or problems that might have occurred, most cats do quite well home alone for the weekend. Owners can simply leave a good supply of dry food in the usual feeding place. Water is best left in more than one bowl, just in case there should be a spill. And, of course, be sure the cat litter is clean or you might return to several signs of protest.

If you're going to be away more than one or two nights, it's even more important (most authorities would say *essential*) to ask a friend or relative to stop by from time to time to check the food and water and to just be sure everything is okay. Some owners also put a radio on the timer with their lights, turning it on at a certain hour and then off again later. Why bother? It's kind of a company thing and is probably not necessary if you have more than one cat.

Some cats, especially those in single-cat households, become anxious if left alone too long. They may claw furniture or chew on fabrics. Other cats will overgroom themselves until they actually lick a spot bare. If you see this kind of behavior once, it will probably happen again. To ease your cat's anxiety, you should make arrangements to have someone your cat knows stop in more often or perhaps house sit for you. Or you can arrange to board your cat outside your home.

Most cats wait patiently for their owners to return.

Photo by Christopher Cronin

Pet Sitting Professionals

Hiring professional pet sitters has become an increasingly popular alternative to boarding pets at kennels, especially for multi-pet households where boarding fees can add up to more than the room rate at a resort hotel. Although some pet sitters actually stay in your home and become de facto house sitters, most practice their trade by stopping by once or twice a day to check on your cat or cats, feed them, and play with them. Most cats, even shy cats, adapt quickly to these new caretakers, partly because they are genuine "animal people" (why else would they have such a job!) and partly because the cats are not being stressed by a forced new residence and life pattern.

It's Been Said
"Nature teaches beasts to know their friends."

—William Shakespeare, *Coriolanus*, act 2, scene 1

But some pet owners worry not only about entrusting strangers with the care of their cats but also about giving these strangers the keys to their homes. In other words, if you've never used a pet sitter before, how can you determine whether he or she is a good one?

Here are some questions you can ask:

➤ How long have you been in the pet-sitting business?

➤ Do you have references? May we call them?

➤ Have you had any previous experience with…? (Name any particular problems your cats may have.)

➤ Are you bonded or insured? What company?

➤ Do you know (name your vet)? Do you know where the office is?

➤ Do you have someone who will take over for you in case of personal illness?

➤ What do you do in inclement weather?

➤ Do you have an answering service or answering machine where we can leave messages?

Rates for pet sitting are negotiable. The most widely used rate across the country is about $10 per visit with the typical visit lasting from 20 minutes to an hour. Rates can vary, however. They might be lower per visit if you choose to have more frequent but shorter visits. They might be higher if you need additional services, such as giving medication or cleaning the litter box. Be sure that you and your pet sitter agree on exactly what is to be done during each visit. Some owners leave a written list; others make arrangements to call home at regular intervals at a time the pet sitter is scheduled to be there.

In addition to regular duties, be sure that your pet sitter knows what to do in an emergency. Needless to say, you'll leave the phone number for your vet. You should also leave the name and phone number of a friend or relative who can make a medical decision if you cannot be reached, and you should arrange with the vet for medical credit if needed. (This can be done with a credit card number or a refundable advance deposit.)

Some Helpful Information

National professional organizations for pet sitters help to maintain standards of service and provide local referrals. You can get the names of members near you by calling:

➤ National Association of Professional Pet Sitters (NAPPS)
1200 G St. NW Suite 760
Washington, DC 20005
(800) 296-7387 or (202) 393-3317

➤ Pet Sitters International
418 East King St.
King, NC 27021
(800) 268-7487 or (910) 983-9222

Cat Carriers

You'll need a cat carrier even if you never plan to travel with your cat. A cat carrier provides a safe place for your pet to wait in the vet's waiting room—a place where she won't be terrified by or terrify the bullmastiff sitting next to you. A carrier will also ensure that your frightened or dissatisfied cat will not jump under the gas pedal while you're driving or leap out the window of the car while it is parked.

How to describe a carrier? There are all kinds! Some are soft-sided and resemble an oversized handbag. Others are actually portable kennels for small dogs and can only be described as cages. Still others are hard plastic with ventilation holes and a door. Some are heavy-duty cardboard.

Most pet supply stores carry a variety of carriers. You can see still others pictured in pet supply catalogs and in the advertising sections of magazines such as *Cat Fancy*. If you attend cat shows, you'll be able to examine the carriers sold by vendors as well as ask exhibitors what type they use and why they prefer it. No matter what style you choose, however, your pet's carrier should have the following characteristics:

➤ An interior dimension large enough for your cat to stand, sit, lie down, and turn around.

➤ Adequate ventilation on at least three sides.

➤ A door or other means of entry and exit that your cat cannot open.

Tales

Cats didn't always travel first class. In ages past, they were quite ignominiously *bagged,* and hardly ever for good reason. This is the story of how the saying *let the cat out of the bag* came to mean someone revealed a secret.

For centuries, farm folk in England took young pigs to market in a tough sack called a "poke." Direct ancestors of our current-day scam artists would often put a "worthless" cat in this bag instead of the "valuable" piglet. Their goal was to get a buyer to pay for the animal without opening the bag.

Of course, the smart buyer would open the bag and the cat would jump out, letting out the trickery too. But the foolish buyer paid for and took home the bag unopened. Buyers who accept goods without testing their value are still said to buy "a pig in a poke."

Boarding Out

Although the American Humane Society has advised that most pets are happiest and least stressed when cared for in their own homes during their owners' absences, there are times and situations when boarding is essential. Many cats are frightened by the new environment of a boarding facility. The vast majority, however, get over their discomfort within a few days and do quite well as long as the boarding facility is well designed and well run.

But what exactly does "well designed and well run" mean? Check these points for your cat's comfort and safety:

Cats in Our Language
Scaredy-cat!
Fraidy-cat!
These taunting words are still commonly heard on grade-school playgrounds. But perhaps the cautious cat and the cautious child are both smarter than those who act impulsively.

➤ Required vaccinations for feline distemper, rabies, and feline leukemia.

➤ An inspection for fleas before admission and a requirement for flea treatments for those cats who are infested.

➤ A separate run for each cat that prevents nose-to-nose contact with other boarded cats, unless the owner requests otherwise (two or more cats from one family boarded together, for example).

➤ Adequate lighting, fresh air, and comfortable temperature maintenance (heating or cooling as needed).

➤ Regular cleaning and disinfecting of floors and other areas in use. (You should be allowed an inspection visit.)

➤ Drinking water available at all times.

➤ Willingness to feed a special diet or give medications.

➤ Record keeping that includes your contact telephone numbers and your vet's number.

To check off each item on this list, be sure to inspect the boarding facility in person. You should feel comfortable while doing so. If you have negative feelings, even if they are non-specific, check out some other facilities for comparison.

On the Road

Some Helpful Information

Many tourist lodgings now accept pets, especially if a pet carrier is being used as a sleeping quarters. To find a pet-accepting lodging and make your reservations, you can call ahead using numbers from tourist bulletins and advertisements, or you can consult a directory of pet-friendly lodgings such as:

➤ *Take Your Pet USA,* Artco Publishing ($11.95)

➤ *Vacationing With Your Pet,* Pet Friendly Publications ($19.95)

➤ *On the Road Again with Man's Best Friend* series, Howell Book House ($14.95)

Although you'll never see a cat hanging out the window of a moving car like a dog with its ears and tongue flying in the wind, cats who are introduced to car travel as kittens often learn to enjoy it. To prevent accidents, however, most experts recommend that cats be kept in carriers while in the car, or at least be restrained by a harness.

New to pet supply stores in this decade are pet seat belts. The best of them consists of a harness that fits comfortably on the cat's body and then attaches through an anchor-belt to the human seat belt fasteners. The anchor belt is long enough for the cat to move around, lie down, and perhaps even look out the window, but not long enough to leave the seat during travel time. Some anchor belts can be adjusted to allow greater length during stopovers so your cat can get out of the car for a bit without the danger of getting lost.

It is better to not feed your cat for about three hours before a trip. During long trips, however, water and small bits of food can be offered at regular intervals during the day. The total food offered should be slightly less than what the cat normally eats and should be offered mostly during a meal at the end of the travel day (in the motel or wherever you are spending the night). Opportunity to use a litter box should be provided at three to four hour intervals.

Sayings and Superstitions
If a black cat crosses your path, it is unlucky—unless you spit and turn your cap around backwards.

Most important of all: do not leave your cat in a closed car on a hot day or an open car on a cold day. Extreme temperatures can kill.

Tales

On April 5, 1996 a Connecticut television station broadcast the story of a cat who took an unusual ride.

Soon after a young woman began her drive to work, she was startled by screeching and scraping from under the hood. It took several minutes of driving before she came upon a service station that had garage facilities. She stopped the car, found the mechanic, and almost frantically began to describe the sounds in her engine. The mechanic opened the hood and a cat jumped out!

Both the engine and the cat were just fine. The cat was placed temporarily in a shelter until its owner heard of its plight on the 6 o'clock news.

Cats at Sea

During the many centuries that the word "ship" brought to mind masts and sails, "traveling" for a cat meant going to sea. Virtually every sailing ship had at least one resident cat. And cats left their mark on our nautical language. Here's a sample:

Cat, catted, catting: To bring an anchor up to the cathead (first used in print in 1769 but commonly used by sailors long before).

Cat back: The hook of the cat block.

Cat beam: The broadest beam in the ship.

Cat block: The block used in catting (hoisting) an anchor.

Cat davit: See cathead.

Catfall: The rope or chain used to hoist the anchor.

Cathead: The projecting piece of timber or iron near the bow of the ship used for hoisting and securing the anchor (first used in print in 1626).

Cat rig: A rig made up of a single mast far forward carrying a single large sail extended by a boom.

Cat-rigged: Having a cat rig—many cat-rigged vessels are called catboats.

Cat schooner: A cat-rigged boat.

Flying Cats

Bet You Didn't Know

You should have with you a current health certificate and a certificate of rabies vaccination, both signed by a veterinarian, whenever you travel from one state to another with your cat. On airlines, you'll need to show these before you board, and you may be asked for them again by baggage inspectors when you land. When traveling by car, you can be asked for both certificates by a police officer who might stop you for a traffic violation or by a hotel owner. For international travel, check with the consulates of the countries you'll be visiting. Some countries require a quarantine.

Cats don't take flying lightly, not on airlines anyway. For most of them, it's a once-in-a-lifetime experience and that's just fine. (In fact, *never* would be better!) But for those who must, here are some safety and comfort suggestions—for their owners:

➤ Federal regulations govern which crates are permissible for handling animals by commercial carriers. These rules change from time to time, however, and they may be added to by the individual airline or other carrier. Ask for printed guidelines several weeks before your intended departure date and be sure your crate complies. You can often purchase an approved crate from the airline.

➤ Find out what health certificates are required and when you must present them.

➤ Be sure that your name, address, and phone number are printed on the crate and on a tag that the cat is wearing.

➤ Print "Live Animal" in large letters on both sides of the crate. Use an arrow to indicate which way is up.

➤ Try to get a direct flight. Changing planes is always a risk for errors that could send your pet in the wrong direction. Layovers without adequate ventilation in the cargo hold are also dangerous, especially in hot or cold weather.

➤ Check with the airline to be sure that your pet will be hand-carried to the plane. You do not want your pet carrier put on a conveyor belt.

➤ Do NOT tranquilize your cat without the advice and help of a veterinarian. Cats respond differently to medications than other animals. An inappropriate medication or an inaccurate dose could cause serious problems or even death.

House For Sale

House hunters almost never open a door with a barking dog behind it. But put a sign on the door that reads "Cat Inside—Please Do Not Open" and many of them will open the door anyway, either to see the room or the cat.

When your home is on the market, other things happen too, such as the real estate agent leaves the entry door open and the indoor cat goes out. Or someone closes a closet door that should be left open and locks the cat inside. Or the house hunters bring their children along and they descend upon and scoop up or chase the cat. Sometimes someone even gets scratched.

Some Helpful Information
While your house is on the market, change the cat litter *very* frequently. Many house hunters, especially those without pets, think they can smell an animal in the house. If they get even the faintest whiff of over-used cat litter, the sale is usually dead.

If you intend to sell your home, try to plan for your cat's safety before you list with a real estate agent. If you will be away from home for short periods only while it is being shown or on errands, you can confine your cat in the cat carrier you will use for the move. If you must leave the cat in the house for the entire workday, however, such close confinement is not advisable. On the other hand, if the cat is left free, there is always the chance the house will be shown without prior appointment.

Some home sellers confine their cat in an area they can lock, such as a garage or storage room. Realtors can be notified that the room or area will not be shown until an interested party comes back for a second showing and the cat is safely elsewhere. Another method, if you're a handy-type person, is to build a pen for the cat in the basement or another out-of-the-way place. Some sellers also leave their cat with friends or family for the daytime hours.

Moving and the Cat!

If you think moving day is stressful for you, try to imagine it from the perspective of about nine inches off the floor. Many a cat has been lost at one end of a move or the other. Why? Sometimes because the owner was so busy he or she forgot about the cat, sometimes because the cat was so nervous he or she ran off to find a safe place, and sometimes due to a combination of these and other reasons. But all are needlessly lost.

Moving companies are most appreciative when owners make provisions to keep cats safely out of the way. A small animal underfoot can be extremely dangerous to people carrying heavy and cumbersome items. For cats, there is also the danger of entrapment. Some have even been known to be packaged in wardrobes!

Take a few minutes to think through in advance what you will do with your cat on moving-out and moving-in days. It is usually *not* a good idea to confine the cat in your car because someone inevitably opens a door. Inside the cat carrier within the car is also risky if the weather is warm enough to make heat stroke a possibility. Also be wary of using a room or closet for the cat unless you can *lock* the door.

Probably the best place for your cat on moving days is with a friend, neighbor, or relative. If you don't have a place where you'll feel comfortable leaving your cat, however, arrange for boarding at a local kennel for a day. Your cat probably won't like it much, but at least she'll be safe.

At the other end of the move, allow your cat to explore your new home only after the movers have left and the doors are closed. Cats have an instinct to return to their home territory and will quickly slip out an open door or window. Some cat owners confine their pet to a single room for a day or two to help with the transition anxiety. After the cat seems to have accepted the new room, they leave the door open so that she can explore the rest of the house but still return at will to her introductory room.

If you have allowed your cat outdoors at your old home, you should suspend that privilege for a while in your new home. How long? You'll have to make a judgment as to when you think the cat is finally feeling at home. Then make the transition to the outdoors a gradual one, allowing brief periods at first with the cat on a leash (or at least closely watched).

It's also important that you establish contact with a veterinarian at your new location *before* you allow the cat out overnight. You may need that vet sooner than you think because your cat will be the new kid on the block and will have to fight for territory and a place in the local hierarchy. No wonder many owners prefer to transform the outdoor/indoor cat into an indoor cat after a move!

The Least You Need to Know

➤ With proper preparations, cats can survive at home alone for several days.

➤ Professional pet sitters can sometimes eliminate the need for boarding.

➤ Traveling with a cat requires documentation of his health and vaccinations, identification tags, and a carrier or crate.

➤ Cats need special consideration when a house is for sale and during a move.

The End of Life

Whether the subject is an 87-year-old man or a 19-year-old cat, writing, talking, even thinking about the end of life is difficult. Yet that time comes to every living being.

If you read that last paragraph and got the feeling that maybe you should skip to the next chapter, it might help to call to mind these familiar words:

> To every thing there is a season, and a time to every purpose under the heaven:
> A time to be born, and a time to die; a time to plant, and a time to uproot;…
> A time to weep, and a time to laugh; a time to mourn, and a time to dance;…
> There is nothing better than to be glad and to do well during life.

> —Eccles. 3:1, 2, 4, 12

Death is not only the end of life, it is a part of life. If we listen to the words from Ecclesiastes, we should give death its time and then strive to be happy and go on doing well during our lives. This short chapter cannot ease the pain of losing a loved companion. But perhaps it can contribute some small amount of understanding that will help in moving onward. And perhaps it will help you to cherish all the precious days you have with your cat.

HEY!

Bet You Didn't Know A female British tabby is on record as having lived to the age of 34.

How Old Is Old?

Like humans, some cats feel old and, in fact, get old sooner than others. Of course, their fur-covered faces don't show the wrinkles, but many aging cats don't hear as well or see as well as they once did. Perhaps they jump less and get up more slowly. Their appetites may fall off as their ability to taste and smell diminishes. And, like humans, many cats become less adaptable and less resilient to changes in diet, routine, and environment.

There's something about pillows…. The longer you've been around, the better they look.

Most cats in the care of a responsible person will live to their mid-teens, and many can make it quite comfortably to age 20. For many owners, these teen years are among the very best. As they age, most cats lose some of their wariness, independence, and aggressiveness. They become both more interested in and affectionate toward humans. And they appreciate security and comfort!

Illness that Won't Get Better

Elderly cats are subject to many of the same health risks as elderly humans, but cats rarely complain. In fact, one of the problems of living with an aging cat is detecting when he or she needs help or medical attention. Let's look at some of the most common conditions:

It's Been Said

"There is no cure for birth and death save to enjoy the interval."

—George Santayana, Spanish-born American poet and philosopher (1863–1952)

➤ *Arthritis:* When aging cats develop arthritis, they usually feel it in several joints. The disease can cause pain and lameness that is usually at its worst when the cat first gets up and that lessens as the cat moves around. Do NOT give aspirin because it is toxic to cats. Weight loss sometimes helps, so does warm bedding. Some owners have found that acupuncture helps.

➤ *Kidney disease:* Many cats have decreased kidney function in their old age. They will drink more and will need to urinate more often. They must therefore have a litter box readily available since they may not be able to retain a large volume of urine for long periods of time. If you suspect that your cat has kidney disease, have your vet check for high blood pressure, which can either cause kidney problems or be the result of them.

➤ *Hyperthyroidism:* When the thyroid gland overproduces, cats will lose weight, have unpredictable appetites, vomit and/or have diarrhea, drink a lot, and urinate a lot. The disease causes high blood pressure and can result in heart and kidney disease. It can be treated with antithyroid drugs, surgical removal of the thyroid gland, or treatment with radioactive iodine-131. Some cats recover thyroid function after treatment, others must remain on medication.

➤ *Diabetes mellitus:* As in humans, diabetes occurs in cats when the pancreas is unable to produce enough insulin to utilize and transport glucose (which is necessary for proper nutrition of body cells). It is far more common in overweight cats. Signs are increased thirst and weight loss despite increased appetite. Insulin to control the disease can be given by injection or orally.

➤ *Heart disease:* Cardiovascular problems can develop at any age, but are far more common in elderly cats. The first sign is usually decreased activity. If your cat seems suddenly tired more often, you should see the vet.

➤ *Tumors:* Both benign and malignant tumors occur in cats, and their likelihood increases with age. Breast cancer is prevalent in both males and females, but seven times more common in unspayed females than in spayed females. Treatment and prognosis depend upon the type and location of the cancer.

Last Days

Despite the old adage, cats have only one life. Every owner hopes that this life will not only be full and fun, but also that it will end quietly and peacefully. Yet some cats suffer from their illnesses and linger on when nothing more can be done to make them comfortable. Fortunately, euthanasia is an option.

Sayings and Superstitions

A woman hath nyne lyues like a cat. Those words appeared in print in 1549! Almost 500 years later, we're still talking about the nine lives of a cat, but women seem to have lost that advantage.

Some owners hesitate to take this step because they cannot bear to part with their much loved companion. But when there is great pain and discomfort and no hope of recovery, it may be the last and kindest gift you can give to your pet.

The decision to end your cat's life is always a difficult one, and you should discuss it with a trusted veterinarian. Do not hold back, however, because you fear that the process will be painful to the cat. Modern technique uses an injection of a high overdose of an anesthetic drug. Many vets allow the owner to remain with his or her cat during the process. The cat falls asleep and death follows quickly and painlessly.

Unexpected Losses

Sometimes young cats are killed in accidents, especially highway accidents. These deaths are unexpected and sudden, and their effect on the cat's family can be devastating.

Sayings and Superstitions

Death does not recognize strength.

—African proverb

Well-meaning friends often suggest that you get a new cat or kitten. Some even bring a newcomer to your home. Most experts suggest, however, that you do not try to replace a cat who has died unexpectedly with another cat. Although the new kitten or cat can be a distraction, it is not "just like" your cat.

Masking grief by remaining busy rarely resolves the pain. It is far better to acknowledge your loss, work through your grief, and then, when the time is right for you, welcome a newcomer for the individual he or she is, not as a replacement cat.

Going through the experience of searching for and accepting the loss of a cat who wanders off one day and is never seen again is in some ways even more difficult than coping with sudden accidental death. Day after day drags on, colored by a mixture of hope and fear. You worry about what could be happening or what could *have* happened. And there is no answer, no closure.

At some point, you must come to terms with the probable fact that your cat is gone from your life, and you must go on. But going on does not mean not grieving. The grieving process can be the balm that heals the pain of loss.

Grief

Grieving for a lost love is genuine and meaningful whether the love be a person, an animal, a home, or a precious possession. The validity and appropriateness of grief is not related to the value of the lost love on some socio-economic scale. For the person grieving, the intensity and duration of grief can only be determined by the importance of the love. Grieving at the death of your cat can be as emotionally intense, and as necessary, as grieving at the death of a beloved friend or relative.

It's Been Said

"Death be not proud, though some have called thee Mighty and dreadful, for thou art not so...."

—John Donne, British poet (1571?–1631)

MEOW!

It is important to let yourself cry. It is important to talk about your pet—what you loved, what was funny, what were the routines, what were his preferences. Some people gather photos together, others write poems. Still others find comfort in just sitting in a place that was often shared with the cat.

Some veterinary hospitals send sympathy cards when a pet dies, as do many friends. In some areas, there are even ongoing pet-loss support groups. Veterinary school hospitals have been among the leaders in establishing and offering this kind of help. To find a group nearby, you can ask at your veterinarian's office and your local animal shelters, or you can contact the public relations office of a veterinary college near you.

Some Helpful Information

The *Directory of Pet Loss Resources* is now available for anyone seeking a nationwide listing of pet-grief help lines, counselors, and support groups. You can order it from:

Delta Society
Ordering Department
P.O. Box 1080
Renton, WA 98057

Include $3 for postage and handling.

About the worst thing you can do when your cat dies is to feel pain on the inside and deny it to the world. Grief can affect the heart, quite literally. In a recent study, Harvard researchers added the death of a loved one to the list of "triggers" for a heart attack. They found that the risk of heart attack was 14 times higher than normal the day after the death, 5 times higher two days after, and significantly elevated for about one month.

Dr. Murray Mittleman, who presented this study on March 14, 1996, said, "we don't know how to avoid this increase in risk." Until more is known about the biological connection between psychological stress and physical illness, however, the best advice psychologists have is to recognize your grief, acknowledge it, and feel it. Time is necessary for recovery, but time does heal.

What to Tell the Children

For many children, the end of a pet's life is their first contact with death. It is important, therefore, that you do not establish behaviors and attitudes that may mask the immediate pain of the pet's loss but cause increased stress in the future.

MEOW!

It's Been Said

"It is as natural to die as to be born."

—Sir Francis Bacon,
British essayist (1561–1626)

Although it may be difficult for you, try to use the words "death" or "died" rather than euphemisms like "passed away" or "put to sleep." Children tend to take words more literally than adults, and they may wonder where the cat passed away to. Using the phrase "put to sleep" can even cause some children to fear going to sleep at night.

Remember that your child's emotions are real and intense. Don't minimize the grief with statements like, "Come on now, she was only a cat. We'll get you another one." When a cat is *your* cat, "only" can never mean unimportant. A significant being in the child's life has died. Give your child the space and time to grieve.

If you can do it, probably the most healing assistance you can give your child is sharing your grief. A child who sees an adult grieving will learn that the expression of emotion can be acceptable and healthy. Parent and child can hold onto each other and form a deeper bond through their grief.

Some Helpful Information

A question children commonly ask is: "Will the cat go to heaven?" Some adults have trouble answering.

If you do have trouble, you might think through this bit of logic: If you believe that heaven is the place in time where all your needs and wants are satisfied, and if you want to be with your cat, then, when you get to heaven, your cat will be there.

In Memoriam

Yes, some cats have funerals. A funeral is a ritual, and the function of many rituals in human society is to provide a means of acknowledging change and the emotional intensity that accompanies it. The ritual of a funeral helps mourners to part company with one they love. The funeral of a cat gives everyone a time and a place to say good-bye and remember.

If you wish to gather your family together to have a funeral for your cat, do so. Don't let anyone tell you it is "silly" or "making too much of this." Love is the most precious emotion of life. It is never wrong to stand tall and acknowledge it.

Tales

The phone rang one morning at 6 o'clock. Startled, Gerrie answered and heard the voice of her neighbor across the street.

"There's been a cat killed down the road. It looks like Napoleon," said the distraught voice.

continues

continued

Paul overheard and was out of bed and heading down the stairs almost before the phone was back on the receiver. Napoleon was curled up on the rocking chair.

So whose cat was killed? Paul dressed and went outside to find out. What he saw was nauseating: the cat had been run over, its skull crushed.

Paul scooped the body into a small box and took it out into the woods to bury it.

Several days later, a distraught teenager from the next neighborhood called about the cat. She wanted to unearth it. "Just to make sure it's really her," the girl said.

Paul wanted to protect the mourning owner from the horrible sight he had seen. So he lied, saying he had buried the cat but he didn't think he could find the place again.

Later, he heard that the girl had been deeply depressed for weeks, and he regretted the decision he had made to try to protect her. He thought that perhaps he should have taken her to the spot and then advised against the unearthing.

Paul was concerned that because of his attempt at kindness, the young cat owner had been deprived of closure—the process and ritual of saying "good-bye." That's true, she was, but she was also spared a horrible sight that she may never have been able to forget.

Some owners choose to bury their cats in their own yards, perhaps with a small marker. If you are considering this, you should be aware that in some areas, burial on residential land is illegal. Check with municipal authorities if you don't know the law in your town.

If you choose to bury your cat in a pet cemetery, you will find many things similar to a human burial, and you will pay many of the same charges, although the actual dollar amounts are far less. Charges include the plot, the casket, and perhaps the digging of the grave. Some cemeteries allow monuments, others do not. For more information on pet burial and the location of pet cemeteries near you, contact the International Association of Pet Cemeteries at 5055 Route 11, Box 163, Ellenburg Depot, NY 12935. Their phone line at (518) 594-3000 is answered seven days a week.

Some pet cemeteries allow markers, others do not.

Photo courtesy of the International Association of Pet Cemeteries

Many cat owners choose cremation rather than burial for their pets. Veterinary hospitals can either do this or arrange to have it done at an animal crematorium. If you wish to have your cat's ashes returned, however, you will have to request a private cremation of your cat's remains. (Some animal crematoriums do mass cremations and then divide the ashes.)

Some owners choose to keep their cat's ashes in an urn. Appropriate containers are available through veterinarians and through private companies that advertise at cat shows or in cat or other animal oriented magazines.

If you prefer not to use an urn, you can bury your cat's ashes in a place of your choosing with or without a marker. Or you can scatter the ashes in a meaningful place—perhaps a corner of the woods near your house where she loved to hunt or along the rock wall where he loved to chase chipmunks.

The Least You Need to Know

➤ Some diseases are incurable and will lead to the cat's death.

➤ The best way to get through the loss of a loved cat is to acknowledge and express your grief.

➤ Children often learn to cope with the concept of death through their experience with the death of a loved pet.

➤ Rituals can help say good-bye.

Part 5
Working with Cats

If we have to work all the livelong day, many of us would prefer to put in those hours with cats.

It's possible to carve out a full-time career or a rewarding part-time job working with cats or other animals. There are numerous cat-related hobbies too, some of which can bring in a small income. For those with higher motives than money, there is volunteer work. As you read the next several chapters you are likely to find some work area or feline-related interest that will draw you like catnip lures your furball, with a more or less equally delightful effect.

Chapter 22

Showing Your Cat Professionally

In This Chapter

➤ The world of the cat fancy

➤ Attending a cat show

➤ "Household" cats can be shown too

➤ Does showing make a profit?

Your cat just has to be the cutest, smartest animal that ever lapped up a tuna delight. His coat gleams. He handles easily. He obeys instructions and has even learned a few tricks. And what a personality!

"Why keep this marvel to myself?" you may be thinking. Well, have you considered looking into the world of the show cat and letting everyone meet your feline wonder and admire him the way you do? Read on. This chapter could help you make that leap—or, after a brief peek into "show" business you might say, "I think I'll pass on this one."

Fancy That

What we are talking about in this chapter is the world of the cat fancy, a term used to cover the areas of cat shows, breeders, and cat clubs. Actually, even if you are merely *interested* in felines, you can consider yourself part of the cat fancy.

"Fancy," as it is used here, is a word of indeterminate meaning. It could be defined as those who fancy cats, since the word dates to the first formal cat show and banding together of feline enthusiasts in England (more about that later). Some in Britain occasionally substitute the word "fancy" for "like," as in "I fancy cats."

Or cat fancy could mean those who like fancy cats, and there are plenty of them in this special interest area.

Just a Bit of Background

The official world of the cat fancy is not that old. In terms of humankind's interest in and devotion to cats, it's probably only a nanosecond back in history.

The first formal cat show was held at London's Crystal Palace in 1871. Organized by the then newly formed English National Cat Club, it was composed of a group of small clubs of cat fanciers who wanted to show, or perhaps more correctly show *off,* their pets. Photographs taken at the exposition show very grandly dressed Victorian ladies, and a few men, accompanying their cats into the judging ring.

It was Harrison Weir who organized that first cat show in London and, as the first president of the English National Cat Club, set the standards of excellence for show cats in 1889. The objective was to find the ideal for a particular breed. Qualities included colors of the cat, whether the tail should be fluffy and how fluffy, and so on. Weir intended those standards to apply around the world, but it didn't work out that way. Today, criteria for winning can vary from one show group to another.

> **CAT TALES**
>
> ## Tales
>
> Writing about the first cat show, Harrison Weir told of taking the train that morning to the Crystal Palace. A good friend came into the car where Weir, the cat enthusiast, was seated. After Weir said where he was headed, his friend launched into a diatribe about the awfulness of cats. Weir, of course, defended them. The friend said, "I see you like cats, and I do not, so let the matter drop." "No," said Weir. "That is why I instituted the Cat Show; I wish every one to see how beautiful a well-cared-for cat is, and how docile, gentle and—may I use the term?—cossetty. Why should not the cat that sits purring in front of us before the fire be an object of interest and be selected for its colour, markings and form? Now come with me, my dear friend, and see the first Cat Show."
>
> The friend did go along and told Weir he was impressed with the variety of cats shown. A few months later, Weir called on the man. "He was at luncheon," Weir wrote, "with two cats on a chair beside him—pets I should say, from their appearance."

America's first cat show was held in 1881 at Bunnell's Museum on Broadway in New York City. What a difference from today's more organized show settings! Cats were brought to Bunnell's in cages, cardboard boxes, and even *bags*. Behavior, at least until the judging took place, could not have counted for much, since there was much hissing, scratching, and wailing coming from the felines, who were understandably outraged at the way they were handled and at the goings-on in general.

The first *major* U.S. cat show was held in New York City at Madison Square Garden in 1895. A male Maine Coon won the honors out of 170 cats exhibited.

Attending a Cat Show

The best way to learn about cat shows is to go to one. It's easy, inexpensive (a few dollars for the entrance fee), and anyone can be admitted. You don't even have to have a cat.

There are several hundred shows held around the country annually. You can check your local newspapers for advertisements announcing a particular one coming near to where you live. You can find show calendars in cat magazines, or you can call one of the registries listed on page 237 for their schedule. Most shows are two- or three-day events over a weekend. Any local club belonging to a national registry can be the sponsor, although who is shouldn't matter to you at this stage because you are going only for a broad overview of what showing a cat entails.

When you walk into the convention center, or similar facility, you will see aisle after aisle of cages in which most cats doze, oblivious (for the time being) of their imminent moment in the sun. Their owners sit next to them, perhaps on folding chairs they've brought along, looking around at the proceedings and perhaps working at a crossword puzzle. Some are grooming their pets. The cages are likely to be decorated, and often there is an award for the best-looking one. Some of those who have already won a prize in the weekend's event will have that ribbon attached to the cage.

Some Helpful Information
If you have cat allergies, you might want to pop an allergy pill before leaving home. Otherwise you could spend your time at the show with eyes watering, digging around for tissues.

1996 Cat Fanciers' Association best cat: brown tabby, American short-hair, male.

Courtesy of Cat Fanciers' Association

Checking out the cats is quite an experience for those new to the world of showing. A sign saying, "You can admire me, but please don't touch me," or something in a similar vein, is often affixed to a cat cage. Cats are very susceptible to disease and having hundreds of strangers petting them after petting other cats is definitely not in their best interest. So it's look, but don't touch.

You might be surprised to see that many of the cats look no different from yours, and certainly no better either. But there are breed standards that must be strictly adhered to for these entries to become winners. This is truly a beauty contest with points awarded for cats that approach the ideal.

MEOW!

It's Been Said

"Vanity...has without doubt been of far more benefit to civilization than modesty has ever been."

—William E. Woodward, writer (1874–1950)

There are cats here as well that are very different from any you have seen outside of magazines or films. This is your opportunity to view a Scottish Fold up close, a Bengal, or any breed that is new to you.

You can talk to the owners, at least in theory. Some of them prefer not to chat with those attending a show. But if others look friendly, go ahead and start a conversation. A few breeders will have a cage of kittens for sale, which, of course, necessitates *some* talking.

There are one, two, or more "rings" in the auditorium consisting of a few chairs (for observers) facing a table and a speaker's mike. These are judging arenas. Periodically throughout the day a loudspeaker will announce a particular judging and where it will be held.

By the way, judges at cat shows are often breeders of pedigreed cats. They are paid their expenses for attending the show, plus a small fee that could be perhaps one dollar per cat per entry.

There are usually several categories of awards. Try to attend at least one judging. It will give you an idea of the qualities and behavior of a champion cat as you watch the judges examine the fur coat, do some measuring, and in general see if that cat adheres to breed standards and is blue-ribbon material.

There might also be a few talks for visitors on one phase of cat care or another. Virtually everything else at an exposition comes under the heading of "commerce"—stuff galore for sale. If it has been manufactured, then at the larger shows you are likely to see it with a price tag. There will be T-shirts, calendars, notepads, books, cat food (free samples from manufacturers), jewelry, and on and on. Nearly everything carries a cat motif.

Bet You Didn't Know Cats sometimes seem to respond better to women than to men. Some say that is because of women's higher voices, which some felines tend to prefer.

You will probably return home with a ton of goodies, some free, others purchases you just could not resist. You will also have had a look at showing that might make you think seriously of entering your puddy for a prize.

Which Cats Are Eligible For Awards

So what makes a pet show material?

Surprise! It's not only for purebreds. Your little old house cat could pick up a blue ribbon, but more about that later.

While many shows have a category for house cats, this is an arena pretty much for the pedigreed feline. That's the one you purchase from a breeder that comes with "papers" tracing its lineage and documenting its purebred stock, physical condition, and so on. (See Chapter 1 about buying a pedigreed cat.)

There are usually three categories for entrants: (1) intact cats; (2) those that are neutered or spayed; and (3) kittens.

To decide if a cat is the best of her breed, she will be checked for a number of checklisted points, such as weight, a visible fault in the tail, any obvious trace of illness, or refusal to be handled easily. There can't be any signs of pregnancy, thinness, or obesity. She can't have constant cross-eyes or a squint. She can't have a shortened tail, unless she is a Japanese Bobtail. There are many other determinants for a blue ribbon. In some shows, declawed cats are not allowed.

Tales

A kinked tail is considered a flaw in a Siamese cat. But legend tells us this flaw had a purpose, which was to serve royalty. Before princesses in Thailand (formerly Siam) bathed, they took off their jewels and put them on the tail of their cat. The cat curved the tip of its tail to keep those gems from falling off.

In the "household cat" showing, which is for mixed breeds, there are standards for judging too. Interestingly, at most if not all shows these days, the cat in this category *must* be neutered or spayed and *cannot* be declawed.

Some cat shows also have lighter categories for winners, such as the cat with the longest whiskers or some similar title that is not a heavyweight one in the cat fancy.

Who Sponsors the Shows

In the early days of cat shows there were no associations for registering felines. The U.S. Department of Agriculture kept studbooks, recording births during a particular year by owner and breed.

Registries

The following are established associations that support and sanction cat shows for pedigreed and household pets. They can send you printed material, including the names of cat clubs near you. When writing you might include a stamped (32 cents), self-addressed #10 envelope for a quick response.

American Cat Association (ACA), 8101 Katherine Ave., Panorama City, CA 91402; (818) 781-5656

American Cat Fanciers' Association (ACFA), P.O. Box 203, Point Lookout, MO 65726; (417) 334-5430

Canadian Cat Association (CCA), 83 Kennedy Rd., Unit 1806, Brampton, Ontario, L6W 3P3 Canada; (905) 459-1481

Cat Fanciers' Association (CFA), 1805 Atlantic Ave., P.O. Box 1105, Manasquan, NJ 08736; (908) 528-9797

Cat Fanciers' Federation (CFF), 9509 Montgomery Rd., Cincinnati, OH 45242; (513) 787-9009

The International Cat Association (TICA), P.O. Box 2684, Harlingen, TX 78551; (210) 428-8046

Today it is possible to belong to a cat club in your area that is a member of one or more national registries (registries do not accept individual members). The largest of these nonprofit organizations is the Cat Fanciers' Association, which was founded in 1906 and is now international in scope. CFA held more than 400 cat shows in 1995 and exhibits an average of 35 different breeds. The second largest is The International Cat Association (TICA). The oldest registry, dating to 1897, is the American Cat Association (ACA).

Each registry has standards for judging cats that are slightly different from the others, as well as its own "feel." You will have to poke around a bit to find the one that best matches your thoughts and feelings on showing cats.

Bet You Didn't Know
"Moggy," sometimes abbreviated to "mog," is the term for a non-pedigreed cat in the United Kingdom. Where the word came from seems uncertain.

Fun? Profit? Let's See

If you want to make money in the cat arena, you might read Chapters 23 and 24 and pick an easier route than cat shows. It is *very* unlikely you will realize anything at all in the way of profit here. Owners who show their cats do it for the fun, the pride they take in their pets, their sense of competition, and the exhilaration they feel—as who does not— when winning. And they love cats, of course. Awards are a ribbon or some other tangible proof of championship.

Why no money in this arena? Let's take a look at the expenses you are likely to incur in the show world.

You will have to pay an entry fee of, let's say, $50 to have your cat judged in a particular show. If that exhibition is some distance from your home—and unless you live in a major metropolitan area, most are going to be from perhaps a few counties away to perhaps the state capital or even a few states away—you will have to pay transportation expenses, whether gasoline mileage or plane fare. If it will have to be an overnight trip, there is a motel or hotel tab, plus meals.

It's Been Said

"A feast is made for laughter, and wine maketh merry: but money answereth all things."

—Ecclesiastes

None of the above takes into account the ongoing expense of maintaining a prizewinner, which is more than the average cat owner spends. You will have a top-of-the-line cage, grooming accessories, and perhaps more frequent visits to the vet and groomer than you would have with a humbler breed of cat.

Then there is time. Having a full-time job outside the home or staying home with small children does not leave much time for making the tour circuit and keeping up with what's going on in the show world. Many who show are breeders, and many are retirees too.

Cat Tales

There is a legend that dates the origin of the Maine Coon cat to the French queen, Marie Antoinette. Afraid for her life in the nearing revolution, she is said to have sent her beloved cats ahead before her planned escape to the United States. She never did leave, of course, but died at the guillotine. However, the cats did well here, and today's Maine Coons are supposedly their descendants.

If you do come across a cat show that offers a small monetary prize, you have probably spent far more than that buying your cat and caring for him. If you want to sell your cat, can you earn big bucks? If he has won many awards you *might* be able to command $7,000 to $10,000, but most sale prices are in the $2,000 to $3,000 range. After all, selling a blue-ribbon male or female for breeding does not guarantee any of their litter will one day be prizewinners. (Breeding is considered in Chapter 23.) If you are a breeder, you might also be able to become a show judge and pick up some money in that capacity.

Tales

A 1993 *Time* magazine article on the lifestyles of America's pampered pets reported the good fortune of Cherry Pop, a 12-year-old prizewinning Persian living in Florida. We won't get into the cat's miniature Rolls-Royces and other over-the-top luxuries. We will mention, however, that a mightily impressed Japanese investor offered the Pop's owners $50,000 for her. They declined, saying she was not for sale at any price.

If the cost of exhibiting does not put you off and you have the time to devote to that pastime, showing your cat will open a fascinating new world to you with ongoing education about cats, keen competition, and an even closer relationship with your pet, if that is possible.

The Least You Need to Know

➤ You can become involved in the cat fancy without showing a pet.

➤ Attending cat shows is the best way to see if you—and by extension your fuzzball—will be comfortable in that milieu.

➤ There are many sponsors of cat shows; criteria for showing varies slightly from one organization to another.

➤ Showing can be costly—travel expenses, grooming and grooming aids for your pet, and so on.

Chapter 23

Careers with Cats

In This Chapter

➤ What's involved in working with animals

➤ The world of the breeder

➤ Medically speaking

➤ Setting up shop in service occupations

Sometimes a love of cats leads to more than just having a few of them in your home life. Sometimes a career can be carved out of that devotion and interest. If you'd like to have your home and work lives overlap, with cats in both, you have many choices for a career these days. You can work full- or part-time. You can opt for a salaried job or, if you are a highly motivated self-starter, open your own business. You can have several years of post-college work to your credit, or you can start work where there are no educational requirements. There's something for everybody here, thanks to people's interest in their furry companions.

It's Not All Petting and Playing

You know that, of course. Work is work, and with many of these occupations you will toil long hours. But there are other considerations with a cat career that ought to give you pause.

Your work will be with creatures that have personalities and can certainly express themselves. But right alongside them are their owners. *They* are your customers/patients too. *They* do the talking—and pay the bills. You very definitely need communication skills for the occupations discussed in the next few pages. If you are not a "people person," you would do well to recognize that fact and seek a career where perhaps co-workers are your primary work contact and not the general public.

The more deeply involved you become in this area, the more you will learn about, and be forced to deal with, its unpleasant side, such as euthanasia, animal abuse and neglect, and vivisection (animal experimentation). You will have to come to terms with the fact that those problems are the often heartbreaking flip side of the cute-cat-living-in-a-good-home view of companion pets that is probably most familiar to you. All of the concerns you will find might indeed outweigh the warm, fuzzy side of animal life.

On the other hand, you could find yourself becoming quite an activist. You may extend your concern beyond household cats to the broader stage of animal rights on the national, perhaps even international, level.

It's Been Said

"Blessed is he who has found his work; let him ask no other blessedness."

—Thomas Carlyle (1795–1881)

As for the pay in all of these work arenas—well, you're not going to see huge incomes no matter what your elected specialty. Still, none of that matters to those who select these fields. They bring the caring that, for most of us, stops with our own pets at home into the workplace where their skills and patience reach so many more animals and make those creatures' lives better.

Do you and your aspirations fit that profile? Then go for it!

The Cat Breeder

Breeding as we know it in the cat fancy is far more complex than mating cats and selling the litter. You are dealing with the delicate area of looks and traits of purebred felines and are trying to maintain the breed and even, if possible, improve it.

It goes without saying that breeders love cats, but most are hobbyists. They are interested in a particular breed of cat and work hard to produce a few kittens a year that fit that standard. Then why do we mention this as a career? Because many think that it *is* a profit-making venture. It usually isn't.

You start by buying a female kitten and waiting a year until she is old enough to breed. A stud cat is also required. If you buy a male kitten, you will wait a year for *him* to mature. Both cats, and all successive ones, must have the very best of care. All the cats will need equipment to keep them happy, such as climbing frames and scratching posts. You will also need a pen to keep the kittens secure when you are not watching them. A breeder's home where he or she keeps kittens and cats in known as a *cattery*.

There is a great deal of paperwork involved in selling kittens. There will be various documentation papers for buyers plus vet certificates (and bills). You will be dealing only with purebreds, incidentally, because there is no money at all in any other kind. You'll join a cat club and might show a cat or two to advertise your business, because you'll just plain enjoy it, and in the hope you have raised a champion who can obtain stud fees from other breeders.

Something else is important here: You are pretty much tied to your business. If you go away at all, you will need someone to replace you, or cat sit, full-time.

How much money *can* you make here? Well, how many cats can you handle in a year? If you sell a kitten with "papers" for, say, $1,500 and make some money "renting" your adult cats for breeding, will that help you pay your running expenses with a little left over for profit?

As suggested in the previous chapter, visit some cat shows. Talk to as many breeders as you can. (Learn where the cat clubs are in your area and contact the registries listed on page 237 to find breeders to speak with.) Nobody knows more about this business—or any other for that matter—than the person engaged in it.

It's Been Said

"No man ever dared to manifest his boredom so insolently as does a Siamese tomcat when he yawns in the face of his amorously importunate wife."

—Aldous Huxley

Unscramble These Words that Help Us Tell One Cat from Another

Can you find the popular cat breeds hidden in these letters?

1. MISEAES   _____
2. XDTEUO   _____
3. SENPARI   _____
4. LORLDGA   _____
5. ARTSOHIHR   _____
6. LTIOSTEHLREOS   _____
7. SNIIBANYSA   _____
8. LOAICC   _____
9. KENONITES   _____
10. LGABNE   _____

1) Siamese   2) Tuxedo   3) Persian   4) Ragdoll   5) Shorthair   6) Tortoiseshell   7) Abyssinian
8) Calico   9) Tonkinese   10) Bengal

Becoming a Cat Sitter

Many pet owners these days leave home not only for vacations, but also for frequent business trips. Kenneling a cat is possible, of course, but it's costly and we all know cats do best in their own environment. And so we have the birth of the pet sitter who also, of course, "sits" with dogs, turtles, birds, and even, sometimes, horses. If you've been in your vet's office lately you may have seen as many as a half dozen fliers on the bulletin board advertising pet sitting by local residents.

Some Helpful Information For many of the careers mentioned in these pages, you will want to talk with local professionals, such as an attorney, accountant, and insurance agent or broker about local zoning, licensing, and tax laws, as well as bonding and liability insurance. Will you have employees? That's more to look into.

Some Helpful Information Do your marketing homework before setting up shop. Does the area where you live have enough residents to support your enterprise? You might have to include a few towns farther afield to have the largest possible number of prospective customers for your service.

Is this for you? If you're willing to do whatever it takes to make those animals happy, from feeding them special foods to dosing them with prescription medicine to playing with them for a while to chase away their loneliness, why not look into it?

Most pet sitters do other chores besides feeding, such as walking the dog, changing the cat litter, watering the plants, taking in the mail, and perhaps turning the lights on and off to deter burglars. Some clients want a visit for their pooch or puddy once a day; others spring for two calls daily. Rates for this usually part-time occupation are about $8 to $15 a visit, which does not, of course, include the pet's food. In large urban areas the fee may be higher for additional services around the house. Sometimes it's higher when there is more than one animal involved.

This is a business where you need no storefront, and you don't even need a home office. Sometimes just a day planner and a file or two will do. Your work is strictly at other people's places.

One point here: It's smart to start a business like this with a backup person who can make your calls if you become sick or some emergency crops up. Naturally, you can't let those animals go hungry. Perhaps you both want to share the business, or you might want that individual just on call. Some sitters have a spouse fill in for them.

Get started by sitting for friends' pets, perhaps for free to build a client base and good word of mouth. You can add your business card or flier to those on vets' bulletin boards, at pet stores, on supermarket bulletin boards, and other local spots where it's likely to be seen by the greatest number of prospective customers.

Pet Grooming

If you have a talent for grooming your own pet, and possibly have friends calling you to take care of *their* pets, you might consider this career move.

There's more to the business than brushing and combing, though. You will have to wash the animal, trim it, and dry it with a dryer. It will probably need its nails clipped, ears cleaned, and perhaps an occasional flea dip.

You should "apprentice" to a groomer for a while or attend a vocational school to learn what's required here. When you decide to open your own place you will want a storefront in a good location, which can be pricey. Take that rent into account as a start-up cost, plus utilities and insurance. You might need to spruce up the shop and buy some furnishings: chairs, lamps, and so on for a small reception area, cages, sink(s), metal grooming tables, a cash register, and so on. Don't forget advertising costs.

If business does well, consider hiring an assistant, allowing you to be open longer hours to accommodate more customers. Some groomers offer related services, such as house-call grooming and boarding animals in the shop while their owners are away. You will need to check for any pet boarding regulations where you live before expanding into that area.

You can determine what the going rates are for grooming and boarding by checking out your competition. They'll probably be from $20 to $35, perhaps higher for a large dog.

Some groomers handle show cats and dogs, but it is hard to make a thriving business on just show animals.

> **Some Helpful Information**
> Depending on where you live and how much income you want to realize from your enterprise, you might have to offer pet grooming, sitting, boarding, *and* taxiing. Or you'll need to furnish at least two of these services.

Taxi! Hauling and Carting Cats

A new service you can offer to time-pressed pet owners is driving those folks' pets to wherever they need to go. That could be the vet, the groomer, to cat shows, the kennel, the airport, and so on. Or you might provide pet food delivery to homebound owners. You will need a reasonably decent looking car (a van or station wagon is preferable, but if you don't have one, you won't want to splurge just yet), a few presentable, but not necessarily expensive carriers, and perhaps a cage. You will also need to advertise heavily. Perhaps you can hook up with a groomer or a pet supply store to offer a service they do not offer. You can leave your business cards on veterinary clinics' bulletin boards and those of groomers, pet food stores, and the like.

Take your pick of a flat fee for a typical "run,"—one-way or round-trip—or an hourly rate that could begin at $10 to $12 (higher in major urban areas).

Some Helpful Information

Doggy day care has arrived. That's a day care center run by one or two dog enthusiasts to keep Fido occupied and amused while his owner(s) are at work. This concept won't work with cats, of course. While they need to be mentally stimulated too, they are more comfortable staying home than being schlepped to another building for the purpose of playing with their peers (if cats can be said to have peers). So cross off opening a *cat* day care center from your list of potential moneymakers.

Today's Veterinarian

Veterinary medicine is a popular choice with those considering a career with animals. That's been increasingly the case as the number of households with pets, multiple pets at that, continues to grow and as scientific advances offer pets the kind of care that had previously been available only to humans—laser surgery, pacemakers, and magnetic resonance imaging, among others.

To earn a veterinary medical degree you must first complete undergraduate preveterinary medical course work. Next comes admission to a college of veterinary medicine, which is highly competitive—the average acceptance rate is 43 percent.

The 27 accredited veterinary colleges in the U.S. are the only schools in this country where a veterinary medical degree can be earned. Each of those colleges is evaluated regularly by the American Veterinary Medical Association.

Some Helpful Information

Another career opportunity for those with an entrepreneurial bent is to open a cat boutique. You can be situated in a small town, as long as you are near a major metropolitan area. Another excellent locale is a popular resort community. Look around for cat shops where you are now and when you travel for vacation or business, and take some notes. With the popularity of furballs these days, a store devoted to cat paraphernalia can do quite well.

About three-quarters of vets are in private practice, most dealing with small animals. A very small percentage—less than 1 percent—work exclusively with cats. (There is an American Association of Feline Practitioners.) If you live in a major metropolitan center with a population of a million or more, you should be able to earn a living confining your practice to cats.

There are many other openings for skilled veterinarians in salaried spots, such as research, teaching, and public health.

There is a good deal of variety in this field. There are poultry vets. There are also "flying vets," who reach their charges by plane and have their own professional association. There are vets specializing in toxicology, radiology, nutrition, emergency and critical care, and more.

Incomes for most entering this field are $20,000 to $25,000. How much you can earn eventually depends on your specialty and the part of the country where you live. A fair range could be from $50,000 to $60,000, certainly more in some instances.

Career Information Sources

The following sources offer career guidance material. When writing, you might send a stamped, self-addressed #10 envelope for a quick response.

American Grooming Shop Association
4575 Galley Rd., Suite 400A
Colorado Springs, CO 80915
(719) 570-7788

American Veterinary Medical Association
1931 No. Meacham Rd., Suite 100
Schaumburg, IL 60173
(847) 925-8070

The Humane Society of the United States
Attn: Center for Respect of Life and Environment
2100 L St. NW
Washington, DC 20037
(202) 452-1100

National Association of Professional Pet Sitters
1200 G St. NW
Washington, DC 20005
(202) 393-3317

North American Veterinary Technicians Association
P.O. Box 224
Battle Ground, IN 47920
(317) 742-2216

Some Other Careers in the Health Field

Men and women who choose to become veterinary care technicians help vets by administering medication, conducting certain tests, taking x-rays, and assisting in surgery (even administering anesthesia). Some handle office work along with those responsibilities, perhaps managing the clinic. Vet-techs, as they are called, also work in veterinary hospitals, zoos, pet stores, pharmaceutical companies, and university laboratories. Thirty-five states require vet-techs to be credentialed. You can look into two-year courses of study at more than 65 accredited colleges and junior colleges around the country.

Entry-level salaries are around $18,000 to $19,000; the ceiling for experienced technicians is around $30,000.

Here is another opportunity: Every animal clinic has a few men and women helping the vet and dealing with patients and their owners. These assistants' jobs include feeding the animals and cleaning their living areas, helping the veterinarian with treatments, and handling the office work: filling prescriptions, billing, setting appointments, and so on.

Some Helpful Information

Working for nonprofit organizations is another career option. You have read about many of them throughout this book. There are opportunities with national agencies or those in your own backyard. You can work directly with animals or with the administrative arm of these groups. The pay isn't great, but the job satisfaction could well make up for that.

What the clinic needs here is a responsible individual who can be depended upon to show up and care for the animals, even when the clinic is not open (the animals have to be fed every day, of course). Another requirement is *very* good people skills. You will often be dealing with worried, sometimes grief-stricken, pet owners. Salaries range from $5 to $6 an hour in rural areas to perhaps $10 or more in large urban areas, especially for the employee who handles more than one of the above-mentioned responsibilities.

How do you find these jobs? Ask at veterinary clinics in your area, and check the newspaper classified advertisements.

The Animal Behavior Therapist, a.k.a. Cat Shrink

A growing development on the career scene over the last few years, this career choice involves helping pet owners with problems that seem to have no medical basis: "Why is Boo Boo Kitty avoiding the litter box, even though it's clean and the vet says he's fine?" "My boyfriend's been spending a lot of time here and Cyclone doesn't like him. What can we do?" (One therapist's prescription for the latter problem: The boyfriend will have to make an effort to win over Cyclone. Also, start feeding the cat her favorite food some distance away from him. Over time move the bowl closer and closer until, it is hoped, he can feed her himself. That's the professional's advice. What would *yours* have been?)

When people are at their absolute wits' end, their friends with cats can't help, and their veterinarian is puzzled, the last resort is often a behavior therapist. Some vets will recommend one.

There are three professional associations here. Two of them—the American Veterinary Society of Animal Behavior and the American College of Veterinary Behaviorists—require that full members be graduates of a school of veterinary science. The third—the Animal Behavior Society—also allows as members those holding a degree in a behavioral science. The ACVB and the ABS offer certification to members who meet certain criteria.

It's true that anyone can hang out a shingle advertising his or her services as an animal behavior specialist. A few folks with an instinctive feel for animals and their behavior, and without a battery of degrees, have become quite skilled in this area over the years and do find clients. Still, it is hard getting recommendations from veterinarians, where many animal behaviorists get much of their business, if you do not have the credentials called for by professional associations.

Tales

In India there is a legend of a young prince who was agitated and nervous. Frustrated by his inability to meditate and enter a peaceful state, he retreated to the forest. While there he met a cat who taught him the elementary relaxation postures of what was to become hatha-yoga, a general term for a rigorous series of physical poses, or asanas, taught in most classes today.

Among other work outlets such as teaching, animal therapists can be in private practice or be associated with veterinary hospitals. Incomes can range from $150 to $400 for a three-hour session with a problem pup or puddy.

In a short *Washington Post* news item a few years ago about this specialty, one therapist was quoted as saying, "There's a reason for everything they [animals] do." A skeptical veterinarian said, "The pets aren't crazy. The humans are crazy."

The Least You Need to Know

➤ A sense of responsibility and good people skills are two important qualities for a successful career with animals.

➤ While some occupations require post-college study, others can be undertaken part-time by high school students.

➤ Entrepreneurial careers such as pet sitting and taxi services require a highly motivated self-starter and plenty of promotion.

➤ Veterinary medicine is very sophisticated these days; it rivals treatment for humans.

For Fun and Profit

Perhaps a traditional, full-time career with cats is not exactly for you. But you want to do *something* with cats, whether as an official hobby, an absorbing occasional pastime, or even—dare we say it—just a bit of a moneymaker.

What could that bit of dabbling be? Hmmm. Read on. Perhaps something will strike a note with you, or you might already know where your interests lie and just need a gentle poke to get started. Cat commerce is huge in this country; billions of dollars are spent annually on products from cat food to…well, as you have seen in the past pages, cat *everything*.

The Novelties Business: Selling and Buying

Let's say you knit handsome "cat" sweaters. Or you make stuffed animals. Or you have created intriguing cat jewelry that friends have admired. Or maybe you have a good idea for a new type of litter pan that solves one or more of the problems owners have with that household fixture. Whatever your specialty, you have either already worked a cat theme into it, or you can do so easily.

If you bake mouth-watering cookies, put up preserves, or have any four-star winner in the food line that others might want to buy, be as clever as a cat and think of some feline connection to that product.

What's next? Start small when trying to sell your item. It is important to know whether there is a market for it, and using local retail outlets is more efficient and far less costly than trying to go national initially.

Some Helpful Information

Do you think your novelty calls for a patent, a trademark, or a copyright? You can call the following offices to have your questions answered and to learn the procedure for securing one. The U.S. patent and trademark office is at (703) 305-8341. For information about copyrights, call (202) 707-3000.

Visit area gift stores, restaurants, supermarkets, or wherever you think buyers might pick up your product to see if those owners will buy a few of them outright or on consignment.

You might also take a table at cat shows that come to your town and at any other exhibitions that seem apropos. Those could be a pet fair, a Christmas crafts show featuring tons of gifts to buy, and a huge area flea market.

If you have some success there, you will have to decide if it is enough for you to stay with regional sales or whether you want to go national with your idea (you can worry about *inter*national down the road!). There are several books that can help the novice with various aspects of setting up a new business. One that might interest you is *How to Market a Product for under $500* by Jeffrey Dobkin (Adams Publishing, $38.50).

Tales

In Belgium there was a medieval tradition of tossing a cat from a church steeple. If the cat landed on his feet, the harvest would be good. In 1938 and again after World War II, the tradition was revived, mercifully with a stuffed velvet cat replacing the live one. The festival is called Kattefest, and it takes place in Ypres. Held each May, it features a parade with floats dedicated to Bastet, Freyjn, and other Belgian cats of legend.

Here's another angle that can help you, both as a source of sales for your product and as a source for *buying* cat clothing, toys, and so on for yourself and for gifts.

You already know how many hundreds of mail-order catalogs are sent out in this country. You might receive some in your home, both requested and unsolicited. Mail order is a great way to check out your competition on the national scene.

There are several catalogs devoted exclusively to pets, although there are pet-related items to be found for sale in others as well. For example, you might find stepping stones with cat faces on them in your gardening catalog, or some cat towels and salt and pepper shakers in a kitchen catalog.

To obtain as many cat- or pet-oriented catalogs as you'd like, check the cat magazines. There are many ads there for products or those companies' catalogs. The latter are either free or available at a small charge. Keep an eye on catalogs selling products in other subject areas to see if your concept fits in with some of them.

Tales

Here's something for the "If-you-think-cats-are-popular-*now*" department: When the West was being settled, it is said cats fled from wagon trains heading in that direction, hightailing it back to their old haunts and homes. No discomfort for them, thank you, they'd leave that to dogs. Western frontier towns infested with rodents purchased cats for as much as $25, which, needless to say, was very big bucks back then.

Catalog companies often sell their mailing lists, so you're bound to find yourself receiving more catalogs without even requesting them. Some folks don't like all that clutter in their mailbox, but if it's about cats, *you* may be just delighted.

When you see a catalog that would be perfect for handling your craft or other novelty, contact that company (their address is always on the booklet) and ask for the name of the person who buys for the catalog. Write him or her, enclosing pictures of your product or the item itself if possible and extolling its marketability. You don't have to say this with pet catalogs, but with those in other interest areas include the fact that cats outnumber dogs in this country as household pets, some 63 million to 52 million, so there certainly are a lot of potential buyers of cat novelties out there. Request that that company consider including your product in their catalog. If they elect to do so, you receive a percentage of dollar sales.

Stamps courtesy of J. Carlson

Collecting Cat Stamps

Stamp collecting is a popular, time-honored hobby, of course, but as a cat aficionado you'll take it one step further: You will collect only cat stamps.

It's possible. You could find yourself with not only an absorbing pastime, but also a profitable one if you make correct choices for your album. There is not likely to be any *big* money in this pursuit, just a few dollars here and there over time.

Some Helpful Information
Would you like to see another American stamp proclaiming the cat? Contact the government office that selects stamp subjects and make that suggestion, perhaps offering some ideas for the kind of stamp as well. Write to the Citizens' Stamp Advisory Committee, c/o Stamp Division, United States Postal Service, Washington, DC 20260.

Most countries of the world have honored the cat at one time or another with a postage stamp ever since the first adhesive postage stamp was introduced by an Englishman in 1840. That gives you plenty of years and many nations from which to make your selections.

For some reason, United States postage stamps have featured cats only rarely. The first cat showed up as recently as 1972. The stamp showed a rural post office of the 1800s with a small black cat sitting on a sack of flour in the foreground. It wasn't what you would call a "cat stamp." In 1988, the U.S. Postal Service issued a four-stamp domestic cat set. Each of the stamps featured two cats, for a total of eight different breeds. And that's all there have been.

You will want to read up on this subject, of course—how to get started, which stamps are potentially valuable, buying unused stamps versus canceled ones, how to trade with other philatelists, and so on. By all means also talk with a local stamp dealer who can offer you valuable advice, and visit stamp shows. Join a national philatelic society, and, obviously, keep up with stamp news from your local post office.

Tell everyone you've started stamp collecting. They'll give you stamps that might not be for your cat collection, but could help you trade for ones that *will* be a nice addition to your album. Here are more sources of information.

John Carlson, a U.S. dealer specializing in cat stamps, has a free price list containing over 500 cat stamps that can be ordered by mail. For that list, plus the free tips he offers novice collectors, call (847) 255-0015 or write to Carlson Stamps, 15 College Dr., Arlington Heights, IL 60004. (In case you're wondering, John Carlson considers his business a part-time job, perhaps just a little more than a hobby, certainly undertaken more for enjoyment than remuneration.)

Cat Mews is a quarterly newsletter published by the Cats on Stamps Study Unit, a subgroup of the American Topical Association where members collect stamps in a particular category—windmills, wild animals, and the like. The Cats on Stamps group has about 170 members. For a sample newsletter, send a self-addressed, stamped (32 cents) envelope to Mary Ann Brown, 3006 Wade Rd., Durham, NC 27705.

Bet You Didn't Know Coin collecting is another hobby pursued by a sizable number of enthusiasts around the world. If you'd like to specialize, you can collect *cat* coins, some of them in gold, which certainly can appreciate nicely. Check with local coin collectors.

Kitty Painting, Photographs, and Cartoons

Cat lovers with an artistic bent have probably worked cats into their specialty many times, both for themselves and as gifts for family and friends.

Is that you? Would you like to take a hobby a step further, perhaps to some sales?

You'll do well to take a course locally in your specialty. You should also talk to someone in your area who is very good and absorb what you can from that individual.

Working in watercolors or oils, photographing cats, and being a clever cartoonist are very different talents, of course, but they do deal with the eye and do offer potential buyers a view of their pets they would not otherwise have. For example, many owners, even though their cat is right there on their lap, enjoy having a picture of that much-loved pet nearby as well.

When starting small, you can offer to paint, draw, or photograph area residents' pets (you'll probably have to expand your base to include dogs, perhaps even other household animals).

Bet You Didn't Know The International Museum of Cartoon Art opened in 1996 featuring, among other displays, several cartoon cats that will be familiar to you: Garfield, KrazyKat, and cats by Kliban. The museum is at 201 Plaza Real, Boca Raton, FL 33432. The telephone number is (561) 391-2200.

Advertise in a local paper or send around a flier describing your service and including photos of some of your work. If you don't already have some artwork on file, do a free sketch or cartoon of some friends' animals to begin a portfolio.

Check to see what "people" art is going for in your area. You might want to charge the same. Your painting or cartoon can be framed by you as part of the transaction if the owner wishes. A photo is usually offered in a cardboard frame.

Speaking of photography, around late October you could investigate renting a portion of someone's store space to take photos of pets. Many owners like to feature their cat's or dog's picture on holiday greeting cards, and they also like to have pictures of their pets for holiday presents.

Tales

There was one noted cat lover and artist who went quite mad. In the late 19th century, and until the outbreak of World War II, Louis Wain was a, and eventually *the,* premier cat artist of England. He was a successful illustrator of many books and drew his charming, mischievous kittens and cats for magazines and newspapers. His personal life, however, was another story. By his own admission he was a strange and frequently unhappy child. His beloved wife died tragically early in their marriage. He fell on financial misfortune and sold quick sketches of cats to pay creditors.

Eventually his interest in cats turned into an obsession. Declared insane in 1924, he was committed to a county asylum. But that period in Wain's life led to even greater success. While being cared for, Wain gradually returned to work but drew in a new style. Ironically, those pictures became famous as excellent examples of schizophrenic art, and when he died in 1939, the nation mourned him.

Another market for photographs is newspapers and magazines. Cat magazines regularly publish readers' photos of their pets, but usually with no payment to them unless they've written an accompanying article. But if you can write a clever caption for a particularly good photo, you can send it to a general interest publication, or your local newspaper, where you *will* be paid. Sometimes if the picture is good enough, the publication will write the caption. Here's an example of good: A year or so ago one of the newspaper wire services published a picture that certainly ran nationally and might even have been seen overseas. It was a head shot of a man in a helmet on a motor bike and his cat in front of him, on the handlebars, also in a helmet. The caption noted the cat loved speed and enjoyed zooming around town with his owner. Great shot! Not your run-of-the-mill cute cat pic.

You might also hook up with area writers, telling them you're there to supply photos to accompany their articles. An animal writer might need a cat photographer for a particular story, although in truth you may find many writers take their own pictures these days.

If you are a *very* good cartoonist, you could look into a career working with one of the established newspaper cartoonists, although those jobs are certainly not common. If you're a clever writer too, maybe you'll come up with the next Garfield-type cartoon strip. However, a more likely career choice could be as an animator at one of the movie studios—Disney, for example. Those folks are *very* much in demand these days with top-of-the-line animators able to write their own ticket at certain studios.

What We Love About Cats

➤ That independence of theirs, freeing us from being worshipped, a state dog owners seem to relish.

➤ That just watching them stretch and sun themselves lowers our blood pressure.

➤ That if you drop a piece of very soft fabric on the floor, a cat will be curled up on it within minutes.

➤ That they can gobble up a new food, savoring each bit, but the next time we serve the same dish, they turn up their noses.

➤ That their favorite spot for a nap is on the spread-out newspaper we're reading or the report we're writing.

➤ That cute way they have of immediately washing the spot we just petted. Was it something we said?

➤ That they don't do tricks for us, or at least very few.

➤ That they let us live with them.

Collectibles: What's Hot and What's Not

Your interests might lie in collecting all sorts of kitty paraphernalia, from figurines to toys to china. Could what you like be a dollar-making investment as well?

It's best to collect what interests you and what you enjoy, but, yes, some stuff is more valuable than others.

What's "in" right now? Postcards featuring cats, particularly Victorian-era cards. Old sheet music illustrated with cats, or with cat songs, could also bring you more money eventually than what you pay for it now.

Bet You Didn't Know

Here's a collection for you. It's of cat artifacts, housed in the Glendale Public Library in Glendale, California. A local couple started purchasing cat-related items 15 years ago. When their collection at home became too huge, the next step seemed to be donating it to the library. There are paintings, books, magazines, posters, and catalogs, including a catalog from the first major American cat show in Madison Square Garden in 1895. Other cat enthusiasts have now also contributed to the collection, which continues to grow. The Cat Collection is in the Special Collections Room at the library at 222 East Harvard St. in Glendale. Call (818) 548-2037 for hours.

Tales

Remember those Garfield the Cat dolls from a few years ago, the ones with suction cups on their feet so you could stick them to your car's rear window? In California, people broke into cars *to steal the cat.* It was a mini-crime wave of $20 doll thefts. When police saw a car with many cats stuck to the windows, they'd stop the driver for questioning, and he or she often turned out to be a Garfield thief.

What's not so hot? Anything that is damaged will not be a good investment, although you might still like to own that item for your own enjoyment. Cat figurines are especially easy to harm because of the animal's ears and tail, which project and can snap off easily. If an antique shop or a flea market dealer offers you a sizable discount for a damaged cat figurine that could be valuable, buy only if you like that item. It will be worthless as an investment.

If you cannot spend the money for expensive paintings or china, you'll be interested to know the far more affordable Calico Kittens, ceramic kitties manufactured by Enesco in Elk Grove Village, IL, appear to be going up in price. You can buy them now in gift shops for $20 to $30 depending on the intricacy of the design. Cat enthusiasts are also beginning to collect present-day cat postcards and greeting cards, obtained from museum stores around the world and card shops anywhere. Others are buying Hallmark's pewter figurines, of cats of course. You can swap some of what you buy with other collectors as well.

A good resource for a beginner and an experienced collector is Cat Collectors, an association with some 1,000 members in this country and abroad. Membership costs $20 a year and brings you a bi-monthly 16-page newsletter of news and buying tips, plus a 12-page catalog of items for sale from the antiques and secondary markets. Write to Cat Collectors, 33161 Wendy Dr., Sterling Heights, MI 48310, or call (810) 264-0285.

Writing About Cats

The cat enthusiast who can string a few words together, whether prose or poetry, can earn a few dollars or perhaps more.

You can sell your work to cat or other pet publications and to national general interest magazines and newspapers. With cats so popular, editors know that your words apply to many of their readers.

What can you write about? Small themes. Write about how taking in a stray cat helped you through a particularly rough spot in your life. Or you might write an article about a local humane society and how some new programs they have initiated are working out.

Try to take pictures, if you can, to illustrate your article. Editors sometimes mark an article "sold" just because of the easily available—and *good*—artwork.

You might want to sign up for a nonfiction writing course offered by many colleges in their adult education departments. Besides helping you refine your work, the course will explain markets and how to find the best spot for what you have written.

Rates are all over the chart here. You can earn $10 for an article in a local paper or over $1,000 for one in a glossy magazine with a large national circulation.

The same tips for articles hold true for poetry—try both local and national markets. Also, don't be afraid of humor in both articles and poems. Editors love a good laugh (so do their readers), and they often complain they don't see humor submitted nearly often enough.

After you have published several articles, you might want to join the Cat Writers' Association, Inc. (CWA).

It's Been Said

MEOW!

"If by chance I seated myself to write, she very slyly, very tenderly, seeking protection and caresses, would softly take her place on my knee and follow the comings and goings of my pen—sometimes effacing, with an unintentional stroke of her paw, lines of whose tenor she disapproved."

—Pierre Loti, French novelist and naval officer (1850–1923)

CWA members are authors, editors, journalists, artists, and others interested in communicating about cats. For more information, contact CWA Secretary Diane M. Smith, CVT, 1759 Lake Cypress Dr., Safety Harbor, FL 34695.

The Least You Need to Know

➤ Try selling your cat-related creations locally before investing time and money going national.

➤ Collecting cat stamps puts a new spin on an established hobby.

➤ Local adult education courses can offer direction and market tips for novice painters, writers, and photographers.

➤ If you're going to concentrate on cat novelties, you might want to try "collectibles" instead and focus on items likely to grow in value.

Chapter 25

It's Better to Give...

In This Chapter

➤ Finding the right volunteer slot

➤ Kids can help too

➤ Monetary donations to your favorite charity

➤ If you see animal abuse or neglect

Lend a hand. Help out. Pitch right in. Give something back. We are a nation of people eager to offer our time for causes we support. Nearly half of all Americans volunteer to make things just a little bit better around this country and around the world.

There are other efforts you can make to aid the cause of animals, even solely cats if you like.

What's Your Volunteer Profile?

So how about joining those millions of Americans engaged in volunteer work?

Just like a full- or part-time paying job, you will want your volunteer work to be something that particularly interests you and is well-suited to your talents and skills.

But what *are* your skills in this area? What exactly should you be looking for in a volunteer slot? Here are some questions to ask yourself:

➤ *Do I want to work with people, or am I truly more comfortable behind the scenes?* Volunteering offers a wide variety of work opportunities in either area, so feel free to choose what's best suited to your temperament.

➤ *Do I prefer office duties or hands-on work with animals?* Here you can also take your choice. It's wise, though, to clarify exactly what you will be expected to do in any position you accept to avoid misunderstandings later.

➤ *Do I want to be with dogs and cats only or tackle a new field?* Maybe you'd like working with a local bird-rescue group you've been reading about. Explore all your options until you find the spot—and the people you'll be working with—where you feel most comfortable.

➤ *Do I have any special skills a nonprofit organization can utilize?* In applying, you could mention your background in accounting, public relations, computers, and so on, unless you want volunteer work to be totally different from your day job.

➤ *How much time do I have to offer?* Calculate not only what hours you can spare, but also which days of the week. Also keep in mind commuting time to your volunteer position. How far are you willing to travel? How will that time on the road cut into your available volunteering hours?

Bet You Didn't Know According to The Humane Society of the United States, there are 3,000 to 3,500 animal shelter facilities in the U.S. The average cost of handling an animal in a shelter is $100.

It's Been Said "The greatness of a nation can be judged by the way its animals are treated."

—Mohandas Gandhi

Finally, clarifying your position in the volunteer world includes keeping seriousness of purpose in mind. Just because you will not be paid for this work does not mean you can be any less responsible than you would with a salaried job. The organization you join has a workable system in place, and it's up to you to fit smoothly into that operation.

You might volunteer to tend cats at a shelter until they are adopted.

Photo by Bm Porter/Don Franklin

Kids Can Help Too

Many humane societies have programs for kids. Some are for children as young as 4 or 6, allowing them to play with the dogs and cats at a shelter. Actually helping with animal care can begin when a child is 8, sometimes 10 or 12. Besides playing with the pets, those older kids wash and groom them, walk the dogs, and handle some cleaning chores. Sometimes they help with fundraising events, promoting them and then working at the affair. The young workers might volunteer during the summer and then cut back, or cut out, work during the school year.

Call the volunteer office at some shelters in your area and ask about a kids' program. If there isn't one, urge them to implement such a worthwhile introduction to being concerned about, and caring for, animals. The kids will feel rewarded by the work they do and feel quite responsible too.

If you're a young person reading this, you might want to contact a nearby shelter yourself. If they have no program for school-age kids, your phone call or personal visit could be just the nudge they need to start one.

Tales

A cat lover from a young age, Winston Churchill signed his untidy letters to his mother from boarding school "The Pussy Cat." Years later, when he married Clementine Hozier, his term of affection for her was "The Cat."

—*The Young Churchill* by Celia Sandys

Where the Jobs Are

Jobs are at animal shelters, of course, including "safe" shelters where dogs and cats are allowed to live out their days if they are not adopted. Sometimes individuals open safe havens for cats or dogs, keeping as many as they can in and around their home. They can always use a hand.

If you live near a major animal hospital, there are likely to be volunteer opportunities. There are opportunities at zoos as well.

You can volunteer without leaving your home by becoming a foster parent to a pet. Many shelters have instituted a foster parent program, which places a dog or cat that is frightened, hyperactive, or seriously injured in a private home. The cure: lots of love and attention with the expectation that when the pet is more settled and confident, it will be more adoptable.

This works very well for the animal, of course, who might have otherwise been euthanized because of shelter overcrowding. It allows the shelter to keep more animals alive with the hope of finding them homes, and it makes the foster parents feel darned good to watch the pet they care for blossom and eventually find a permanent home.

The shelters provide medical care, a collar and tag, a crate if you need one, and lots of advice. You supply food, a litter box, and plenty of play and hugs.

If this interests you, ask about the program at a local shelter. Many of them also foster out rabbits, turtles, and birds.

Finally, there are a number of local volunteer jobs created to meet a specific need. In coastal states, for example, there can be groups formed to save the turtles or the manatees or to look out for the seals. In any state there will be folks who get together to care for injured birds. You don't have to look far for volunteer opportunities; there's so much to be done.

HEY!

Bet You Didn't Know

Anthropomorphism is not a word we come upon every day, but we often put its definition into practice with our cats. It means to attribute human form or personality to that which is not human. We do this when we dress up our pets or say things like "Doodad is upset because Helen went back to work and now he thinks...and he's trying to tell us that...." Of course, cats do have some feelings that are the animal equivalent of human feelings, primarily the ability to give and receive affection.

Humane Organizations

The following are some of the leading national organizations involved in various aspects of animal welfare. They can provide you with information about their association and can direct you to agencies in your area concerned with cat welfare:

American Humane Association
Animal Protection Division
63 Inverness Dr. E.
Englewood, CO 80112
(303) 792-9900

Animal Protection Institute of America
P.O. Box 22505
Sacramento, CA 95822
(916) 731-5521

Friends of Animals, Inc.
777 Post Rd., Suite 205
Darien, CT 06820
(203) 656-1522

American Society for the Prevention of Cruelty to Animals
424 E. 92 St.
New York, NY 10128
(212) 876-7700

The Humane Society of the United States
2100 L St. NW
Washington, DC 20037
(202) 452-1100

The Pet Savers Foundation/Spay USA
750 Port Washington Blvd., Suite 2
Port Washington, L.I., NY 11050
(516) 944-5025

Turning Volunteer Work into a Paying Job

It helps to already have your foot in the door when seeking full-time employment at any company or nonprofit association. That could be a part-time job, temp work, and, yes, volunteering too.

Most volunteers aren't looking for a paying position where they spend those hours helping out, but some wouldn't mind at all if one came along. They'd try for it.

If that sounds like you, you are probably already doing a good job so that you can apply for a paying slot expecting a good reference from the volunteer coordinator. Naturally, you'll also keep an eye on bulletin boards and read the newsletter of that association to see what's opening up and where you might fit in.

Bet You Didn't Know Albert Schweitzer devoted his life to the well-being of human-kind. He was also a cat lover and showed that same care and concern to his cat, Sizi. The doctor was left-handed, but often would write with his right hand so as not to disturb Sizi, asleep on his left arm.

Be sure you are up to the job you apply for, though. Although it is wise in most instances to say, "I'll take anything to start," you ought to be sure you can do that entry-level work and are not relying only on your love of animals and desire for that paying job. Many of those positions call for special education or other skills. One man who had been trying for a permanent job at the zoological gardens near his home where he had done volunteer work took an entry-level position as a zookeeper. That job involves feeding and exercising the animals and cleaning their living quarters. Fine, he thought. But the man had back trouble and was forced to resign in two weeks. He did not recall that part of the job description was lifting heavy tubs of water.

Other Ways to Help

There are several small steps you can take locally to ensure the well-being of cats. For example, periodically take food and litter to veterinary clinics that collect those provisions for cat owners who cannot always afford them.

When there's a natural disaster in your area—a hurricane, tornado, flood, and so on—contribute cat food to the several agencies that will be collecting for animal welfare.

MEOW!

It's Been Said "It is better to light one candle than to curse the darkness."

—old Chinese proverb

Usually it is only the cat and dog owners who think of these things in the understandable overwhelming swell of concern for humans. But cats are hungry, frightened, and sometimes homeless too. You might also offer your time to distribute that food to those who need it.

Here's another thought. How about chipping in with a neighbor to have a few local strays spayed or neutered? You'll be doing that cat a favor and will not have to witness the sad sight of litter after litter showing up around your home to meet who knows what end. Check around at area veterinary clinics. Many offer discounts to folks who bring in neighborhood strays.

Bet You Didn't Know

Each spring there is a week set aside in April designated as National Volunteer Week to recognize and thank all of our country's volunteer workers.

Donating to Your Favorite Animal Group(s)

Money, it is said, is a perfect gift. It's always the right size and color. Just as most of us appreciate some greenery for a birthday or special occasion, so do charitable groups involved in animal welfare. But while we may think, "Mmmm, Aunt Edna didn't send what she did last year," the charity just says, "Oh, thank you, thank you, thank you" no matter what amount falls out of the envelope.

Some well-known humane organizations are listed earlier in this chapter. If you'd like to know more about others you might be considering, there's a way to learn their history; programs; policies; use of funds; tax exempt status, if any; percentage of fundraising that goes toward programs and percentage used for administrative costs; and more. The National Charities Information Bureau's "Wise Giving Guide" is published quarterly to help those making donations make informed decisions. A single copy is free. You can call (212) 929-6300 to request a copy. Located in New York City, NCIB is a nonprofit organization founded in 1918 to foster informed giving.

If you have a favorite animal-related charity, you might want to remember that group in your will too.

Some Helpful Information

If you're considering donating to a *local* organization, a good way to see if you agree with its policies and how the group spends its money is to volunteer to work there.

It's Been Said

"Dogs look up to you/ Cats look down on you/ Pigs is equal"

—from England, an old Gloucestershire proverb

What to Do if You See Abuse or Neglect

What can you do about the dog down the street who seems to be always chained to a fence with no shelter from the weather? Or what about animal abuse on a national or international scale? How do you fight back when you see heartbreaking stories on television or read them in the newspaper? Someone has to *do* something.

Maybe that someone is you taking just one small step to right a wrong.

Tales

The movement to protect animals from overwork and cruel treatment began in early 19th-century Britain. It was led by a wealthy landowner and member of Parliament, Richard Martin (nicknamed "Humanity Martin" by King George IV). In 1822 the first preventive law against cruelty was passed, and two years later Martin organized the world's first humane society. In 1840, by command of Queen Victoria, the society's name became the Royal Society for the Prevention of Cruelty to Animals (RSPCA). Similar organizations were formed in France in 1845, the United States in 1866, Canada in 1869, and then elsewhere.

On the local level, you can contact your animal control officer. A phone call might be all that is needed, although in some instances you will have to lodge a more formal complaint.

If you are traveling and are concerned about the mistreatment of animals, the Boston-based World Society for the Protection of Animals (WSPA) has offered several tips. Among them are:

➤ Consider making a donation to the humane society in the country you visit to support their work there.

➤ If you see an instance of cruelty to animals, note the date, time, place, and a description of the incident, and then report it to local authorities and a humane society.

➤ Do not attend events that exploit animals or cause suffering, such as bullfights, circuses, zoos, or aquariums.

➤ Do not pay to have your picture taken posing with a wild animal.

➤ If you are at a hotel or resort that displays wild animals, report your disapproval in writing to the management.

➤ Send copies of all your notes and correspondence with local authorities and humane societies to WSPA at P.O. Box 190, Boston, MA 02130, or call them at (617) 522-7000.

The Least You Need to Know

➤ Volunteering a small amount of your time can aid local humane associations, which are almost always in need of assistance.

➤ There are volunteer programs targeted at kids too.

➤ Being on the spot and doing good work might lead to a paying job where you volunteer.

➤ If you can't afford a large monetary donation, even a small one will be appreciated by a nonprofit group working for the better treatment of animals.

Part 6
Even More than You Wanted to Know!

Due to some oversight somewhere in the scheme of things, cats didn't get the body mechanics necessary for making and recording words, numbers, visual images, and musical compositions. Pity. Think of the libraries, the data banks, the galleries, and the recordings that would be collections of the cat's view of planet Earth.

Well, it just can't be. But we hope you'll enjoy this brief overview of the cat in history and in the arts from a human perspective. We'll leave it to your imagination to guess what the cat would have written.

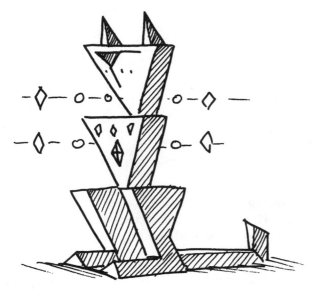

Way, Way Back

The earliest ancestors of the cat appeared on Earth about the same time as the earliest ancestors of mankind—right after the disaster that killed off the dinosaurs. That was 65 million years ago. Ancestors, however, that we would recognize as having a family resemblance to the cats we live with today appeared about 10 million years ago. They were completely wild, though, and had no associations with the early humans.

Archeological evidence suggests that some of these wild felines became tame and began to live in our company about 8,000 years ago, which isn't very long in geological time. (Just to give you a standard of comparison, it's estimated by some authorities that dogs have been keeping company with humans for almost 50,000 years.) Since those first cats came in from the cold, the cat/human relationship has hit the extremes of love and hate.

If one were to write the cat's version of the history of western civilization, it would be packed with enough passion, hate, fear, and bloody gore to qualify for a prime-time TV series. Cats have been worshipped as gods and persecuted as devils. And they have survived.

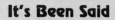

MEOW!

It's Been Said

"What sort of philosophers are we, who know nothing of the origin and destiny of cats?"

—Henry David Thoreau, American philosopher and writer (1817–1862)

Cleopatra's Relatives?

In George Bernard Shaw's play *Caesar and Cleopatra,* Cleopatra tells Caesar that her grandmother's great-grandmother was a black kitten born of the sacred white cat. No, she's not putting herself down or making a joke, she's claiming kinship to divinity. The Egyptians worshipped cats.

In the fifth dynasty in Egypt, about 3,000 B.C., the Egyptian goddess Bastet was depicted with the head of a lioness and symbolized light and warmth from the sun. But over a millennium, she gradually came to be depicted with the head of a cat and was associated with the night and the moon. The Egyptians believed that she controlled fertility, cured illnesses, and protected the dead. She was also worshipped as the Corn Spirit that assured healthy crops and a good harvest. Farmers believed that to dream of a big cat foretold an abundant harvest.

One of the many images of the cat goddess Bastet.

By the year 950 B.C., Bastet took precedence over all other goddesses in Egypt. A magnificent red granite temple was built in her honor in the city of Bubastis. "Divine" cats were kept in the shrine and tended to by monks and maidens. Pilgrims came to the shrine by the thousands during April and May and participated in music making, feasting, drinking, and naked orgies. Many victims were sacrificed; others were injured in the frantic reveling when the statue representing the goddess was brought out from the temple.

The punishment for killing a cat in Egypt was death. Household cats were treated with the greatest respect for almost 2,000 years. They ate the same food from the same plates as their owners. Many wore jewels and slept on cushions. When a cat died, it was often mummified in the same way as a human and then placed in a casket with a mummified mouse or two and water for its journey to the afterlife. Diggings in the cat cemeteries that were laid out along the banks of the Nile have produced a variety of bronze cat effigies and hundreds of cat amulets in gold, silver, amethyst, lapis lazuli, agate, quartz, marble, and other stones. Experts believe these figures were hung on necklaces worn either by cats or by humans.

Bet You Didn't Know When a cat died in Egypt, every member of the family shaved off his or her eyebrows as a sign of mourning.

Tales

There is a legend that the Persians (present-day Iran) won a major military victory because of the Egyptian reverence for the cat. In 522 B.C., the Persian army attacked the city of Pelusium in the Nile delta. As an attack strategy, Persian King Cambyses II ordered each of his lead soldiers to tie a cat to his shield. When the Egyptian soldiers saw the struggling cats, they feared killing or even wounding their sacred animals and threw down their weapons.

Ancient Greek and Roman Cats

In Greek mythology, Apollo, the god of the sun, created the lion; Artemis, his sister and goddess of the moon, created the cat. Artemis was the Greek version of the Egyptian goddess Bastet; Diana was the Roman version. Neither had a cat head, however, and cats were not worshipped in either country.

Cats were primarily pets and kept in the home in Greece and Rome where weasels, skunks, and small snakes were used to kill mice outdoors and on farms. They are depicted in domestic situations of wealth and comfort on the vases and statuary that has survived.

Bet You Didn't Know When Mount Vesuvius erupted in A.D. 79, it destroyed the city of Pompeii. An archeological dig into the lava found the remains of a woman clutching a cat.

Although associated with domestic comfort, cats in the Roman empire were also used as the symbol of liberty. (They were probably just as independent then as now.) A cat was very often shown at the feet of Libertas, the Roman goddess of liberty. Cats were also the emblems depicted on the flags of several legions traveling over Europe. One legion marched under a banner with a green cat on a silver ground, another with a red cat on a pink shield. A legion bound for the Alps carried a cat with one eye and one ear. It's interesting that later in time, the Swiss also used the cat to symbolize liberty. And the first French Republic placed the cat at the side of the statue of liberty and added a cat to its shield of arms.

 Tales

Cats appear often in the 6th century B.C. fables of Aesop, usually personifying human traits of wit, trickery, dishonesty, and deceit. Versions of one of the most famous fables, *The Cat Maiden,* appear in literature throughout the world. Here's the gist:

A beautiful cat who had fallen in love with a young man asked Aphrodite for help. This goddess of love changed the cat into a fair maid. Needless to say, man and maid were married.

But Aphrodite tested the cat maiden's respect for love by setting a mouse free in the room while the couple were, well, copulating. The woman jumped up to chase, pounce upon, and eat the mouse on the spot. Aphrodite, angered at the lack of reverence, changed the woman back into a cat.

The moral is: What is bred in the bone will never be absent from the flesh.

Cats on the Deity Staff

In Nordic mythology, Freyja is the goddess of youth, beauty, sexual love, and fruitfulness. She was believed to travel through the countryside in a chariot drawn by two white cats. (Some versions say the cats were gray.) Her passing presence caused seeds to swell and sprout. She gave special benefits to those farmers who left pans of milk out in their fields for her divine cats.

Freyja also blessed all lovers, and the presence of the divine cats at the blessing led to the belief that cats can foretell whether or not a marriage will take place. This belief grew and spread into the many cat and wedding superstitions in our culture. Freyja's day (Friday) was considered the best day for a wedding.

The Cat and the Bride

Cats seem to get mixed up with weddings in people's minds, and there are many sayings and superstitions in western culture about cats and weddings. Some are contradictory. Here's a sample:

➤ A girl who cherishes a cat is sure to marry.

➤ Keeping a black cat in the house will ensure that all your daughters will marry.

➤ If you keep black cats at home, you'll never marry.

➤ If you step on a cat's tail, you will not marry during the year.

➤ Whether or not to accept a suitor can be "left to the cat." Three hairs from the cat's tail are carefully folded into a piece of paper and left on the girl's doorstep. In the morning the paper is unfolded. If the hairs are crossed, the girl should marry the suitor. If not crossed, she should reject him.

➤ In northern Europe, young girls are told to feed the cats well so that the sun will shine on their wedding day.

➤ If a cat washes her face near a crowd of people, the one she looks at first will be the next to marry.

➤ If two young women shake a cat in a quilt, the one whose end it runs out of will marry first.

➤ If a bride feeds the cat before she goes to church, she will have happiness in her married life.

➤ If a cat is sitting on the bride's doorstep on the wedding day, it is considered a bad omen indicating that the bride did not care for the cat and might therefore not be a good housekeeper.

➤ It is lucky to see a black cat on the way to church to be married.

➤ A black cat as a wedding present means good luck.

continues

---

continued

➤ In Thailand the breed of cat we call Korat and the Thai people call Si-Swat is considered a symbol of good fortune. A pair of them is traditionally presented to a bride to ensure a happy marriage.

➤ It is lucky to have cats turn up at a wedding.

➤ In eastern Europe, family members bring newlyweds a cradle with a cat in it to ensure children.

The Relatively Bright Dark Ages

The cat population seems to have declined in western Europe from the fall of the Roman empire in the 5th century through early medieval times up to the 10th century. But there is evidence that cats were living quietly with humankind on farms and in religious communities.

In Wales in 936, King Hywel Dda set down as law many practices that were in common use. Many of the new laws mentioned the cat, for example:

➤ In order to qualify for the legal designation of a Welsh hamlet, a settlement had to include nine buildings, a plow, a kiln, a churn, a bull, a cock, a herdsman, and a cat.

➤ If a husband and wife separated, the wife got the cat.

➤ A newborn kitten's value was one cent; when its eyes were opened the value was two cents; and when it had caught its first mouse its worth climbed to four cents. (Four cents would buy you a calf or a filly in those days.)

Cats were welcomed in monasteries and convents throughout Europe and the British Isles both as mousers and companions. Nuns in British convents were not allowed to possess any animal except the cat. Gregory the Great, a pope at the end of the 6th century, loved cats, and when he retired from his papacy to a monastery, he took with him only his cat. Saint Patrick in 5th century Ireland raised cats, as did many Irish monks after him.

Dark Centuries For the Cat

From the turn of the first millennium into the 18th century, many pagan rituals survived despite Christianity's best efforts, and many included the torture and sacrifice of cats. In springtime when crops were being planted, cats were routinely burned alive in wicker (and later in iron) cages. They were also buried alive in the fields to protect the crops from evil spirits. On the eve of St. John-in-June (the feast day of John the Baptist is June 24) great cat fires were lit every year, sometimes by heads of state, to celebrate fertility, long days, and growing crops. Although most of these ritual "midsummer" rites were declared illegal by the middle of the 18th century, some survived. The last documented occurrence took place in 1905!

Cruelty to cats cannot be blamed solely upon superstitious farmers and peasant folk, however. In 1231 Pope Gregory XI created the Inquisition, one of the most pervasive and murderous tribunals in the history of humans and their cats. Cats got caught up in the investigations because Gregory believed that the devil took the form of a black cat. It became dangerous to show affection or even attention not only to black cats but to any cat. The Roman Catholic Church initiated and supported centuries of punishment, persecution, and even death to those who befriended a cat.

Bet You Didn't Know

In 1305 the Archbishop of Coventry was accused of worshipping the devil in the form of a cat. He was arraigned before Pope Clement V, but it was felt the charge was not proven so he was not burned at the stake.

Sayings and Superstitions

East European legend tells that cats' bodies are inhabited by devils during thunderstorms. So of course, cats were routinely put out of the house to protect against a lightning strike. Believers thought that with each clap of thunder, the angels pray to God while the devils in the cats' bodies mock and taunt the angels. Lightning bolts are the shafts the angels throw at the devil-possessed cats.

Near the end of the 15th century, Pope Innocent VIII turned the power of the Church against women who practiced magic and women who dared to be different. They were called "witches" and were grouped together with people who chose to worship the spirits of evil. Since many of these solitary and/or unconventional women chose cats as their companions, the cat became known as the "familiar" (close companion) of the witch and was thought to be either the devil himself or his empowered representative. Many people also believed that a witch could change herself into a cat at will. Cats sat beside their mistresses in the dock at witchcraft trials and were often burned alive with them too.

It took a long time for the evil image of the cat and its association with witchcraft and the devil to dissipate, but by the middle of the 18th century, the British poet Christopher Smart could write:

> For I will consider my cat Jeoffry.
> For he is the servant of the Living God, duly and
>   daily serving him.
> For he keeps the Lord's watch in the night against the
> Devil, who is death, by brisking about the life.

In France, cats had already come back into family life in the early 18th century; England and the rest of Europe were not far behind. But small scale torture of cats continued well into the 19th century, including such atrocities as hanging two cats together to fight to the death and throwing a cat from the church steeple to see if the harvest would be good. In 1750 the English artist William Hogarth depicted this mistreatment of the cat in his series of engravings titled *The Four Stages of Cruelty*.

Detail from The First Stage of Cruelty *by William Hogarth in 1750.*

Bet You Didn't Know

HEY!

The cat is mentioned only once in the Bible. In the Apocrypha, the Letter of Jeremiah (Chapter 6) describes the gods of Babylon. Verse 22 reads "Bats and swallows and birds of all kinds perch on their bodies and heads, and cats do likewise." (*Revised English Bible*, Oxford University Press, 1989) The Apocrypha, however, is excluded from the Jewish and Protestant canons of the Old Testament.

The Cats of Islam

The prophet Mohammed who founded Islam early in the 7th century was a lover of cats, and the cat is described as a pure animal in the Koran. The followers of Mohammed therefore respect cats and treat them kindly. There is no history in the nation of Islam of burning cats, burying them alive, or projecting on to them the spirits and personifications of evil.

In fact there is even a legend about the prophet's favorite cat, Muezza. It seems the cat once fell asleep in the sleeve of his master's robe. Rather than wake him when it was necessary to leave, Mohammed cut the sleeve off.

In the Company of Saints and Leaders

Despite medieval Christianity's apparent fear of cats, some saints and respected religious leaders were known to love and cherish them. And some legends give them important roles. Let's take a look at a few of the stories that have come down to us:

➤ Legend has it that a cat gave birth to kittens in the same stable and at the same time that Jesus was born. Many paintings of the Annunciation and some of the Madonna and Child include a cat.

➤ St. Agatha is said to reprimand women who work on her saint's day (February 5) by appearing as an angry cat. She is called Santo Gato (Saint Cat) in the north of Spain. A martyr, she is called upon for help with diseases of the breast, which are common in both cats and humans.

➤ In Sicily the cat is sacred to St. Martha, the patroness of home and hearth.

➤ St. Ives, the patron of lawyers, is pictured with a cat.

➤ St. Gertrude of Nivelles is the patroness of cats and of gardeners, widows, and travelers.

➤ Cardinal Wolsey (Henry VIII's lord chancellor) ate dinner with his cat at the table and said mass with the cat in attendance.

➤ Cardinal Richelieu (chief minister to Louis XIII) had dozens of cats according to one story, but he had 14 according to another version. They sat on his desk while he worked, and they played with the wigs of his visitors.

➤ Leo XIII (pope from 1878 to 1903) found a kitten in the Vatican. He named him Micetto and kept him as a companion for the rest of his life.

 Tales

St. Francis of Assisi is the patron of animals. Many legends have been told about his ability to communicate with birds and beasts alike. Among them is a cat story.

While St. Francis was praying and fasting for 50 days in his solitary cell on Mt. Alverna, the devil tried to plague and distract him by sending hundreds of mice. The mice were everywhere about the good-hearted monk, gnawing at his clothes and nibbling at his feet. Francis was about to give up his prayers and give his attention to dispelling the mice when suddenly a cat jumped out of the long, loose sleeve of his robe. The speed and intensity of the miracle was so great that only two of the mice escaped by hiding in a crack in the wall.

Legend has it that the descendants of this miraculous cat still sit motionless before holes and crevices, waiting to catch the mice that got away.

The Least You Need to Know

➤ Cats were worshipped in ancient Egypt.

➤ In the middle ages people believed that cats were the "familiars" of witches and sometimes the devil in disguise. Some people believed witches could transform themselves into a cat and then back into a woman at will.

➤ Cats were tortured, burned, and buried in pagan rites that persisted into the 18th and, in some places, even into the 19th centuries.

➤ Cats were, and still are, respected and well treated by the nation of Islam.

Cats Around the World

The feline species is native to every continent except Australia and Antarctica. That means cats of one size or another, ranging from lions, the largest, to black-footed cats, the smallest, (both native to Africa) have lived there just about as long as humans.

But ask about the creature we live with and know as *the cat* and you will get some conflicting answers about its origin and history. The ancient Egyptians have the best documentation of early domestication, including a cat portrait that is dated way back to 2,000 B.C. and an abundance of cat mummies and cat statues. In the Andes Mountains of South America, however, fragments of ancient Mochica pottery show cat figures doing the work of men. Cats then were probably a part of the culture that predated and gave rise to the Incas.

Although there are neither mummies nor pottery to substantiate the current theories, there are writings in Chinese and Sanskrit that also place the cat in the home, or at least associating with humans, in China and India at about the same time as in Egypt. So cat history and human history are inextricably entwined over the millennia of recorded history. Let's look at some of the results of that worldwide association.

Cats and the Sun

When the cat is likened to the sun in the mythologies of the world, the moon is often likened to a white mouse. Ancient West African natives, for example, explained an eclipse of the moon by saying the sun cat was eating it. One native ritual tried to help the moon by using a slow hand clapping to persuade the solar cat to release her.

On the other side of the Earth, the Chinese once believed that the size of the pupils in cats' eyes were determined by the height of the sun above the horizon. It was said that these people lifted up a cat's lids to tell the time.

This figure shows the first step in the game cat's cradle. In this game a string is looped in a pattern like a cradle on the fingers of one person's hands, then transferred to the hands of another person so as to form a different figure.

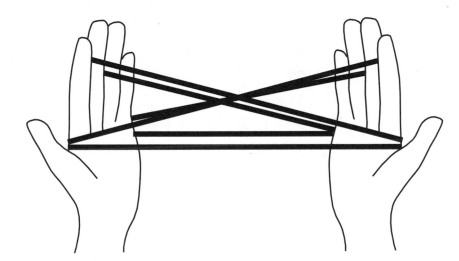

In a children's game called *cat's cradle* (it's always called cat's cradle even though it's played in many different countries around the world), a web of string is sometimes thought of as a means to catch the sun, but for many different reasons. Eskimo children play the game after the summer solstice trying to entangle the solar cat and thus hold back the long winter setting. Children in central Africa make cradles of string to encourage the sun to rest from its heat-producing activities. And in New Guinea, cat's cradles are made to help the sun promote the growth of the crops. (Sometimes they're also used to tie up the yam plants.)

Do You Think We'll Get Some Rain?

In Egyptian mythology, Bastet was the Great Nourisher. In the form of the white moon-cat, she sustained vegetable life by nourishing it with the necessary rain. And as civilization developed elsewhere, cats were associated with rainmaking in many parts of the world. One ritual practiced on the island of Celebes in Indonesia called for the cat to be tied to a sedan chair and carried three times around the parched field while the observers chanted for rain to fall. In Malaysia and Java, cats were bathed or dunked into pools to produce rain. In Sumatra, a black cat was used so that the blackness would darken the sky with rain clouds.

Is There a Cat in Your Garden?

Have you been thinking that all the cats in your garden have four feet, two eyes, and one tail? Think again!

If the cat has meant the sun and rain to humans, why would they not name some products of the garden with cat names? Here's a selection:

Catberry: Mountain holly

Catbrier: A prickly climbing plant of the lily family

Cat-chop: Fig marigold

Cat-clover (cat-in-clover): Bird's-foot trefoil

Cat foot: Biennial cudweed

Cat grape: Missouri grape

Cat haw: Hawthorn fruit

Catkin: Scaly spike

Cat-locks: Cotton grass

Catnip (catmint, catwort): Herb with whorls of small blue flowers

Cat pine: White pine

Cat's-cradle: Ribwort or ribgrass

Cat's-faces: Pansy

Cat's-foot: Ground ivy

Cat's grass (cat's-hair, cat's milk): Sun spurge

continues

---

continued

Cat-spruce: White spruce

Cattail (cat's-tail, cattail rush, cattail grass): Tall marsh grass

Cat's tongue: Velvet bur

Puss clover: Rabbit-foot clover

Pussytoes: Wooly or hoary with small, usually white, flower heads

Pussy willow: Small willow with silky catkins

Catkins from the poplar tree

Catbrier

Pussytoes

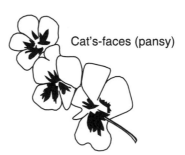

Cat's-faces (pansy)

In ancient China, it was said that when a cat winked, rain was on the way. Japanese fishermen and sailors took calico cats to sea because of their ability to foresee storms and guide ships to safety. Cats were kept more often on Japanese ships than on the ships of any other country in the world.

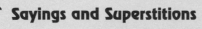

Sayings and Superstitions

Cat on its brain, it's going to rain. This British saying refers to the sleeping cat curled in such a way that the part of its head between the ears touches the ground or floor.

"Cat on its brain, it's going to rain."

A Powerful Talisman

Cats are considered lucky or protective in many parts of the world. In Chinese mythology, cats were looked upon as the living assistants to the hearth god, who was the protector of the home. Ceramic pillows molded in the form of a cat were slept upon by the emperor and peasants alike so as to ward off evil spirits. In Buddhist households, it was believed that there would always be silver in the house that owned a light-colored cat, and gold in the house that owned a dark-colored cat.

Chinese shopkeepers also kept collared and chained cats in their stores to ensure prosperity. The older the cat, the greater luck it could bring the business owner. The cats were kept chained because the businessmen believed that if the cat escaped, all prosperity would go with it.

But the prize for "Cat as Talisman" goes to Japan and the beckoning cat. Even today, the ceramic beckoning cat is often seen in homes, shops, and temples. It is considered a symbol of welcome, but it is also thought to be a charm that brings good luck and prosperity. The legend of its origin goes back to the days of the samurai.

Tales

The monks of the temple of Go-To-Ku-Ji were very poor in ancient Japan, often having barely enough to eat. But the master priest kept a cat that he loved and shared his food with.

This cat was sitting by the roadside one day when a group of samurai riding on magnificent horses came by. Legend says the cat looked up at them and raised one paw to its ear as if beckoning. Enchanted, the samurai stopped and followed the cat to the temple.

Once everyone was inside, the master priest served tea. Then torrential rains fell and kept the samurai longer, giving the priest time to talk about Buddhist beliefs. In the years that followed, one of the samurai known as Lord Li returned regularly for religious instruction. He was generous and endowed the temple with a large estate. Neither monks nor cat went hungry again.

Today the temple grounds are rich with towering trees and beautiful gardens. In the cemetery of the Li family, there is the little shrine of the beckoning cat.

In India, people still recognize the name *Patripatan,* a legendary cat who brought gentleness and beauty to the land. He was said to have found his way to Devendiren, the land where 24 million gods and 48 million goddesses reigned. A favorite there, Patripatan "forgot" to come back for 300 years. During that time, however, everything stayed the same in the land of his birth (no one even got older). When he finally returned he brought in his paws a heavy branch of the rare talisman-flower *Parasidam.* From then on there was well-being in the kingdom.

French folklore also includes the belief that a cat can show a person the way to wealth. The French directions say: *Tie a black cat to a post at a spot where five roads meet. After it has been there for a while, let it loose. It will lead you straight to treasure.* With a legend like that in the national repertoire, it's not surprising that someone who suddenly becomes wealthy in France is said to have "found the silver cat."

In the lowlands of Brittany, the idea of the lucky cat goes yet a step further. There it is said that in the fur of a black cat there is one hair of perfect white. The person who can find that hair and pluck it out without being scratched will hold a powerful talisman. That person can choose to be either extremely rich or very fortunate in love.

Evil Demons and Bad Luck

The black cat is associated with evil and misfortune more than any other cat. For centuries in eastern Europe, peasants feared meeting a black cat at night. They believed black cats were really demons that could (and would) seize and destroy a man, woman, or child traveling alone. In China, black cats were considered an omen of sickness and poverty. Even today, a black cat crossing one's path is considered an omen of impending bad luck in many parts of the United Kingdom and the United States.

In Hungary and Russia, the evil image of the cat was not restricted by coat color. During the middle ages and beyond, many Hungarians believed that most cats became witches between the ages of 7 and 12. To prevent this metamorphosis, they made a cut in the cat's skin in the form of a cross. In Russia, Jewish boys were not allowed to pet a cat because it was thought they would lose their memories.

In parts of Scotland and in the American south, cats were routinely shut up in a separate room whenever someone died because it was thought extremely unlucky for the family to have a cat come near the corpse. In Holland, it was believed that a person who disliked cats was quite certain to be carried to the cemetery in the rain.

Sayings and Superstitions
In Japan, catlike demons depicted with two tails or a single forked tail were thought to have doubly strong powers of bewitchment.

Death and the Journey to the Afterlife

Just like humans, cats always seem to have a good and a not-so-good side. Since they are associated with both good luck and misfortune, cats are associated not only with fertility and new life, but also, inevitably, with death. In Germany, it was believed that a black cat jumping on the bed of someone who is ill foretells his or her death. The Germans also believed that the sight of two cats fighting was a sign of death. In Italian Tuscany this belief was embellished by denoting the two cats as an angel and a devil fighting over the soul of the soon-to-be-deceased.

In the folklore of Finland, the epic *Kalevala* tells the story of a group of men who were enchanted by a sorcerer. They were put into a sledge drawn by a strange-colored cat. The cat speedily bore them off to the land of Pohjola, the world of darkness and evil spirits. In Finland myth says that cats transport humans from the outer world to the inner world, which may not, of course, be death, but it is certainly a change of state.

HEY!

Bet You Didn't Know
In Scotland the many single standing stones thought to have come from Neolithic pre-recorded history are called *cat stanes*. No one knows why.

In west coastal Africa, some tribes believe that when people die their souls pass into cats. In 6th century

Sayings and Superstitions

In some parts of Asia it is said that if you are afraid of cats, you must have been a rat in your last incarnation.

HEY!

Bet You Didn't Know

The Hindu word for cat means "the cleanser."

MEOW!

It's Been Said

"The real objection to a great majority of cats is their unsufferable [sic] air of superiority."

—P. G. Wodehouse, British novelist (1881–1975)

China, it was believed that, after death, some people chose to return to Earth as cats in order to take revenge on their enemies.

The Malaysian Jakurs people venerated the cat. They believed that when they died, a cat would lead them on their journeys through hell to paradise. Legend said that the cat would spray the infernal atmosphere with water to lower the temperature and make it more bearable.

The Exorcising Cat

The ancient Chinese believed that cats had the power to detect evil spirits and put them to flight. They used clay pictures of sitting cats with staring eyes to drive out and keep bad influences away. These "pictures" were placed on top of the walls surrounding a house or beneath the eaves of the house itself. A cat spirit was even worshipped in some parts of China.

The Japanese believed that a black cat could cure spasms if placed on the stomach of a sick person. The cat could also cast out the evil spirits that were causing melancholia and even epilepsy.

In Scotland at the end of the 19th century, some people believed that a sick infant might be cured by taking a cat by its four feet, swinging it around and around the baby, and then throwing it out the hole in the roof for letting out smoke. It was said that if the cat dies, the baby will live because the witches or evil spirits have left the baby's body and gone into the cat.

Russian peasants used to put a cat into a new baby's cradle to drive away any evil spirits from within the infant.

Unconventional, Uncommitted, and Fickle Too!

The independent attitude of the cat is legendary around the world. In Chinese Buddhism the cat appears as the symbol of self-possession. In fact, it's said that the cat was just too self-possessed and disrespectful to get itself included in the Chinese zodiac. The chief disgracing behavior supposedly took place at the Buddha's funeral.

Tales

The ancient Buddhists advocated the protection of all animals except the cat. Why? Legend says it was because of disrespect at the Buddha's funeral. But there are several versions of the story:

➤ It is said that the cat was the only animal that did not attend the Buddha's funeral because it had disgraced itself by having killed the rat that had been sent to fetch healing medicine.

➤ It is said that the cat decided to take a nap on the way to the funeral and slept right through it.

➤ It is said that only the cat and the snake did not weep at the funeral.

➤ It is said that while all the other attendees were beset by the deepest sorrow, the cat saw a rat quietly licking up the oil leaking from a lamp burning by the catafalque. The cat pounced upon and killed the rat. But to kill another being was to transgress against the teachings of Buddha.

Whether all or any of these transgressions caused the cat's disgrace is irrelevant, however, because in the Buddhism of today, the cat joins all other beings in being capable of attaining Nirvana.

The Japanese word for "cat" is sometimes applied to the geisha. The grace and beauty of these lithe and sinuous women dedicated to providing entertainment for men is easily compared to the cat. Ironically, the man a geisha captures has been depicted in art and legend by the catfish.

The reputed fickleness of cats and perhaps their nymphomania when in estrus led to their sharing the punishments of unfaithful wives in Iceland. A woman caught cheating on her husband was tied up in a huge body sack, a cat or two was put in with her, and then the sack was tied shut and flung into a "drowning pool."

Bet You Didn't Know

In the Vietnamese zodiac, the cat replaces the rabbit used in the Chinese system. It is a cat year once every 12 years. The last was 1987, the next will be 1999. Cat people are a lot like cats: kind, aloof, lovers of habit and tradition, clever, and loving. They can also be devious and over-sensitive.

Cats in Our Language

Turn cat in pan means to become a traitor. At the turn of the 16th century, Francis Bacon in his essay "Of Cunning" said, "There is a cunning which we in England call the turning of a cat in the pan...." The phrase probably comes from the French *tourner cote en peine,* which means to turn sides in trouble. If you were English at that time and couldn't read French, the spoken French phrase would sound like "turning cat in pan." Many paintings of the Last Supper show Judas with a cat at his feet.

Real Jobs

Cats haven't always had it easy in human employ. In Paraguay, for example, they have been used for snake hunting. Some accounts describe struggles with rattlesnakes that lasted for hours.

In China, cats were widely used to protect silkworms from rats. When the season came for feeding the worms, silkworm farmers gathered up all the cats they could find. In the absence of live cats, they hung "silkworm cat" pictures on their walls thinking that the images had the same power as the live cat to protect the worms. It didn't work.

Sayings and Superstitions
The rat stops still when the eyes of a cat shine.

—a proverb from Madagascar

In Japan, cats were kept in temples to guard sacred papyrus rolls from mice and rats. They were also used as guards against vermin in mortuary chambers. The famous wood carving *Cat Among the Peonies* hangs over the doorway of the Temple of Nikko. The cat depicted was said to have driven all the vermin from that temple.

In addition to real cats, at one time ceramic cat statues were used in Asia to frighten away mice. Small oil lamps were lit behind the statues' hollow eyes so that rodents would think the cats were real.

More Alike than Different

"All cats are gray in the dark" is a saying heard in many languages. It speaks for the similarity in size and shape shared by cats throughout the world. But beyond appearance is the essence of the cat, which hasn't changed much over time and doesn't seem to be affected by location. Perhaps the Spanish say it best. *Un gato es un gato*—a cat is a cat.

The Least You Need to Know

➤ World mythology puts the cat into many positions of power including providing the light and warmth of the sun and the crop-nourishing rain.

➤ Cats are considered both lucky and unlucky. They are seen as both demons and protectors against demons.

➤ The independent nature of the cat has given it a reputation for nonconformity and even fickleness.

➤ In the history of humankind, cats have performed some essential services.

Chapter 28

V.I.C.s (Very Important Cats)

In This Chapter

➤ Leading nations

➤ Help for writers

➤ Cats in art and music

➤ Cat books for kids

Certainly with tongue in cheek, for he is both a great cat lover and a great satirist, Garrison Keillor once said, "Cats are intended to teach us that not everything in nature has a function."

The line got a good laugh. But perhaps in a more serious moment, Keillor really wanted us to think about the possibility that cats are with us for something more than "function," something intangible like feelings, beauty, inspiration, and other factors of the soul.

A lot of people who have influenced our world and our lives have kept cats in *their* lives. In fact so many that we could do a whole book about cats in the lives of the rich and famous (and maybe we will). But here we can only give you the equivalent of a wine tasting at a party featuring many of the world's greatest wines.

Politically Correct Cats

Cats in Our Language

Sitting in the catbird seat is an American expression that means holding a position of prominence and often power. Red Barber used it often while announcing baseball games in the 1940s. James Thurber also wrote a short story called *The Catbird Seat.* The catbird is a real bird. It is gray with a call that sounds like a cat's meow.

Cats have a long tradition in the American presidency. They go back to the very beginning—George Washington. Several well-loved cats lived with the Washingtons at Mount Vernon. Not too far away at Monticello, favorite cats also lived with Thomas Jefferson. And several cats called the White House home during Abraham Lincoln's term in office.

In 1878 President Rutherford B. Hayes received as a gift the first pair of Siamese cats in the United States.

Rough rider Teddy Roosevelt had two favorite cats in the White House, Slippers and Tom Quartz. If cat-lover Adlai Stevenson had won his campaign against Harry Truman, there surely would have been presidential cats in the '50s.

Some Helpful Information

A sign seen inside London's Parliament Buildings reads, "No Dogs Allowed! Animals leading blind persons will be deemed cats." *Only the British!!!*

John F. Kennedy's daughter Caroline briefly had a White House kitten, but the president's allergy to cats proved too difficult and the kitten was adopted by a friend. Susan Ford's pet, Shan, was another White House Siamese. Amy Carter continued the Siamese-in-the-White-House tradition with a Siamese called Misty Malarky Ying Yang. And then, of course, there's Socks.

Socks is the Clinton family's tuxedo cat and probably the most photographed of all the White House cats. He's even had his portrait painted by American artist Todd Mallett.

In the United Kingdom, queens named Elizabeth don't seem to take to cats. Elizabeth I burned them in a wire cage at her coronation celebration as a symbol of the papacy, and Elizabeth II favors the Welsh Corgi and, in fact, all dogs over cats. But Queen Victoria had a favorite white cat named Heather. This beautiful feline outlived her mistress and was sadly mourned by Edward VII and the other people of Buckingham Palace when she finally died during his reign. During World War II, Winston Churchill's ginger tom, Jock, was present at cabinet meetings and state dinners. Somewhat later, Harold Wilson's

Siamese, Nemo, made frequent unannounced appearances.

The British have the expression "a cat may look upon a king," which certainly crossed the channel at least once. Louis XV of France had a white cat who was the first to enter his bedroom each morning. A royal medal inscribed with the words *Chat Noir Premier Ne en 1725* (Black Cat I—born in 1725) was also struck during his reign. Later in the century, Marie Antoinette was said to have sent several of her pet cats to America, and some legends say they were influential in establishing the Maine Coon breed. Napoleon, however, hated and feared cats.

In Russia at the beginning of the 19th century, Czar Nicholas I had a favorite cat named Vashka, who was an aristocratically beautiful Russian Blue. A century later, Lenin loved all cats, purebred and plain.

Writing Cats

Whether swatting at the feathers of a quill pen or pushing the mouse about, cats have been helping writers almost as long as there have been words. Images of cats are wound in among the flowers in early Irish illuminated manuscripts, and an Irish monk wrote:

> I and Pangur Ban my cat
> 'Tis a like task we are at;
> Hunting mice is his delight
> Hunting words I sit all night...

In France in 1727, Auguste Paradis de Moncrif published the first book dedicated to cats, called, appropriately, *Les Chats.* The book catapulted him to fame (or perhaps infamy) as he was known everywhere as the "chronicler of the claw" and teased with meows and purrs. But he was elected to the prestigious Academie Francaise, and cats were firmly "in" among French society.

France's love affair with the cat continues to be documented by its writers right down to the present day. Victor Hugo, author of *Les Miserables* and *The Hunchback of Notre Dame,* built a chair in the shape of a throne and lined it with crimson satin for his cat, *Chanoine.* Baudelaire and Gautier found time to champion the cat. George Sand was said to drink from the same cup as her cat. Colette wrote of cats in many of her works, including *La Chatte.* Jean Cocteau who knew Colette and her cats said of himself that he was not "one of the maniacs," but he

It's Been Said

"As an inspiration to the author, I do not think the cat can be over-estimated."

—Carl Van Vechten, American novelist, journalist, music critic, and photographer (1880–1966)

MEOW!

kept and carefully cared for many cats and left us many quotable words about the cat.

The Brontë sisters are among the early cat fanciers of English literature. Charlotte, who wrote *Jane Eyre,* was captured by the helplessness of the small animal; Emily, who wrote *Wuthering Heights,* loved its fierce, wild, and intractable nature. Charles Dickens, who so vividly depicted the struggles of the weak in British society, didn't especially like cats until his daughter's cat deposited her kittens at his feet. He had them taken away. The determined mother brought them back. He tried again. She brought them back again and won him over. One of those kittens adopted Dickens and followed him everywhere.

Mark Twain, Edgar Allan Poe, Henry David Thoreau, and Ralph Waldo Emerson are perhaps the best known 19th-century American writers who loved cats, but no one loved them better than Edward Lear, whose companion for 17 years was a cat named Foss. Lear's nonsense song *The Owl and the Pussy-cat* is still a favorite in our culture.

As the 19th century ran into the 20th century, American cat-loving writers were led by two men as different as men can be, Henry James and Ernest Hemingway. James is said to have written his social-mores novels, such as *Daisy Miller* and *The Portrait of a Lady,* with a cat sitting on his shoulder. In the company of cats, Hemingway wrote novels of men trying to maintain grace under pressure, such as *For Whom the Bell Tolls, A Farewell to Arms,* and *The Old Man and the Sea.* His last novel, *Islands in the Stream,* includes a beautiful tribute to the intelligence and character of the cat.

A descendant of the Hemingway cats at the Hemingway house in Key West, Florida.

Among contemporary American cat fancier writers, you'll certainly recognize the names Cleveland Amory, Truman Capote, Garrison Keillor, Doris Lessing, Anne Morrow Lindberg, and Tennessee Williams. There are many, many others!

The Owl and the Pussy-cat

I

The Owl and the Pussy-cat went to sea
    In a beautiful pea-green boat,
They took some honey, and plenty of money,
    Wrapped up in a five-pound note.
The Owl looked up to the stars above,
    And sang to a small guitar,
'O lovely Pussy! O Pussy, my love,
    What a beautiful Pussy you are,
            You are,
            You are!
What a beautiful Pussy you are!'

continues

continued

II

Pussy said to the Owl, 'You elegant fowl!
How charmingly sweet you sing!
O let us be married! too long we have tarried:
But what shall we do for a ring?'
They sailed away, for a year and a day,
To the land where the Bong-tree grows
And there in a wood a Piggy-wig stood
With a ring at the end of his nose,
His nose,
His nose,
With a ring at the end of his nose.

III

'Dear Pig, are you willing to sell for one shilling
  Your ring?' Said the Piggy, 'I will.'
So they took it away, and were married next day
  By the Turkey who lives on the hill.
They dined on mince, and slices of quince,
  Which they ate with a runcible spoon;
And hand in hand, on the edge of the sand,
  They danced by the light of the moon,
        The moon,
        The moon,
They danced by the light of the moon.

Tales

The cat has appeared as a character in fables around the world since the time of Aesop in 5th-century B.C. Greece. In 17th-century France, La Fontaine often used both the cat and the fox to depict human faults such as hypocrisy, wily scheming, and mean spiritedness.

Although usually shown as smarter than the fox, the cat is used as the dupe in some tales. Perhaps the most famous is the story of the monkey who persuaded the cat to reach into the fire to extract roasting chestnuts. Of course the cat's paw was singed. As a result, we have our expression "asked to pull chestnuts out of the fire," which means being duped into doing someone else's dirty work.

There is another foolish cat in the Japanese version of our fable *The Tortoise and the Hare*. It's called *The Cat and the Crab*. Here's how it goes:

A cat and a crab decided to have a race. The cat, thinking himself fast and strong, was quite certain that the crab, who had to run sideways, could not beat him. So he decided to take it easy. What he didn't realize was that the crab had attached itself to his tail.

As the cat approached the finish line, he began wondering how the crab was doing and turned around to have a look. Just at that moment, the crab let go of the tail and called out, "Hey cat, are you just now getting here?" When the cat turned back, the crab had one foot over the finish line. The cat had disgraced himself because of his pride and complacency.

Puddy in Poetry

Cats made their debut in English poetry in a rhyme about the cat as a mouser in Chaucer's "The Maunciple's Tale," published in 1388 as part of *The Canterbury Tales*. Before Chaucer, however, the Italian poet Francesco Petrarch, who would influence the form of the sonnet for generations of poets (including Shakespeare), loved both a woman named Laura and his cat. He dedicated his sonnets to Laura, and he also preserved his cat for all time. After the animal died, he had it embalmed as the Egyptians did and buried it in the lintel above his doorway to keep it near and to prevent evil spirits from entering his home. The skeleton is still preserved in the town of Padua.

The list of cat-loving poets writing in English goes on and on: Thomas Gray, William Cowper, John Gay, Christopher Smart, John Keats, William Wordsworth, Sir Walter Scott,

Matthew Arnold, Lord Byron, W.B. Yeats, Carl Sandburg, Marianne Moore, Elizabeth Coastworth, and May Sarton to name only some of the most famous. But the person who probably contributed the most to cat poetry is the American-born British poet T. S. Eliot. More about that in just a bit.

Framed and Hanging

The oldest example of the cat in art that civilization has preserved is an Egyptian rendering dated at about 3000 B.C. It depicts a cat with a hunting party in a marsh jumping out of a boat to seize a bird. From that time on, it seems that wherever in the world cats have been, cats have been in art.

Among the greatest artists of the Renaissance who loved cats, Leonardo da Vinci stands tallest. His drawings of cats are still awesomely beautiful, and one of his paintings is indeed called *The Virgin of the Cat.* Da Vinci also wrote a book of fables, one of which is titled, "A Mouse, A Weasel, and a Cat."

Most of those French Impressionists whose reproductions currently decorate millions of homes have painted cats. One of the most famous paintings of this period is Manet's *Olympia,* now in the Louvre in Paris. Unless you are a true ailurophile, however, you might miss the wonderful black cat in the right corner because you're focusing a bit more on the beautiful (naked) woman on the left. Renoir, Courbet, Millet, Bonnard, the American-born Mary Cassatt, Toulouse-Lautrec, and Gauguin have all left favorable and flattering renditions of cats as well.

It's Been Said

"Cats in general have always had as their chief assignment our aesthetic satisfaction."

—Roger Caras, American animal authority and writer

Bet You Didn't Know

The cat as the subject of art is almost as popular as the cat itself in France. In 1983 (declared the year of the cat), the Musee de l'Art Naif in Paris put on an exhibit of the cat in art. It was a huge success.

The giant among painters of the 20th century, however, was not always flattering to cats. Picasso includes cats in his works, but they are often almost frightening in their raw animal power, as in his *Cat Eating a Bird.* But that is just what the artist intended. Picasso said, "I want to create a cat like the real cats I see crossing the streets, not like those you see in houses. They have nothing in common. The cat of the streets has bristling hair. It runs like a fiend, and if it looks at you, you think it is going to jump in your face."

Tales

When George Stubbs, the celebrated English painter of horses, did the memorial portrait of the great Arabian stallion, Godolphin, he included in the composition the black cat who was his stablemate. Legend has it that the cat kept a vigil over the horse's body until the stallion died and then went off to die its own death alone in a hayloft. Godolphin died in 1753, but cats are still found in stables around the world.

Among Western artists, no one has produced a more prolific collection of cat drawings than the Parisian artist Theophile-Alexandre Steinlen (1859–1923). Every day he dedicated himself to capturing his favorite animal in all its moods and motivations. His cats leap, cavort, tumble, stalk, and sleep. They catch mice and frogs; they play with yarn, cigars, fish, and lampshades; and they keep company with children, adults, and each other. A book of these drawings titled *Steinlen Cats* can be ordered from Dover Books through your local bookstore. The price is $3.95.

Steinlen was much in demand for his graphic art and posters featuring cats to advertise coffee, tea, entertainment, events, services, and other products. In fact, some of the posters have now been reproduced and are being marketed in museum shops and catalogs.

A Steinlen poster created in 1894 for the Guillot Brother's Dairy. The artist did many posters featuring Steinlen's daughter, Collette, and the family pets as models.

Classically Musical Cats

In addition to Bastet, the cat goddess who was the dominant deity in ancient Egypt, the Egyptian god of music also had a cat's head. So we can at least guess that cats had communicated to humans their sensitivity to sound and their love of music as early as a millennium or two B.C. Today many cats help with piano lessons, and many owners have learned that an agitated cat can be calmed by a little Brahms or Chopin.

In the 18th century, the cat was first rhapsodized in a classical composition, *Fuga del Gatta* (Fugue of the Cat) by the Italian composer Domenico Scarlatti. In the 19th century, the celebrated opera composer Gioacchino Rossini wrote *Duetto Buffo due Gatti,* a comic duet attempting to mimic the sounds of two cats through a musical depiction of meowing in tuneful ecstasy.

With a more sensitive touch, Russian composer Peter Tchaikovsky wrote the wonderful clarinet music that portrays the cat in his orchestral piece *Peter and the Wolf.* Tchaikovsky also wrote the music for the figures of Puss in Boots and the White Cat in the ballet *The Sleeping Beauty.* Besides keeping the beat for the dancers in the scene they share, the orchestra attempts to reproduce mewing and spitting.

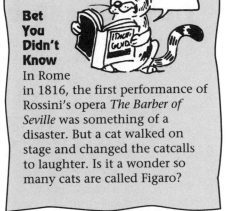

Bet You Didn't Know In Rome in 1816, the first performance of Rossini's opera *The Barber of Seville* was something of a disaster. But a cat walked on stage and changed the catcalls to laughter. Is it a wonder so many cats are called Figaro?

In the early 20th century, Maurice Ravel attempted to orchestrate cat sounds in *L'Enfant et les Sortileges.* (Colette was the librettist for this work.) And later in the century, Igor Stravinsky composed music for Edward Lear's *The Owl and the Pussy-cat.* Also among the world's most famous cat lovers is the Spanish cellist Pablo Casals.

If cats can listen to music and be portrayed in music, why not also have them dance to music? It's been tried. According to biographer Bernard Taper, George Balanchine, the great Russian-born American choreographer, trained his cat to do brilliant *jetes* and *tours en l'air.* When asked how much time he had spent on this training, he replied evasively that at last he had a *body* worth choreographing for.

Bet You Didn't Know *Cats* became London's longest-running musical on May 12, 1989. In 1996 *Cats* surpassed *A Chorus Line* in the United States to become the longest-running Broadway big-theatre musical. And it's still going!

There was also plenty of cat-like choreographing going on and plenty of musical renditions of the sounds and movements of cats when Andrew Lloyd Webber created the musical *Cats* using the poems in T.S. Eliot's *Old Possum's Book of Practical Cats.* Cat lovers

307

(and even cat haters) of the world are still enjoying the beauty and excitement of this happy combination of words and music.

Cats in Our Language

Even English slang has associated the cat with music. From the 1920s to about 1945, a *hep cat* was a jazz or swing music enthusiast. After 1945 that same person was a *cool cat*. By the late 1950s, *cool cat* meant a rock 'n' roll enthusiast. Today *cool cat* means a self-assured male, one who is accepted by the group ("one of us").

From Mother Goose to Dr. Seuss

Cats can't keep up with bears and rabbits in children's literature, or even with dogs for that matter, but they have made their mark. We all know about the pussycat going to London to visit the queen, about the pussy in the well, and about the cat and the fiddle. Some of us, especially in the UK, have been caught by the nursery rhyme multiplication riddle:

> As I was going to St. Ives,
> I met a man with seven wives,
> Each wife had seven sacks,
> Each sack had seven cats,
> Each cat had seven kits;
> Kits, cats, sacks, and wives,
> How many were there going to St. Ives?

The Cheshire cat "who vanished quite slowly, beginning with the end of the tail, and ending with the grin, which remained some time after the rest had gone" is one the most unforgettable characters in Lewis Carroll's *Alice's Adventures in Wonderland,* which was first published in 1865. We've even coined the phrase "grinning like a Cheshire cat" to mean a big smile that lasts a long time.

Most of us think of Peter Rabbit when we hear the name Beatrix Potter, but in fact the British author wrote of many animals. In 1907 she published *The Tale of Tom Kitten,* which was actually about Tom and his three sisters. And in 1909 she told the story of *Ginger and Pickles,* a yellow farm cat and a terrier who kept a shop.

In the 1930s and '40s, cats were a popular subject for children's books. Kathleen Hale wrote a series of books about the adventures of Orlando, the marmalade cat, who lives with his dear wife, Grace, and their three children, Pansy, Blanche, and Tinkle. Between

1942 and 1963, Diana Ross wrote five books about Miss Pussy, a spinster cat with seven brothers and seven sisters, all married with children.

Cats also make their appearance in Elizabeth Coatsworth's series of stories about the orphan girl Sally Smith who lived in post-Revolutionary War Boston.

In 1966 *Sam, Bangs and Moonshine* by Evaline Ness told the story of a girl named Samantha and Bangs her cat. Sam was trying to cope with the death of her mother and often told fanciful stories (her father called them "moonshine"). Bangs, her cat, was a great listener. The book was highly praised and is still available in many libraries.

It's Been Said
"There are no ordinary cats."

—Colette, French writer (1873–1954)

Still available in bookstores and libraries everywhere is the book that allowed the cat to lead the juvenile best-seller lists. In 1957 Theodor Seuss Giesel (known forever hence as Dr. Seuss) introduced *The Cat in the Hat* as a Random House Beginner Book. This whimsical creature who walks on two legs and talks in rhyme has led the series to sales of over 30 million copies and is now working on his second generation of admirers.

This drawing of Alice and the Cheshire cat by Sir John Tenniel has become one of the most reproduced illustrations of all time.

The Most Important Cats

So the world is full of very important cats. But the most important cats are *your* cats. They're important when they greet you at the door, tail high and eyes bright. They're important when they curl up on your lap purring. They're important when they take a playful swat at your hair and when they wash so carefully after a great meal.

Your cats are important because they're with you, sharing your life. When you're together feeling each other's warmth, you catch moments when, finally, words and money are unimportant.

The Least You Need to Know

➤ Some cats have had inside information on decisions that affect the world.

➤ There are many writers who say it's impossible to write without a cat.

➤ Artists and composers have tried to capture the essence of the cat.

➤ Kids love cats!

Colleges of Veterinary Medicine in the United States and Canada

Colleges of veterinary medicine often have associated veterinary clinics with specialists available for consultation. Many also make pamphlets, research papers, and books available to the general public. Here's a list for those who want to explore academic information or seek help from a recognized authority. It is in alphabetical order by state, followed by Canadian provinces.

Alabama

Auburn University
College of Veterinary Medicine
Auburn University, AL 36849
(334) 844-4546   Fax (334) 844-3697

Tuskegee University
School of Veterinary Medicine
Tuskegee, AL 36088
(205) 727-8174   Fax (205) 727-8177

California

University of California
School of Veterinary Medicine
Davis, CA 95616
(916) 752-1361   Fax (916) 752-2801

Colorado

Colorado State University
College of Veterinary Medicine and Bio-medical Sciences
Fort Collins, CO 80523
(303) 491-7051   Fax (303) 491-2250

Florida

University of Florida
College of Veterinary Medicine
Gainesville, FL 32610
(904) 392-4700 ext. 5000   Fax (904) 392-8351

Georgia

University of Georgia
College of Veterinary Medicine
Athens, GA 30602
(706) 542-3461   Fax (706) 542-8254

Illinois

University of Illinois
College of Veterinary Medicine
2001 South Lincoln St.
Urbana, IL 61801
(217) 333-2760   Fax (217) 333-4628

Indiana

Purdue University
School of Veterinary Medicine
1240 Lynn Hall
West Lafayette, IN 47907
(317) 494-7607   Fax (317) 496-1261

Iowa

Iowa State University
College of Veterinary Medicine
Ames, IA 50011
(515) 294-1242   Fax (515) 294-8341

Kansas

Kansas State University
College of Veterinary Medicine
Manhattan, KS 66506
(913) 532-5660   Fax (913) 532-5884

Louisiana

Louisiana State University
School of Veterinary Medicine
Baton Rouge, LA 70803
(504) 346-3100   Fax (504) 346-5702

Maryland

See listing under Virginia.

Massachusetts

Tufts University
School of Veterinary Medicine
200 Westboro Rd.
North Grafton, MA 01536
(508) 839-5302   Fax (508) 839-2953

Michigan

Michigan State University
College of Veterinary Medicine
East Lansing, MI 48824
(517) 355-6509   Fax (517) 336-1037

Minnesota

The University of Minnesota
College of Veterinary Medicine
Saint Paul, MN 55108
(612) 624-9227   Fax (612) 624-8753

Mississippi

Mississippi State University
College of Veterinary Medicine
Mississippi State, MS 39762
(601) 325-3432   Fax (601) 325-1498

Missouri

University of Missouri
College of Veterinary Medicine
Columbia, MO 65211
(314) 882-3877   Fax (314) 884-5044

New York

Cornell University
College of Veterinary Medicine
Ithaca, NY 14853
(607) 253-3000   Fax (607) 253-3708

North Carolina

North Carolina State University
College of Veterinary Medicine
4700 Hillsborough St.
Raleigh, NC 27606
(919) 829-4200   Fax (919) 829-4452

Ohio

The Ohio State University College of Veterinary Medicine
1900 Coffey Rd.
Columbus, OH 43210
(614) 292-1171   Fax (614) 292-7185

Oklahoma

Oklahoma State University
College of Veterinary Medicine
Stillwater, OK 74078
(405) 744-6648   Fax (405) 744-6633

Oregon

Oregon State University
College of Veterinary Medicine
Corvallis, OR 97331
(503) 737-2141   Fax (503) 737-4245

Pennsylvania

University of Pennsylvania
School of Veterinary Medicine
3800 Spruce St.
Philadelphia, PA 19104
(215) 898-5438   Fax (215) 898-9923

Tennessee

University of Tennessee
College of Veterinary Medicine
Knoxville, TN 37901
(615) 974-7262   Fax (615) 974-8222

Texas

Texas A&M University
College of Veterinary Medicine
College Station, TX 77843
(409) 845-5051   Fax (409) 845-5088

Virginia

Virginia Tech and University of Maryland
Virginia-Maryland Regional College of Veterinary Medicine
Blacksburg, VA 24061
(703) 231-7666   Fax (703) 231-7367

Washington

Washington State University
College of Veterinary Medicine
Pullman, WA 99164
(509) 335-9515   Fax (509) 335-6094

Wisconsin

The University of Wisconsin—Madison
School of Veterinary Medicine
Madison, WI 53706
(608) 263-6717   Fax (608) 263-6573

Ontario

Ontario Veterinary College
University of Guelph
Guelph, Ontario
N1G 2W1 Canada
(519) 823-8800   Fax (519) 767-0440

Prince Edward Island

University of Prince Edward Island
Atlantic Veterinary College
Charlottetown, Prince Edward Island
C1A 4P3 Canada
(902) 566-0800   Fax (902) 566-0958

Quebec

University of Montreal
Faculty of Veterinary Medicine
Saint Hyacinthe, Quebec
J2S 7C6 Canada
(514) 345-8521   Fax (514) 773-2161

Saskatchewan

University of Saskatchewan
Western College of Veterinary Medicine
Saskatoon, Saskatchewan
S7N 0W0 Canada
(306) 966-7103   Fax (306) 966-8747

Index

nose, 52-53
paws, 48-50
skeleton, 46
spine, 46-47
swollen, 170
tongue, 50
whiskers, 54
ancestors, 273-275
Chinese, 286
Egyptian, 273-275, 285
French, 280
Greek, 275
Islamic, 282
Roman, 275
Roman empire, 278-279
South American, 285
anestrus cycle, 190
anger, communication, 65
Animal Legal Defense Fund,
105
Animal Medical Center, 169
Animal Protection Institute of
America, 265
animal shelters
adoption screening, 8
cats as gifts, 8
costs, 262
donations, 8, 266-267
littermates, 9
medical histories, 9
neutering, 8
petmobiles, 9
purebreds, 8
returning a cat, 9, 12
selecting a cat, 8-9
spaying, 8
state of health, 9
strays, 21
vaccinations, 8
volunteering, 263-264
Antarctic cats, 285
anxiety
caused by being left alone,
208
communication, 59-60
pregnancy, 199
purring, 55
apartments, pet restrictions,
105
arched back, 62
area rugs
fleas, 160
taping, 127

The Aristocats, 147
art, 305-306
arthritis, 174, 221
artists, 255-257
Asian beliefs, 292
aspirin, administering to cats,
170, 221
attending cat shows, 233-235
attention span, 94
attentiveness, 60
attributing human emotions/
personalities to cats, 176, 181,
264
audiocassettes, 147-148
Australian cats, 285

B

bacterial infections, 154, 170
balance, 47-48
balconies, 99
The Barber of Seville, 307
barn cats, 82
bathing, 156-157
fleas, 156
pregnancy, 200
skin problems, 156
beds, 34-35
costs, 123
fleas, 123, 160
play time, 133
sleeping, 162
training to stay off of, 122
behavior
aggression, 176-177
behavior problems, 175
changes in, 160
clawing, 177
destructive, 179
fear of humans, 179-180
hormone-related, 183
instinct, 176
manipulation, 181-182
mind games, 180-182
not using the litter box,
177-178
punishment, 176, 183-184
spraying, 178
sterilization, 194-195
symptoms of illness, 169

behavior therapists, 185-186
careers, 248-249
bells on collars, 52
The Best Cat in the World, 144
Bible, 282
bi-color, 70
biodegradable litter, 35
birth weight, 200
birthing box, 198-199
birthing process, 199-200
The Black Cat, 146
black cats, 213, 279, 290-291
bladder infections, 177
blindness
communication, 26
determining, 24
kittens, 200-201
nutrition, 114
blinking, 59
boarding, 211
costs, 5
day care, 246
body language, 62-63
see also communication
body rhythms, sleeping, 162
body type
heredity, 71-72
purebreds, 71
bones, 46
in food, 116
books about cats, 144-147
boosters (vaccinations), 204
boutiques, 246
Breakfast at Tiffany's, 147
breathing
as a determinant of health,
24
difficulties, 169
kittens, 50
symptoms of poisoning, 96
breeders
adopting from, 11-12
careers, 242-243
choosing, 12
breeding
personality, 192
Scottish Folds, 77
success, 47
see also purebreds
breeds
Abyssinian, 79
American Shorthair, 76

319

When You're Smart Enough to Know That You Don't Know It All

For all the ups and downs you're sure to encounter in life, The Complete Idiot's Guides give you down-to-earth answers and practical solutions.

The Complete Idiot's Guide to Buying Insurance and Annuities
ISBN: 0-02-861113-6 ▪ $16.95

The Complete Idiot's Guide to Managing Your Money
ISBN: 1-56761-530-9 ▪ $16.95

The Complete Idiot's Guide to Buying and Selling a Home
ISBN: 1-56761-510-4 ▪ $16.95

The Complete Idiot's Guide to Doing Your Income Taxes 1996
ISBN: 1-56761-586-4 ▪ $14.99

The Complete Idiot's Guide to Making Money with Mutual Funds
ISBN: 1-56761-637-2 ▪ $16.95

The Complete Idiot's Guide to Getting Rich
ISBN: 1-56761-509-0 ▪ $16.95

Y o u   c a n   h a n d l e   i t !

Look for The Complete Idiot's Guides at your favorite bookstore, or call 1-800-428-5331 for more information.

The Complete Idiot's Guide to Learning French on Your Own
ISBN: 0-02-861043-1 ▪ $16.95

The Complete Idiot's Guide to Dating
ISBN: 0-02-861052-0 ▪ $14.95

The Complete Idiot's Guide to Cooking Basics
ISBN: 1-56761-523-6 ▪ $16.99

The Complete Idiot's Guide to Hiking and Camping
ISBN: 0-02-861100-4 ▪ $16.95

The Complete Idiot's Guide to Learning Spanish on Your Own
ISBN: 0-02-861040-7 ▪ $16.95

The Complete Idiot's Guide to Gambling Like a Pro
ISBN: 0-02-861102-0 ▪ $16.95

The Complete Idiot's Guide to Choosing, Training, and Raising a Dog
ISBN: 0-02-861098-9 ▪ $16.95

The Complete Idiot's Guide to Trouble-Free Car Care
ISBN: 0-02-861041-5 ▪ $16.95

The Complete Idiot's Guide to the Perfect Wedding
ISBN: 1-56761-532-5 ▪ $16.99

The Complete Idiot's Guide to Getting and Keeping Your Perfect Body
ISBN: 0-286105122 ▪ $16.99

The Complete Idiot's Guide to First Aid Basics
ISBN: 0-02-861099-7 ▪ $16.95

The Complete Idiot's Guide to the Perfect Vacation
ISBN: 1-56761-531-7 ▪ $14.99

The Complete Idiot's Guide to Trouble-Free Home Repair
ISBN: 0-02-861042-3 ▪ $16.95

The Complete Idiot's Guide to Getting into College
ISBN: 1-56761-508-2 ▪ $14.95

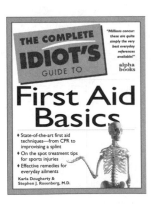

You can handle it!